Indian Business, Economic Development, and the Jobs Dilemma in the Twenty-first Century

PRAISE FOR: *Indian Business, Economic Development, and the Jobs Dilemma in the Twenty-first Century* by Anthony P. D'Costa

"India stands at a pivotal moment in its economic journey. As the nation grapples with transforming into a high-productivity, skill-driven economy, a fundamental question emerges: Will India successfully accelerate this transition, or will progress stagnate, leaving millions of young people trapped in fierce competition for scarce opportunities? Anthony D'Costa delivers an unflinching examination of the complex dynamics between business and state, exposing critical vulnerabilities while illuminating pathways toward prosperity. His analysis reveals how India could emerge as a high-income, more equitable society by 2047—the centennial of its independence—if it can navigate the challenges ahead."

Tony Addison, Non-resident Senior Research Fellow, UN University-World Institute of Development Economics Research (UNU-WIDER), Helsinki.

"Anthony D'Costa wonderfully weaves the wide-ranging empirical material on Indian business into an interesting analytical tale to illuminate our understanding of the role that business plays in advancing development in a country like India. His in-depth knowledge of Indian business, which is rather unusual among the majority of development scholars, uniquely privileges him to develop a synthetic perspective drawing from two apparently unbridgeable disciplines, namely, development studies and business strategy. The book is a must-read for those who are interested in seeing Indian business through a development lens."

Achin Chakraborty, Former Director and Professor, Institute of Development Studies, Kolkata.

"In this insightful book, Anthony D'Costa provides a fresh look at the path of Indian economic development through the lens of the relationship between state and business. Anyone interested in whether and how private corporate enterprise can address the crucial problem of employment generation will find this of great interest."

Jayati Ghosh, Professor of Economics, University of Massachusetts, Amherst, USA.

"Professor Anthony D'Costa's new book addresses the challenging question of creating productive jobs for India's growing labor force by looking into the role of the business sector in manufacturing and services. A theoretically informed analysis in Asia's historical context, it focuses on India's post-independence experience.

A lucid text that distils the author's deep and varied research and teaching experience. I highly recommend it for students of business, development studies, and non-specialist intelligent readers."

Nagaraj Rayaprolu, Former Professor, Indira Gandhi Institute of Development Research, Mumbai.

"Anthony D'Costa's innovative book breaks fresh ground in the analysis of the structural employment challenges that currently characterizes the Indian, and indeed the global economy, namely, job-less or job-loss growth. This phenomenon has been much studied but almost invariably at the aggregate macroeconomic level. The especially valuable feature of this excellent volume is that it constructs its overall perspective from a wide-ranging spectrum of insightful disaggregated industry-specific assessments of the interplay of technological, institutional, policy and employment factors that influence business and their impact on economic development. I strongly recommend the book that will be of great interest to students, scholars, policy makers, business leaders, and the wider community of engaged lay readers."

Ashwani Saith, Former Dean and Emeritus Professor at the International Institute of Social Studies, The Hague, Erasmus University Rotterdam.

"Anthony D'Costa's book is about *the* central challenge confronting the Indian economy currently – the lack of good jobs for India's increasingly educated working-age population. Combining rich political economy analysis with detailed industry level case-studies, the book is a *tour de force*, with deep insights on the nature of state business relations in contemporary India. The book is a must read for students of political economy, and for scholars who would like to understand both the promise and peril of India's future economic trajectory."

Kunal Sen, Director, UNU-WIDER and Professor of Development Economics, University of Manchester.

"The understanding of the Indian labor market remains limited due to the wide range of employment: from informal to formal, subsistence-level to well-paid, and unskilled to highly skilled work. Anthony D'Costa, who has extensively researched Indian and East Asian development and taught in development studies and business programs in a number of universities around the world, offers a pioneering perspective on the intricate relationship between India's business landscape, economic development, and employment. Covering micro and traditional enterprises, modern industry, and the wider economic sectors of agriculture, manufacturing, and services, the author through both historical and comparative perspectives skillfully analyzes the employment conundrum of a high-growth economy with persistent surplus labor. Written in a lucid and nontechnical style, this book is a must-read for students, scholars, and policymakers seeking to understand India's complex labor markets in the twenty-first century."

Alakh N. Sharma, Director, Institute for Human Development, New Delhi, and President, Indian Society of Labour Economics.

Indian Business, Economic Development, and the Jobs Dilemma in the Twenty-first Century

Anthony P. D'Costa

OXFORD
UNIVERSITY PRESS

OXFORD
UNIVERSITY PRESS

Great Clarendon Street, Oxford, OX2 6DP,
United Kingdom

Oxford University Press is a department of the University of Oxford.
It furthers the University's objective of excellence in research, scholarship,
and education by publishing worldwide. Oxford is a registered trade mark of
Oxford University Press in the UK and in certain other countries.

Published in the United States of America by Oxford University Press
546 Fifth Avenue, New York, NY 10036, United States of America

British Library Cataloguing in Publication Data
Data available

Library of Congress Control Number: 2026936030

ISBN 9780198948377

DOI: 10.1093/9780198948407.001.0001

Printed and bound by
CPI Group (UK) Ltd., Croydon, CR0 4YY

MIX
Paper | Supporting
responsible forestry
FSC® C013604
FSC
www.fsc.org

The manufacturer's authorized representative in the EU for product safety is
Oxford University Press España S.A. of Parque Empresarial San Fernando de Henares,
Avenida de Castilla, 2 – 28830 Madrid (www.oup.es/en or product.safety@oup.com).
OUP España S.A. also acts as importer into Spain of products made by the manufacturer.

To my parents, Celine and Vincent D'Costa

Contents

List of Figures

List of Tables

List of Boxes

Preface and Acknowledgments

As we enter the second quarter of the twenty-first century, the world appears to be at a turning point. Old alliances are dissolving, liberal democracies are becoming authoritarian, and the global economic and political outlook deteriorates daily. Artificial intelligence is on the threshold of destabilizing labor markets, while pervasive uncertainty engenders a climate of nervousness all around. The rise of Big Tech and the oligarchic partnerships between the state and private business are also altering state–society relations; in the larger scheme of things, these are impacting ordinary citizens in untold ways through the pursuit of narrow economic and political interests.

This, of course, is not the primary subject of this book—or rather, it is, albeit in a different context. The focus is on India, a large, diverse country striving to find its place in a hyper-competitive and uncertain global economy. As a development scholar with one foot in the understanding of business as integral to capitalist dynamics and the other in the appreciation of a good society made possible through economic development, this book examines the relationship between business sectors and economic development. The purpose here is not to offer a research monograph for specialists, although the analysis is research-informed. Rather, through the lens of business sectors, the goal is to provide for the interested reader an accessible account—a window to the vexing question of why creating jobs in India is so difficult today. The paradox is that the country displays one of the highest growth rates in the world and is projected to become one of the top three economies.

This employment problem is not an Indian one *per se*; everywhere, young job-seekers are increasingly frustrated with the limited options available to them. Automation and AI have become real threats, but the Indian story is infinitely worse. As an aside, in 2024, there were 10.8 million job applicants for 32,438 positions—or 333 applicants per opening—in the Indian Railways, the world's largest single employer. There are many other horror stories about job scarcity in India. The absence of social protections in a market where the competition for jobs is mind-boggling is an open invitation to mass despair. While it is true that India's workforce is larger than most, it is also the youngest workforce that is brimming with private aspirations. The hard reality, however, is that lofty official pronouncements are unable to narrow the deep divide between the formal and informal labor markets. In India, only 10% of the workers are employed in "regular," decent jobs, while the 90% bound to informal jobs have little social protection. How to process this twenty-first-century dilemma has flummoxed even experts.

This book is a modest attempt to raise awareness of the scarcity of jobs in India. It is also inspired by the many young students in my international business and economic development classes who have been discouraged by the limited employment opportunities available to them. I have taught these as separate subjects throughout my academic career at the University of Washington (Tacoma and Seattle), the National University of Singapore, Copenhagen Business School, Bordeaux School of Management, the University of Melbourne, and the University of Alabama in Huntsville. To my knowledge, this may be the first effort to relate business dynamics to the broader realm of economic development without taking development for granted. Popular perception is that business is the building block of development; however, on closer examination, what business does, how it operates, and the results it achieves are dependent on a host of factors. These include, but are not limited to, the inherited structures of compressed capitalism and the political economy of the state's mediating role. I have had the privilege of using these ideas to converse about the job question through lectures, seminars, and conferences in Kyoto, Urbino, Rio de Janeiro, New York, Seattle, Tacoma, Honolulu, Wellington, Auckland, Sydney, Melbourne, Copenhagen, Plzeň, Boston, and York. I am grateful to all the participants for their engagement and constructive feedback.

In this book, I survey a mix of Indian business sectors to assess their contributions to economic development—including growth, employment, economic diversification, and exports—in an ever-changing world economy. Notwithstanding some of the business successes, when perceived through a political economy lens, the prognosis for employment as a development outcome is far from rosy. I have relied on the vast scholarship on Indian industrial development and labor markets, including my own political economy research over the last thirty-five years, the business press and other media outlets in India and abroad, government and private consulting reports, and many conversations over the years with knowledgeable people.

I have deliberately stayed away from policy recommendations. That was never the intent, though readers will observe that in the course of the discussions, I have expressed some possible interventions. There are many others who are better placed than I am for this task, although the solutions offered by most seem to be repetitive and cohere around a long list of supply-side factors—such as more investment, building technological competence, quality education and skill upgrading, and infrastructure spending. Aligned with the many well-wishers of India, I too want these efforts to be directed toward labor-intensive industries in manufacturing and services, with adequate social protections; however, the reality is something else. There is a diverse range of business sectors in India: some older and heavier, others tottering, still others are emerging, and a few others that are globally shining. Each one of these sectors has something to offer to the Indian economy, hopefully with greater dignity to those who are already toiling to sustain livelihoods and to new job-seekers. But it is an inescapable fact that each of these sectors will have to expand several-fold to make a dent in India's surplus labor and growing workforce. Furthermore, new geopolitical realities are beginning to subvert the business-as-usual approach. India needs to go back to the drawing board as much as possible.

This is the second major project that I undertook at the University of Alabama in Huntsville (UAH), where I taught from 2018 to 2024. For a project like this, one is indebted to many individuals and organizations. In Huntsville, Dr Gurmej Sandhu, originally from Punjab, as a successful entrepreneur and a community leader, generously endowed my university position as an Eminent Scholar of Global Studies and Professor of Economics at the College of Business. The position provided the intellectual freedom and the financial resources to pursue my ongoing research on economic matters pertaining to India. I am grateful to UAH's College of Business for providing a congenial environment to undertake this research.

Over the nearly thirty-five years of my academic career, I have learned a great deal from many of my Indian colleagues, several of whom are also close friends. For the sake of brevity, I cannot mention everyone, but I would like to acknowledge their inspiration and the knowledge they have shared. I would particularly like to mention Amiya Kumar Bagchi, the founding Director of the Institute of Development Studies, Kolkata (IDSK), who is no longer with us, and Achin Chakraborty, also a former Director of IDSK, for our long, continuing conversations—or *addas*, as we call them in Bengali. I also acknowledge the many research materials provided by Sushil Khanna, formerly of the Indian Institute of Management, Calcutta and Jayan Jose Thomas of the Indian Institute of Technology, Delhi.

Very specific to this book project, I talked to a number of colleagues, many of them for the first time, both in person and online. I had the good fortune to meet Ajit Ghose, formerly of the International Labour Organization, at Cambridge University, who is also no longer with us. As a leading labor economist of India, my interactions with him in Copenhagen and Delhi opened my doors to engage more with India's employment challenges.

For this project, I traveled to India on two occasions, occurring both before and after the pandemic of 2020. The first field trip was in 2019 to gather data from business cases at the Institute of Chartered Financial Analysts of India (ICFAI) Business School in Hyderabad; the second field visit was in 2024 to Delhi, Kolkata, and Bengaluru to meet in person people I consider knowledgeable about the Indian economy. For this segment of the research, I thank Achin Chakraborty and Surajit Mazumdar of Jawaharlal Nehru University (JNU) for suggesting people to meet.

Both in person and online, I talked to the following academics: Aditya Bhattacharya, formerly of Delhi School of Economics, Surajit Mazumdar and Ravi Srivastava, JNU, Nitya Nanda and Biswajit Dhar, Council for Social Development, Delhi, Rishikesha Krishnan and Chetan Subramanian, Indian Institute of Management Bangalore, Pratik Kumar, CEO WIPRO Infrastructure and Engineering, Bangalore, Amit Basole, Azim Premji University, Bangalore, Mritiunjoy Mohanty and Parthapratim Pal, Indian Institute of Management Calcutta, Saibal Kar, Centre for Social Science Research Calcutta, Nagaraj Rayaprolu, formerly of Indira Gandhi Institute Development Research Institute, Mumbai, and Pronab Sen, Chief Statistician, Standing Committee on Statistics of the Government of India. I am grateful to all these individuals for taking the time to speak to me.

Yaryna Zhurba, my former teaching assistant at UAH, created an annotated bibliography based on all the business cases that I had collected from ICFAI. It was always a pleasure to work with her. I thank David Morris and Amanda Gilbertson for reading the very first draft of the first chapter for some non-specialist feedback, while Camille D'Costa helped rework some diagrams. As an Honorary Professorial Fellow of the University of Melbourne, I gratefully acknowledge the online access to the university's fantastic library resources for this book.

Lastly, I am ever grateful to Janette Rawlings for her love and patience in wading through pretty much all my manuscripts for the last several decades before they see the light of day! This was no exception.

Anthony P. D'Costa
Kirkland, Washington
March 2026

List of Acronyms

AI	Artificial Intelligence
AICTE	All India Council for Technical Education
APIs	Active pharmaceutical ingredient
ASEAN	Association of Southeast Asian Nations
BHEL	Bharat Heavy Electricals Limited
BHIM	Bharat Interface for Money
BJP	Bharatiya Janata Party
C-DOT	Centre for Development of Telematics
CMC	Computer Maintenance Corporation
COSL	Citicorp Overseas Software Limited
DPE	Digitalization and the platform economy
EDB	Ease of doing business
EDO	Economic development outcomes
ESDO	Economic and social development outcomes
EVs	Electric vehicles
FAME	Faster Adoption and Manufacturing of (Hybrid and) Electric Vehicles
FDI	Foreign direct investment
FERA	Foreign Exchange Regulation Act, 1973
FIRE	Finance, insurance, and real estate
FMCG	Fast-moving consumer goods
GATT	General Agreement on Tariffs and Trade
GERD	Gross expenditure on research and development
GFCF	Gross fixed capital formation
GHGs	Greenhouse gases
GST	Goods and services tax
HCL	Hindustan Computers Limited
HDI	Human Development Index
HL	Handloom
HM	Hindustan Motors
IBEF	India Brand Equity Foundation
IBM	International Business Machines
ICL	International Computers Limited
ICT	Information and communications technologies
IMF	International Monetary Fund
INR	Indian Rupee
IoT	Internet of Things
IPOs	Initial public offerings
ISI	Import substitution industrialization
IT	Information technology
ITES	Information Technology Enabled Services

JAM	Jan-Dhan, Aadhar, and Mobile Connectivity
KYC	Know your customer
LGD	Lab-grown diamond
M&M	Mahindra & Mahindra
MC	Mature capitalists
mcts	Million carats
MIC	Made in China
MII	Make in India program
ML	Machine learning
MNREGA	Mahatma Gandhi National Rural Employment Guarantee Act
MRTP	Monopolies and Restrictive Trade Practices Act, 1969
MSMEs	Medium-, Small-, and Micro-sized Enterprises
NASSCOM	National Association of Software and Services Companies
NCR	National Capital Region
NITI	National Institution for Transforming India
NPAs	Non-performing assets
NPCI	National Payments Corporation of India
NREGA	National Rural Employment Guarantee Act
OECD	Organisation of Economic Co-operation and Development
ORG	Operations Research Group
PA	Primitive accumulation
PAL	Premier Automobiles Limited
PCP	Petty commodity production
PLI	Productivity Linked Incentive Scheme
PMP	Phased Manufacturing Program
PwC	PricewaterhouseCoopers
RCEP	Regional Comprehensive Economic Partnerships
SaaS	Software as a Service
SAL	Sipani Automobiles Limited
SMP	Standard Motor Products
STPI	Software Technology Parks of India
TCS	Tata Consultancy Services
TELCO	Tata Engineering and Locomotive Company
TISCO	Tata Iron and Steel Company
TNC	Transnational corporation
TRIPS	Trade-Related Aspects of Intellectual Property Rights
UNDP	United Nations Development Programme
UPI	United Payments Interface
VOC	Varieties of Capitalism
WTO	World Trade Organization

1
Is the Business of Business Economic Development?

1.1 Introduction

Many young readers of this book will be unfamiliar with the Bombay Plan of 1944. It was a social contract that resulted from a meeting between eight leading Indian business heads, a few technocrats, and political leaders who were seeking India's independence from Great Britain. In this gathering, the tacit understanding between business and would-be leaders of the independent state was that a "mixed economy" would best serve India's economic development needs (Bhattacharya and Guha Thakurta 2019: 196). Eighty years later, India still has a mixed economy, except that the constitutive roles of business and the government have shifted away from a state-commandeered economy to a more private-sector-led process. While the role of the Indian state and economic development outcomes between 1950 and the 1990s have been comprehensively scrutinized, the purpose of this book is to investigate how commercial activities are contributing (or not) to India's capitalist economic development in the twenty-first century.

Without getting into the huge debate about what constitutes capitalism, for the sake of clarity, I take a simple definition. First and foremost, it is an economic system that is driven by businesses and entrepreneurs (capitalists) who invest capital to make profits. It does not matter what they produce as long as the returns are greater than zero. These profits, along with borrowed capital, are reinvested to expand the individual business; collectively, these businesses and entrepreneurs contribute to macroeconomic growth. The systemic imperative of capitalism is growth. Lack of growth for sustained periods of time results in an economic crisis and a high rate of business failures. The second aspect of capitalism is that capitalists hire workers as needed to undertake production at an agreed-upon wage, typically what the local market will bear. Workers with little bargaining power must accept what is offered, which is sometimes below the official minimum wage set by the government. A third characteristic of capitalism is that the

Indian Business, Economic Development, and the Jobs Dilemma in the Twenty-first Century. Anthony P. D'Costa, Oxford University Press. © Anthony P. D'Costa (2026). DOI: 10.1093/9780198948407.003.0001

state typically plays a mediating role between capitalists and workers without undermining the system of capitalism. In other words, it does not kill the golden goose. Instead, the state provides the institutional architecture, legal and otherwise, such as contract enforcement, the settlement of labor disputes, and investment regulations by which business operates and invests in physical and social infrastructure, such as roads, ports, and education. As a general rule, this tripartite interaction generates business profits, jobs for workers, and other economic development outcomes, such as technological development, a supplier industry, infrastructure development, and revenues for the government.

The central issue examined in this introductory book is the understudied relationship between business and economic development in India. Both are situated in contemporary capitalism that is global in scope. As a development scholar with one foot in the understanding of business as integral to capitalist dynamics and the other in the appreciation of a good society that is possible through economic development, I examine the relationship between business sectors and economic development. The purpose here is not to offer an account for specialists; there are plenty of such sources available, which can be found in the references cited. Rather, my goal is to provide an accessible account for the interested intelligent reader by opening a window into the vexing question of why creating jobs in India is so difficult today.

Instead of jumping straightaway into a discussion of labor markets, I begin the exploration by using the lens of business sectors to identify what it is that they do and how that contributes to different facets of economic development, especially employment. I adopt this approach because India displays one of the highest growth rates in the world, a growth that is driven by corporate (big) business but which also relies on the supplies provided by small and medium enterprises. The economy is projected to become one of the three largest in the world. But the paradox is that high growth is also supported by a large underbelly of medium-, small-, and micro-sized enterprises (MSMEs) of informal or unorganized workers that experience little mobility toward decent jobs that are typical of the formal corporate sector.[1] Decent work, as outlined by the United Nations International Labour Organization (ILO), calls for access to quality jobs that incorporate dignity,

[1] I acknowledge that the "India" narrative misses out on the substantial differences in economic performance, and thus the nature of employment, at the state and regional levels. However, we are stuck with the nation state as a unit of analysis and most data is collected at the national lever. Furthermore, even with state level differences, the narrative of the persistence of the informal sector is unlikely to be significantly altered.

equality, fair incomes, safe working conditions, rights that protect workers from exploitation, inclusivity, and sustainability of jobs (ILO 2025).

In this book, I use the terms informal and unorganized labor or sectors interchangeably. Informal workers include those employed in the informal sector and those workers in the formal sector who do not receive any employment and social security benefits. Informal or unorganized work in India includes casual work and self-employment, along with short-term, poorly paid, insecure jobs (see Government of India, National Commission on Enterprises in the Unorganised Sector 2007). Typically, enterprises with fewer than ten workers are defined as part of the unorganized sector, but unorganized or informal workers can be found in both informal and formal sectors; however, they have no legal right to social security benefits (Government of India, National Commission for Enterprises in the Unorganised Sector (NCEUS) 2009: 134). Further, unorganized enterprises have low capital intensity and labor productivity, and often use family labor, "concealed as self-employment under different forms of putting out systems" (Government of India, National Commission for Enterprises in the Unorganised Sector 2009: 357).

However, not all informal labor in the unorganized sector is poorly paid. There are different levels of workers within the informal sector (see Sen 2025).[2] While the distinction between the formal and the informal sectors is legally defined, in actual practice, the dividing line between them can be blurry, with various degrees of interdependence between the two sectors. However, all said and done, most of India's jobs are in the informal sector. In a surplus labor context, the market-clearing wages are low for informal workers. Their exclusion from any formal, legal, or regulatory protective schemes means these jobs are not highly sought after. In practice, however, surplus labor in the economy compels severe competition. The place of informal labor in capitalist economic development can be optimistically viewed as the best possible market outcome or condemned as a failure of (Indian) capitalism to resolve the surplus labor problem. The informal labor market can be viewed as a permanent feature of contemporary capitalism in which both formal and informal, modern and archaic production technologies and institutions coexist.

Job scarcity is not an Indian problem per se, although the circumstances influencing it are quite unique. Young job seekers everywhere are increasingly frustrated with the limited options available to them. Automation and

[2] The literature on India's informal labor is vast, the discussions and debates varied, and much of the analysis are derived from data collected from government surveys. See Azim Premji University (2023, 2018) and Chapter 6 for some elaboration.

artificial intelligence (AI) have become real threats. But the Indian story is manifold and far worse. The absence of social protections in a market where the competition for jobs is mindboggling is an open invitation to mass despair. While it is true that India's workforce is larger than most, it also has the youngest workforce, which is brimming with individual aspirations. But the hard reality does not match up with such aspirations and neither government efforts nor private business strategies are able to narrow the deep divide between the formal and informal labor markets. In India, only 10% of the workers are employed in formal "regular" decent jobs, while the 90% are bound to precarious, informal jobs with little social protection. Resolving this twenty-first-century economic and social fissure has flummoxed even policymakers and experts because the problem, as we will see, is structural and not amenable to simple interventions.

In this book, the Indian context provides concrete links between commercial activities undertaken by private businesses and their developmental outcomes. The focus is on Indian business, including foreign business in India. The book is different from most accounts of the Indian employment market. It begins with a survey of a mix of Indian business sectors to understand what they do and how their operations impact economic development, including the types of employment they create and their future potential (Chapters 3–5). In Chapter 6, we confront the larger question of job scarcity and its underlying proximate causes. Putting the two parts together, that is, the set of chapters that analyze individual business sectors and the bigger narrative of labor markets in India, allows us to appreciate the coexistence of old, successful, big, and domestic; small and new; emerging, international, and critical; and vulnerable and precarious business sectors that lie at the heart of the Indian economy. The jobs they create are also varied, with few formal ones compared to the vast informal work found in the economy. The survey of business sectors undertaken in this book anticipates that the overall contribution of these sectors to economic development thus far and into the near future is positive, especially when it comes to economic growth. However, it also shows that the mix of jobs, when put together along with the agricultural sector, points to a depressing labor market.

I have not attempted to disaggregate business into domestic and foreign actors in this analysis, making the assumption that domestic businesses greatly outnumber foreign ones by a long shot, and the latter, like their domestic counterparts, are also expected to have more or less similar developmental outcomes. For example, foreign companies concentrated in particular sectors, such as automobile production and information technology (IT), just like their domestic counterparts, have contributed to employment, technology transfer, supplier industries, and export markets (D'Costa 2005, 2025a). However, in the absence of certain mitigating factors that regulate the behavior of multinational corporations, specific sectors can be dominated by foreign enterprises; if that has negative repercussions for the economy, a case can be built to regulate foreign enterprises. The erstwhile complex accounting of the impact of transnational corporations (TNCs) through inflows and outflows of resources in the form of net retained value (Jenkins 1987) has been abandoned because of the deliberate and desirable internationalization of economies by business and governments, leading to complex supply chains created across the world.

However, as local industries are hollowed out and unemployment and underemployment rise, governments may be prompted to regulate TNC behavior through tariffs and other policy instruments. The ownership question centers around whether TNCs displace (substitute) domestic firms or complement them. Powerful foreign firms could merge with domestic firms, but this is quite consistent with the adage: "the big fish eat the small fish"; or, in Marx's view, the centralization (mergers and acquisitions) and concentration (internal growth) of firms. If these businesses continue to employ people and resources and do all the things that benefit economic development, it does not matter, as Deng Xiaoping's metaphor suggested, if the cat is black or white as long as it catches mice (in Speake 2015). China attracted foreign investments and know-how in exchange for access to its large and growing domestic market. Besides, capital is by definition global, and its mobility is determined by the most attractive economic and political conditions for its expansion. This logic suggests that mature Indian capitalists could also invest elsewhere, as they have done, should profitability or other commercial goals, such as access to technology and markets, be better outside of India (see Nayyar 2008). But if local businesses are outcompeted by imports and become dependent on them, there could be negative repercussions on the economy and employment.

Any business activity is likely to contribute to jobs and income, the two critical outcomes of economic development.[3] The ultimate litmus test of development is the rising average material standard of living and social well-being, outcomes that are significantly dependent on how large and fast a dent is made to reduce India's massive labor surplus through growing employment in diverse economic activities. Here, surplus labor is used to indicate that due to the massive population, there are a lot of people/workers in the country who cannot find adequate work or opportunities where they are adequately

[3] We only consider those activities that are socially sanctioned and legally permissible.

compensated for their work. At the same time, surplus is also taken to mean that the economy is unable to create good jobs for various reasons, consequently leaving more people either looking for work or underemployed, meaning they could be working more and earning more.

Surplus labor refers to "excess" workers relative to jobs, resulting from the systemic inability to create lots of jobs. It would be difficult to put a precise number to this surplus. But if we consider the number of jobs estimated to be needed to absorb the *new* entrants to the workforce, we have some idea of the magnitude involved. One meticulous estimate in 2015 shows that at least 16 million *new* jobs must be created each year for the next fifteen years to absorb just the *new* workers entering the labor force and exhaust the labor surplus (Ghose 2016: 83–87).[4] That is an order of 240 million jobs needed over a fifteen-year period. This estimate is likely to be higher today, given that the workforce has increased and the backlog of people seeking work is assumed to have risen as well. The workforce for 2021–2022 stands at 493 million, with over one billion people of working age, and 35 million estimated to be unemployed (Table 1.1).

The low unemployment rate relative to the total number of workers—about 7.5%—is largely due to the fact that poor people cannot afford to be unemployed. This suggests, and as Chapter 6 will illustrate, that there are many

Table 1.1 Recent Key Labor Market Indicators (in millions) and Participation Rates (%, in parenthesis)

Indicator	2017–2018	2018–2019	2019–2020	2020–2021	2021–2022
Working-age population	968	985	1000	1022	1021
Labor force	468 (48.4)	478 (48.5)	512 (51.2)	525 (51.4)	528 (51.7)
Workforce	427 (44.1)	436 (44.3)	467 (46.7)	486 (47.5)	493 (48.3)
Unemployed	41 (8.7)	42 (8.7)	45 (8.8)	39 (7.5)	35 (6.6)
Out of labor force*	500 (51.6)	508 (51.5)	488 (48.8)	489 (47.9)	493 (48.3)

Notes: * mostly women at home, older children in school/college, the elderly, and discouraged workers. Labor force includes everyone aged sixteen and over who is employed or actively looking for work, whereas the workforce includes only those who are currently employed.

Source: Periodic Labour Force Survey (PLFS), various rounds and others in Azim Premji University (2023: 46)

[4] For assumptions behind this estimate, which is based on the employment data available from 1999–2000 to 2011–2012, see Ghose 2016). This figure does not include the unemployed or underemployed.

workers who toil in the low-wage, precarious informal sector as a desperate coping mechanism. Not seen in the table is also a massive decline in female labor participation, a phenomenon that has multiple explanations (see Azim Premji University 2023: 30–31, Deshpande 2023). This is a reversal of the progress made with female participation in the labor force until recently.[5]

There are different policy options for tackling this development challenge, but they are not the subject of this book, although some references to policy directions are unavoidable (see especially Chapter 7 for a discussion). Instead, this book examines Indian businesses through a sectoral lens to see the type and volume of employment generated by these sectors and assesses the broader developmental impact. A sector consists of an "industry" of firms producing similar goods and services. For example, the automotive manufacturing sector includes companies that produce both components as well as companies that assemble vehicles, while the IT sector includes all businesses that produce services using digital technologies and technology professionals.[6] The extent to which the state is able to work with business to accomplish employment and economic diversification and not be politically beholden to big business is also part of the development discussion (see Chapter 6).

The rest of the chapter is divided into two parts. Section 2 discusses the importance of job creation in India and offers some reasons why the process of economic development as experienced in the previous century may be difficult to match in the twenty-first century. Section 3 provides chapter descriptions for the rest of the book.

1.2 Tackling Surplus Labor for Development

The biggest challenge for the government, and by extension business if they are to play a constructive role in development, is to figure out how to employ millions of people looking for decent or good jobs. In low-income countries such as India, and consistent with ILO's guidelines, good jobs are those that

[5] A few of the possible reasons for this regression are the availability of few jobs (with women being secondary in a patriarchal society), rising incomes of the household (which may lead women to withdraw from the labor market as caste (*jati*) status would dictate), and increased enrolment in education.

[6] This approach is less precise than using the industrial classification system, which is a fine-grained categorization of all output in the economy. I use this approach since the objective of this book is to provide a quick qualitative assessment of employment in selected business sectors at the aggregate level and draw some implications for surplus labor. The Ministry of Statistics and Programme of Implementation of the Government of India lists the economic activities at the five-digit level, https://mospi.gov.in/classification/national-industrial-classification/alphabetic-index-5digit. See also Annual Survey of Industries (ASI) Reports, https://mospi.gov.in/download-reports?main_cat=Nzg1&cat=All&sub_category=All. However, informal activities that could fall under the official classification scheme may not be adequately reflected in these statistics.

offer an income above subsistence level and social protection against unemployment to avoid precarity (Azim Premji University 2018: 92). Surplus labor can be conceptualized as the gap between the large stock of workers plus its incremental increase through population growth and the number of actual jobs the economy can create to employ those looking for work. As a rule of thumb, the smaller the surplus labor becomes, the better it is for workers and the economy as a whole, up to a point, as relative shortages of workers bid up the price of labor through higher wages and incomes. Both contribute to a higher material standard of living and relative freedom from the everyday struggles, such as access to adequate food and nutrition, basic healthcare, children's schooling, running water, uninterrupted power supply, and so on.

Employment creation on a sustained basis in a labor surplus economy begins to tighten labor markets and puts upward pressure on wages.[7] As workers become relatively scarce, businesses, to maintain their profitability, are expected to diversify to more capital- and skill-intensive production, adopt innovations, and attain economies of scale (producing more output with the same equipment and therefore reducing the per unit cost). With this virtuous cycle of rising wages through employment, surplus labor is reduced, which by logical extension should contribute to depleting, if not exhausting, surplus labor. In theory, with some empirical evidence, economic development thus entails the quantitative and qualitative expansion of output. Depletion occurs when employment of more and more workers shifts away from unskilled to skilled and highly trained professionals that match the needs of ongoing investments, new technologies, and new markets (domestic and foreign). In this evolving development process, sustained value addition is the name of the game by which surplus labor could become a thing of the past.

Of course, there is nothing mechanical about this process. In fact, this is an abstracted narrative from the experiences of "successful" countries ranging from early (Western Europe, North America, and later Japan) to more recent late industrializers (East and Southeast Asia, and later China), who are endowed with vastly different institutional settings, experiencing change at different time periods. The oft-repeated mantra that India should not have pursued heavy industrialization of the 1950s as it violated its comparative advantage (World Bank speak) is correct only in hindsight. That it could have followed the Japanese and East Asian approaches of labor-intensive industrialization is a non-starter since the East Asian "miracle" had not occurred in

[7] We omit the possible macroeconomic effects of inflation and monetary policy responses under this wage-cost scenario. The assumption remains that there are more people looking for work than openings available (an inexhaustible reservoir of labor), hence, inflationary pressures, while inevitable under jobs growth and economic expansion, are expected to be either slight or politically manageable.

the 1950s.[8] Japan began its economic modernization after the Meiji Restoration of 1868, when India was a British colony, and Japan later colonized parts of China (Manchuria), the Korean Peninsula, and Taiwan. It could extract resources (rice at low costs) to keep Japanese industrial wages low to support its industrialization drive. The East Asian countries were ethnically homogeneous with powerful (soft and hard) authoritarian states that were buttressed by the United States during the Cold War. Land reforms to increase agricultural productivity were part of their industrial drive, an option that was tried piecemeal in India but was mostly blocked by the local landlord classes.

Notwithstanding the desire and policy efforts of governments to transform their economies, it is unlikely that India and other developing countries of today could follow this "neat and clean" development trajectory. This is due to timing, let us call it "lateness." This means that other countries have already industrialized and gone through some of the processes behind the quantitative and qualitative expansion of output, leading to material, technological, and institutional gaps between the forerunners and late developers. In addition, a country's institutional legacies and their subsequent evolution in late industrializers may facilitate or hinder economic change. Business strategies and far-sighted policy interventions are helpful but not enough to overcome the structural barriers of lateness and institutional hangover. Timing of intervention, global economic conditions, crisis, and serendipity all have their influences as well in a path-dependent way.

The relationship between business and economic development needs to be contextualized in the process of late industrialization. Economic development results from the interactions between private commercial pursuits, state mediation, and societal expectations of better jobs and an improved standard of living. Late industrialization suggests that the process of independent modern economic development in India is relatively recent compared to the United Kingdom, Western Europe, and later the United States, and Japan. Lateness also suggests that the political autonomy or national sovereignty to pursue an independent policy for economic change has been both facilitated and constrained by the structural presence of more advanced economies and, more recently, and pertinently, by contemporary China. To take an example, foreign technologies could be imported from advanced economies

[8] A priori, it is hard to know where a country's comparative advantage lies. Generally, such advantages are revealed through exports. As a former colony, India at that point decidedly went against engaging wholesale with the world economy. Dominant development ideas then in vogue relied on Keynesian fiscal spending and "big push" industrialization. The industrial experience of the former Soviet Union also had an impact on India's development aspirations. A couple of decades later South Korea, the paragon of practicing comparative advantage went against the World Bank's advice and established its steel (one of the world's most efficient) and other heavy industries in the 1970s (D'Costa 1999).

and assimilated for local development. However, the competitive pressure from mature businesses in advanced economies could limit the profit space for latecomer firms.

Additionally, lateness also means that the colonial hangovers in terms of institutions and administrative and legal practices can limit the formation of an internally coherent and competent state. New or existing institutions may need to be designed or repurposed since they were originally created for the needs of colonial interests. Such a delayed entry into the modern economic development process suggests many initial teething problems before a well-functioning system of business and state could be established and coordinated toward generating economic development. In other words, pre-capitalist social relations are stubbornly reproduced by and are in conflict with the forces of contemporary capitalism in late industrializing societies.

To put it differently, economic development does not begin with a clean slate, nor does the world stand still. We can make the case that the development trajectory is influenced by the past—history if you will—in a path-dependent way. As Figure 1.1 illustrates, hypothetical positions on a development trajectory, A, B, C, D, and "actual" outcome are all linked, albeit with the past receding more into the background, while new developments or interventions, such as a changed global environment with new competitors, impinge on future outcomes.[9] An early industrializer will face a different set of conditions than a later one. Path-dependent development is similar

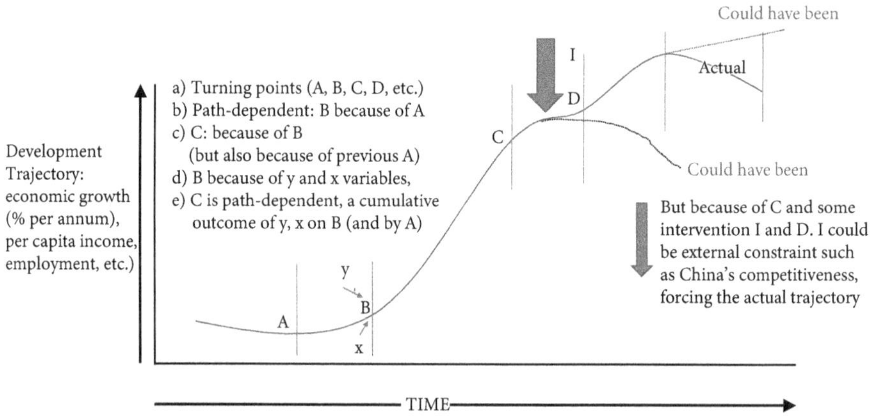

Figure 1.1 Path-dependent Economic Development in a Changing World
Source: Compiled by author

[9] Nayyar (2019: 468, 486) notes that the "world has changed" with reference to the rise of the services sector in the process of structural change that is similar to the analytical category of industry in terms of

to cumulative causation (Myrdal 1957), which could generate a virtuous circle of growth, development, and diversification or a vicious cycle of poverty, low savings, low investment, low growth, and continuing poverty. As it will be shown, India is somewhere between the two possibilities, closer to the vicious cycle when it comes to the jobs dilemma, meaning not enough jobs are created, even as it has made considerable progress in economic growth and diversification. Chapter 6 shows that India's path-dependent development is determined by the evolution of endogenous institutions and exogenous factors imposed by lateness, leading structurally to a development stalemate that limits job creation.

In practice, India and Indian businesses must continue to negotiate past economic legacies, both colonial and post-colonial, while at the same time, as the past becomes more distant, forge new paths that could either be virtuously facilitated or viciously constrained by a changing world at home and abroad. To illustrate changing conditions in simple terms, consider that seventy-five years ago, when India became a Republic, China's economy did not matter to anybody other than its own people. Now, if China had remained unchanged, India's economic and business opportunities today might have been different. Consider also the size and diversity of the Indian business. Some of the enterprises under the Tata Group or Reliance Industries rival their global counterparts. Yet, India is also home to nearly 64 million MSMEs (Tambe 2024), suggesting continuing legacies of pre-industrial cottage enterprises and massive expansion of some businesses. This uneven developmental outcome is theorized and introduced as compressed capitalism in this chapter and further elaborated in Chapter 6 to understand why exhausting labor surplus by way of creating plenty of decent jobs is as good as impossible.

Today, China, as a global manufacturing powerhouse and India's geopolitical rival, is one of India's major trading partners with which it has the largest bilateral trade deficit of about $100 billion. Except in tradable services, Indian businesses are unable to compete with China's manufacturers or, for that matter, even Bangladesh's textiles and garments industries. Indian manufacturing has become dependent on industrial and electronic components from China. It goes without saying that businesses everywhere must compete with China.

Lamenting over "the path not taken" (Mody 2023: 35–37), meaning India should have followed the Japanese experience of labor-intensive industrialization at the time of its independence, while well-intentioned, is a counterfactual that has no merit. The circumstances today are fundamentally different.

growth, employment, exports, and its extensive and intensive forms. He also sees protectionism, technological change, automation, and AI as part of change, all of which have a bearing on late industrializers who missed the manufacturing bus.

This is what lateness comes with, although that does not mean that labor-absorbing production activities, whether in basic manufacturing or services, should be dismissed. The problem is a structural-institutional one, which does not offer easy solutions even if labor is abundant and cheap in India. The geopolitical, historical, sociocultural, and institutional circumstances surrounding Indian and Japanese developmental processes, one as a former colony and the other as a colonizer, respectively, separated by an industrial head start of seventy years by Japan, could not have been more different than what India faces today. Besides, the East Asian industrialization experience had not yet happened in the 1950s, so the lessons of that experience were unavailable at the time of India's independence. Similarly, following the South Korean and Taiwanese experience of the 1960s and 1970s in the second quarter of the twenty-first century appears unrealistic (Rodrik 2016) (see also Chapter 6).[10]

The reasons that India cannot replicate the success of Japan, South Korea, or Taiwan include: a) India's evolving institutions differ from those successful Western and East Asian cases; b) India's massive workforce and the diversity of the challenges confronting it, in the presence of China's industrial might, is an unfolding challenge when it comes to reducing surplus labor of India's magnitude; and c) lateness to development also means contending with new changes at home and in the world economy that could foreclose many of the earlier options that were available for economic development for early industrializers.

This is not an excuse for India not pursuing a labor-intensive type of industrial effort or for not learning the lessons from the East Asian experience and adopting corrective actions. But any historically grounded institutional understanding of the development process must take into account the initial conditions, the path-dependent nature of economic change, and the political economy of institutional inertia. Lateness offers the advantage of knowledge diffusion of best practices and leapfrogging in select technologies and organizational practices. It also imposes new constraints on smaller businesses in labor surplus economies, resulting from the rise of big business and

[10] On this point, I touch upon the significance of capital-intensive industrialization in India (see Chapter 6). Celso Furtado (1963, 1964, 1976), a brilliant structural economist from Brazil, had already noted in the 1950s and 1960s that developing countries are likely to get locked into capital-intensive industrialization without addressing the problems of surplus labor in the countryside (pre-capitalist) and economic dualism. Industrialization in many countries has been an elite, middle class project under the rhetoric of national development that catered to a narrow consumer base. Systemic inequality suppresses aggregate demand and limits scale economies in small markets. This according to Mazumdar (2025) and Nagaraj (2025) is the current Indian stalemate. Chapter 6 shows, these challenges that were anticipated in Latin America more than half a century ago, continue to plague India today. How to address them in a world where industrial production and competition has changed dramatically is the twenty-first-century question.

big tech firms at home and abroad. In a general sense, this lateness offers both opportunities and barriers to the development process. For example, India does not need to reinvent the wheel. It has moved very swiftly on a massive scale from landlines to mobile phones, today estimated at 1.15 billion subscribers (Government of India, Ministry of Communications 2024). Similarly, globally oriented Indian businesses, to maintain their international competitiveness, are compelled to adopt innovations, automate, and rely on modern methods of lean production systems, which have dampening effects on jobs.

Lateness has also introduced sharper business, economic, and labor divides and a polarized distribution of wealth and income in the world economy. To offer one example, in mid-2025, Nvidia—an American company that produces high-end semiconductor chips and computers for AI, co-founded by Taiwan-born Jen-Hsun Hwang—had a market capitalization of $4.102 trillion. To put it in perspective, India's nominal GDP for 2025 was estimated at $4.19 trillion (International Monetary Fund (IMF) 2025). This illustrates that the size of firms and their technological clout are immense enough to possibly influence public policy. Witness the big tech CEOs hobnobbing with the US administration. India likewise has big companies, such as the Tatas, Ambanis, Birlas, and L&T, albeit it does not boast cutting-edge innovation-driven firms such as Nvidia, Google, Apple, and Microsoft in the United States. The point is that technologies under proprietary knowledge have become highly specialized, monopolized, and expensive. They also tend to be labor-displacing in many manufacturing activities. Deploying them in the midst of heightened international competition from Asian economies could be strategic for access to global markets, but they could also seriously dampen local employment growth for India.

Therefore, the generalized process of economic development experienced in the past cannot be expected to be replicated in India today. A movement of labor from agriculture to industry to absorb surplus labor of India's magnitude has become increasingly unviable because the typical avenues to replace rural jobs (such as industrial development) are closed off; meanwhile, the informal services sector has become a de facto sink for low-wage and self-employed, insecure workers. India's economic transformation, beginning in the 1990s, has already deviated from the traditional route. It has become a service-oriented economy with low per capita income without having experienced industrial maturity (Nayyar 2019).[11] The middle-income trap (Griffith 2011) or premature deindustrialization (Rodrik 2016), two

[11] Per capita incomes in 2024, in current dollars, in China and India were $13,303 and $2697, respectively (World Bank 2025a). https://data.worldbank.org/indicator/NY.GDP.PCAP.CD, accessed September 29, 2025.

interrelated empirically grounded concepts, suggest that countries across the developing world stop growing at low levels of per capita income due to globalization, declining competitiveness, rising costs, and innovation challenges. These difficulties could be linked to policy or governance issues (Lewin, Kenney, and Murmann 2016). It also suggests that lateness introduces its own handicaps, thereby limiting replication of the earlier process of development. Putting it more colloquially, it is easier to pick low-hanging fruit now than those higher up on the tree later.

Today, based on the actual developments in India, it is not absolutely clear whether to go the traditional way by fostering industry or ride the wave of opportunities in tradable and other high-value services. No doubt both will be needed, but in what proportion and in what types of sectors is difficult to answer. Only very small countries have survived on services. Tourism and financial services in tax-free havens could potentially drive an economy based on services. However, based on global experience, there is a general consensus that without industry, a country cannot be prosperous. But India has already missed the manufacturing bus. Late developers, such as India, by default could get pushed into mostly low- but some high-value tradable services that have low entry barriers. The problem is that there is little certainty about the prospects of which sectors to focus on since markets, technologies, the global economy, and geopolitics are quite unpredictable.

Moreover, the persistence of low-wage, precarious work in agriculture, manufacturing, *and* services is evident from the size of the unorganized sector (90% of workers) (Sharma and Mehta 2024: 49). This suggests that neither manufacturing nor services can absorb a near-infinite supply of workers from the countryside.[12] The vast majority of Indian businesses and households that continue to hire and offer labor services belong to the informal sector. The resulting dystopian condition of workers and employment prospects, as described by Mody (2023), is on the mark. The dire situation is not only because of the lack of accountability, corruption, and callousness on the part of the political and business establishments to seriously address the country's employment crisis, but it is also a product of structural inheritance, which both the government and business must contend with.[13]

Most business/commercial entities fall under MSMEs that absorb the bulk of informal workers. Medium-, small-, and micro-sized enterprises (MSMEs) rely on outdated technologies and small-scale production, which limit output

[12] This outcome is also part of "compressed" capitalism, briefly introduced below and elaborated in Chapter 6.

[13] Chapter 6 sketches out an integrated understanding of the complexities of the challenges in creating jobs today. See also Azim Premji University (2023: 27).

expansion, diversification, and the hiring of skilled workers. Informal workers can be found in both the informal (unorganized) and formal (organized) sectors. Informal workers do not have access to employment and social security benefits and thus do not constitute regular jobs. Workers and owners in this sector include small-scale operators and petty capitalists engaged in food processing, garments, shoes, and household goods, and self-employed "footloose" vendors (no fixed place for conducting business), as well as contract and casual wage workers.[14] A sizeable number of informal workers survive at the subsistence level and are mostly underemployed. To this must be added the large number of people dispossessed of their rural lands and displaced from the countryside and are excluded from the formal orbit of modern economic development. They represent a "dark space" that is a product of but external to the circuits of capital (Sanyal 2007: 249, also Abraham and Kesar 2025: 2).

Conversely, "regular" jobs are found in the organized (formal sector). They are "regular" jobs and come with one or more benefits such as social security, pension, or healthcare. The best type of a good job in the Indian context is when regular employment comes with benefits and is bound by a written contract (Azim Premji University 2018: 96). These jobs can be found mostly in the modern, corporate sector. These enterprises tend to be more capital-intensive in their production. However, with deregulation and the concomitant rise of business power, there is growing pressure on labor and enterprises to be flexible to the demands of the market (see Chakraborty, Chowdhury, Banerjee, and Mahmood 2019, and Chapter 6 on labor rigidity). Consequently, with business restructuring, privatization, and retrenchment of workers, formal labor in the organized sector is also being informalized as workers are increasingly hired in contract, temporary, and insecure (informal sector) positions (Azim Premji University 2023: 63).[15]

The cumulative process of technological and organizational leapfrogging by big business using formal workers and the coexistence of low-productivity MSMEs reliant on the vast informal labor market is what I call "compressed capitalism" (D'Costa 2014a, 2014b, 2016a).

[14] Many of these self-employed sellers are often referred to as petty commodity producers who have a small scale of production, do not generally hire wage workers and instead rely on family labor.

[15] Contract labor is different from a "worker having a contract." The former refers to an enterprise that supplies workers under contract to another enterprise, typically for a fixed duration, after which the terms may be renewed or renegotiated for a new contract cycle. Here the contract is between the supplier and buyer firm and the supplier firm pays the wages to the workers. These contract workers generally do not have a written contract, their wages are likely to be lower than those who perform similar tasks with a formal contract, they do not have any social protection (although the contractor could offer some benefits), they are temporary, and precarious. A good or formal job would entail a formal contract between the worker and the employer and is bound by all regulatory and labor laws.

The simultaneity of the presence of the advanced and the archaic employment markets and sectors is not about technologies alone; they also encompass institutions and social norms, all of which vie to negotiate between India's pre-capitalist past and its ongoing quest for dynamic capitalism. Businesses are not immune to these contests. They pursue their commercial interests where workers are poorly trained, government regulations are cumbersome, and the power of business is often unchecked, simply due to their social and economic position in a hierarchy- and status-conscious society.[16]

Japan and Korea, in the second half of the twentieth century, have worked through their particular mix of old and new institutions through rapid industrialization and agricultural development. Labor was absorbed productively, and formalization of workers went hand in hand with the flexibility to hire and fire workers. A particular type of group ethos (ethnic-national), accompanied by a favorable external environment, allowed rapid industrialization that ultimately exhausted their surplus labor. The internal organization of top-down states in homogeneous societies in East Asia, including China, is different from the state established in 1947 in pluralistic, independent India. The structural transformation in East Asia was possible through rapid, export-driven, labor-absorbing industrialization with increasing agricultural productivity to release rural workers for urban industry. The increase in rural incomes led to higher demand for industrial products, which fostered the classic agriculture-industry virtuous development nexus (Lewis 1954, Kaldor 1967).[17] In the twenty-first century, with open economies, it is much harder to establish such virtuous linkages between agriculture and industry in large, populous countries.

In India, attaining the Lewisian turn, meaning exhausting the surplus labor, has now become an impossibility since industrialization, even its extensive form, has already run out of steam, let alone the intensive kind. Extensive refers to the linear expansion of low-value economic activities, while intensive industrialization refers to higher-value economic production entailing investments in technology and capital equipment. Labor productivity tends to be higher in the latter than in the former. As was noted earlier, the competition from China in a global setting forecloses many of the manufacturing avenues that India could have taken with its competitive wage rates. What is becoming clear is that Indian capitalism has become a "hybrid" (Saez 2014), in contrast to "advanced" or "mature" capitalism, due to limited diversification in the

[16] In Chapter 6 the framework of compressed capitalism is deployed to structurally analyze the political economy of job creation.

[17] The debates surrounding the agriculture-industry relationship for economic development can be found in Bhattacharyya, Abraham, and D'Costa (2013).

types and size of business and persistent and polarized labor markets. High growth rates are no longer a guarantee that a large and growing workforce can be absorbed through economic growth.[18] And yet, India (and even China), despite their many economic and technological advancements, are unable to create plenty of regular jobs (Sharma and Mehta 2024, D'Costa 2014a).

What then have Indian businesses been doing to shape development? The conundrum is that compressed capitalism introduces new business elements such as advanced production and organizational innovations well before the old problems of outdated education systems, educated surplus labor, inadequate infrastructure, and the unethical and counterproductive social hierarchies disappear. In the absence of a dynamic agriculture industry interface, with rising agricultural productivity and industrial expansion, the migration of rural workers for urban jobs is slow. There are not enough decent manufacturing or services jobs in urban areas, compelling many to hold onto low-productivity agricultural and rural work as a backup. This was most visible during the COVID-19 pandemic in 2020–2021, when tens of millions of urban migrant workers returned to their villages under severe physical and emotional duress. What is incontrovertible is that despite many areas of progress, India's late-development trajectory has been stymied by the persistence of labor surplus, informal labor markets, and worsening inequality. It is unable to structurally break free from the consequences of compressed capitalism.

1.3 Chapter Descriptions

Chapter 2 introduces a general framework to discuss the key relationship between business and economic development in India. In broad brushstrokes, it works with four interrelated questions that are designed to bring out the dynamic relationship between business and economic development. They revolve around a) what it is that businesses do, b) how they might contribute to economic development directly, c) how they might contribute indirectly through the mediating role of the state or government (and its many arms), and d) what some of the tangible results of economic

[18] Hybridity suggests that there is a "purer" form of capitalism. But there is only one unified global economic system that is spatially and temporally heterogeneous at the national and local levels. The institutional legacies are part and parcel of really existing, as is, capitalism and not some distorted version of some ideal system. The coexistence of modern competitive business with suppliers from the low productivity informal sector is not an anomaly but a result of the necessary interdependence and survivability of people under compressed capitalism. Breaking free from some of these legacies in a large and diverse India is difficult due to the vast labor pool and the cost- and price-sensitive business and market environment that keep reproducing this interdependence.

development could be. The discussion is foregrounded in the Indian context, but the key interpretive arguments are fairly general in nature. It does not dispute that businesses contribute to economic development but asks under what institutional contexts their commercial activities could transform the economy. It assumes that the business of business is not to solve societal problems such as economic development; rather, business–state and state–society interactions collectively determine economic-development outcomes. At a fundamental level, desired economic-development outcomes include production diversification, both in its extensive and intensive forms, with public investments pulling in complementary private investments, especially in an economy where the capitalist classes are hesitant to make large investments with long-gestation periods. How this materialist transformation impacts the quality of life remains key to understanding the relationship between business and development. This framework discussion liberally uses examples from the business world, particularly economic and industrial sectors, to drive home salient points of tangible economic development outcomes such as job creation, output growth, and spillover effects.

In Chapter 3, some of the early leading business sectors are showcased to illustrate how they evolved in the Indian context, especially in terms of their interactions with the government, and to capture in broad brush strokes their contributions to some aspects of economic development. The backdrop to the discussion presented in Chapter 3 is the double movement of ongoing structural shifts in the Indian economy as well as the wider restructuring of the global economy. The latter entails a movement toward a services-based economy and offshoring of manufacturing (and tradable services) activities in an interconnected global economy with a highly dispersed global division of labor. India participates actively in the global IT and software services sectors, but it also has foundational industries—such as steel, automobiles, and pharmaceuticals—that are a mix of public, private, and foreign-owned. These sectors are analyzed in a global context to assess their developmental impact on the Indian economy and society.

There are other business activities that are less conspicuous than these, but quite critical for employment, livelihoods, and export revenues, such as agriculture, textiles—particularly the handloom sector—and diamond polishing. These are discussed in Chapter 4 in terms of labor absorption and possible spillover effects. The discussion underscores the difficulties for late industrializing, labor-surplus countries to transition to a modern, vibrant, and organized economy. The three distinctive sectors—agriculture, handlooms, and diamonds—are all characterized by labor-intensive production, and all are linked to the rural economy in one way or another, with considerable engagement of informal workers. Most of these businesses are family-owned or are owner-operated enterprises that secure low economic returns. Of the three, agriculture is the most important economic activity for the rural poor, but also for the urban economy. Increased incomes and productivity growth, accompanied by expansion in nonagricultural activities in both rural and urban areas, are critical to both the welfare of the rural poor and to long-term economic development.

The handloom sector comprises manual textile weaving by artisans located in both rural and semi-urban areas. It has been vulnerable to factory-based, fashion-conscious, urban markets. Both handlooms and the diamond industry are good examples of rural surplus labor absorption in nonagricultural activity in rural and urban areas. The diamond industry is deeply integrated with the world economy, but it does not have a large economic multiplier, as seen in other manufacturing industries, and therefore, may not be a good staging ground for major economic diversification. In the absence of branded retail products and the limited presence of handloom products in high-income markets, India's handloom and diamond industries are expected to find diversification by moving up the value chain challenging. Domestic demand for gems and jewelry, including diamonds, remains high, but both rely on imported raw materials. Handloom markets at home remain vulnerable to machine-made products for fashion-conscious consumers seeking convenient and cheaper products.

Taking off from the previous discussions of the contributions of older business sectors such as steel, automobiles, IT, the diamond industry, and pharmaceuticals to output, employment, and exports, Chapter 5 summarizes the characteristics and new developments in these sectors and then turns our attention to new types of businesses emerging in India's economy. These include the new frontier of the Indian retail sector, digitalization and the platform economy (DPE), and diversification of energy sources for development. These are analyzed to bring out state and business initiatives as necessary responses to economic development challenges such as employment, productivity, fossil fuel consumption, health, and climate change.

Retail and energy sectors represent a transition process of economic development whereby services and commodity sectors take on new global formats and best industry practices, but they also coexist with older systems. Building on and breaking out from existing business sectors is DPE. The DPE is part of the "new economy" convergence technologies, namely software, the internet, and satellites that enable high-density interconnectivity for digital applications and link customers and sellers or service providers through large online networks by applying Industry 4.0 innovations.[19] Digitalization and the platform economy represent transformative applications of digital technologies in business and societal spheres with new firms, new occupations, restructuring of existing economic activities, increased efficiencies, foreign partnerships, and new wealth. However, the development implications of these activities remain inconclusive at this juncture. While they help lay the foundation for new, related sectors, the question remains of their capacity to generate a large volume of decent employment that is not part of the informal sector.

Chapter 6 takes stock of the role of Indian business by acknowledging its contribution to economic development, but it also notes that the development outcomes are lopsided. The structural legacy of late-industrialization, as discussed under the framework of compressed capitalism, and the dysfunctionality of the business–state relationship generate highly uneven economic development and employment prospects. The economy appears to do well in terms of business growth, but not in terms of growth of quality jobs, as a vast number of workers and would-be job seekers are stuck in precarious, informal jobs. The persistence of the informal sector is the source and outcome of worsening inequality that has other implications for economic development, such as depressed demand. On top of the employment dilemma, Indian business has become heavily dependent on imports for its economic activities, which is reinforcing premature deindustrialization that began more than a decade ago. This chapter offers a more sober assessment and a less sanguine picture of the future of jobs.

Chapter 7 concludes with a quick assessment of key government initiatives aimed at addressing India's manufacturing woes and employment challenges. These policy schemes are yet to show visible results. This is followed by a review of the jobs dilemma by highlighting some of the looming technological and tariff threats confronting India's labor-intensive manufacturing and services sectors, covered in this book. Lastly, the book ends with a quick recap of the employment narrative as seen through late industrialization and the relationship of Indian businesses and their contributions to economic development.

[19] There are other emerging "new" sectors. This is largely the state-led outer space sector in India. For lack of "space," the under-studied, state-dominated space industry is not included in this book. For details of this emerging outer space sector—which has on-earth and outer space commercial implications such as satellite launches and the sale of remote sensing data, including India's place in it—see D'Costa (2025b). The economic development implications are both immediate and long term. Aside from skill development, innovations, and employment of engineers and other technically trained professionals, there are many applications of satellite imagery and global positioning services for consumer, business, government, and defense markets. These are long-term developmental outcomes, including environmental sustainability, monitoring deforestation, predicting weather, preventing flooding, and ultimately getting some grip on climate change with responsive policies to name a few.

2
How Business Contributes to Economic Development

2.1 Introduction

The central objective in this book is to capture the relationship between Indian business and economic development. Analyzing business dynamics in the Indian context is expected to provide concrete links between commercial activities undertaken by private businesses, their interactions with the state, and their joint developmental outcomes. The ultimate litmus test of development is the rising average material standard of living and social well-being. These outcomes are significantly dependent on how large and fast a dent is made in reducing India's massive labor surplus through expanding employment opportunities and rising wages in diverse economic activities.

In this chapter, I develop a simple analytical framework to understand business contribution to economic development. The chapter assumes that the business of business is not to solve societal problems; however, their investment activities could contribute to meaningful employment and other social goals, such as responsible investing in green technologies. For these to occur, business–state and state–society political interactions are expected to collectively lead to economic and social development outcomes (ESDO). Commercial activities undertaken by businesses could be channeled through regulatory guardrails of the state for economic transformation. At a fundamental level, ESDO entails production diversification both in its extensive and intensive forms, which becomes the basis for job creation, output growth, and spillover effects.

The rest of the chapter is divided into five sections. Section 2 briefly reviews two recent approaches that study modern business as a society-embedded institution. The chapter acknowledges that the Indian economy comprises not just large modern firms but also the estimated 64 million medium-, small-, and micro-sized enterprises (MSMEs) and a large household-based agricultural production sector with nearly 50% of the workforce under it. Both MSMEs and the agricultural sector are repositories of precarious informal

Indian Business, Economic Development, and the Jobs Dilemma in the Twenty-first Century. Anthony P. D'Costa, Oxford University Press. © Anthony P. D'Costa (2026). DOI: 10.1093/9780198948407.003.0002

workers representing industry, services, and agriculture. Therefore, the performance of these two types of business enterprises has huge implications for future economic development (see Chapter 4). Hence, a more rudimentary understanding of typical business behavior under capitalism is outlined to capture the general workings of business before getting down to the specifics of Indian business. Section 3 outlines how business activities with the mediation of the state contribute to development, while Section 4, using some real-life examples, illustrates how economic diversification through business activities can lead to economic development. The final section is divided into two parts. The first part looks back on the evolution of Indian business to capture the salient elements of Indian business development since the country's independence in 1947. The second part, using the lens of economic and industrial sectors, looks ahead to the subsequent empirical discussions on the relationship between Indian business and economic development.

2.2 Understanding Business in Society

The idea of modern economic development has been an attractive one. After all, what is there to dislike if development means material prosperity and the freedom from the struggles of everyday existence arising from poverty, malnourishment, ignorance, and servitude? However, translating the idea of economic development into tangible outcomes—such as reduced poverty, access to reliable basic healthcare and education for all, and decent roads to transport crops from agricultural fields to the nearest market—is a challenging activity. The question is what might be the role of business in meeting some of these challenges. And more importantly, as the rest of the book explores, to what extent have different business sectors contributed to the employment challenge for economic and social transformation.

There are different ways to study business activities and their impact on the economy and society. The most convenient way is to aggregate individual businesses under specific "sectors" and capture the salient aspects of their impact on economic development, especially employment. Since reducing labor surplus (or meeting other economic developmental goals) is an enormous macroeconomic challenge, it is impossible that a single individual business or even a business sector will be able to accomplish this herculean task. For example, it is estimated that the Indian IT industry, as a whole, employs about 5 million people (India Brand Equity Foundation: IT and BPM 2025), which is indeed a large and by many global standards an envious number but in the Indian context it is less than 1% of India's 2024 workforce of 608 million (World Bank Group 2025b). Analyzing business sectors allows us to examine, even if incompletely, the kind of economic development contribution they make and why. In addition, how businesses as a group or sector politically engage with government policies and vice versa also aids in our understanding of their role in the wider society.

Two interdisciplinary approaches that could be the starting points for studying business, not necessarily economic development, are the "varieties of capitalism" (VOC) (Hall and Soskice 2001) and the "business systems" (Whitley 1999) approach. Both approaches focus on the coordination of economic activities, but neither of them explicitly treats the contribution of business to the development process. It is either assumed away or not explicitly acknowledged since the focus is to analyze the coordination mechanisms among institutions to regulate a particular "version" of advanced or advancing national capitalism. Discussion of impoverished countries, which incidentally are also part of capitalism, is left out. To their credit, however, these approaches offer a large canvas to position business in the wider economy, polity, and society. In both approaches, the state is an important actor in a matrix of other institutions that constitute the larger capitalist system and "business system." Unfortunately, these are incomplete frameworks, as they are more about modern firms and industry—and their coordinating mechanisms—and not directly about economic development.

The varieties of capitalism (VOC) framework rests on national institutions and their coordination in advanced capitalist countries. They do not engage with the impact of internationalization and the changing global economy on these institutions. Over the years, this approach has expanded to include other less wealthy regions of the world. But imposing a framework and its constituent parts that were formulated using wealthy-country experiences with relatively stable coordination mechanisms is out of place for societies that are still trying to get the development ball rolling. The business systems approach overlaps with the VOC approach by explicitly analyzing stakeholders, their interactions, and the underlying economic organization at the national level. The framework includes eight sub-systems. These are the roles of the state, the financial system, ownership and governance, internal structure of firms, employment relations, education and skills formation, inter-company relations, and social capital (Witt and Redding 2014: 1–8).

Such disaggregation of an economy is no doubt useful for an overview of national institutional structure and the interactions among the sub-systems (Saez 2014). Both frameworks analyze the formal corporate sector as part of capitalism, which is understandable, but if a large part of an economy is informal and noncorporate, how useful will these frameworks be to understand the evolution of late capitalism? The business system framework does not address why business systems are unable to overcome the continuing structural challenges, such as the persistence of a low-productivity agriculture sector, the massive informal sector, and worsening economic and social disparities that are integral to compressed (or late) capitalism.[1] Compressed capitalism, as further elaborated in Chapter 6, offers a historical structural framework to situate late industrializers in a global context without diluting their national characteristics. As the Indian case suggests, these mainstream institutional frameworks do not account for informal household economic activities such as India's vast agricultural sector, which is a source of survival for hundreds of millions of people. The agricultural sector is a deep reservoir of surplus labor that seems to weigh down the economy with precarious employment conditions, low purchasing power, and inequality. What happens to this sector has huge implications for the transformation of agriculture as a harbinger of industrialization and economic development. Historically, in the evolution of capitalism, in the early stages, the supply of rural migrants has met the urban demands for industrial workers. Knowing whether this is the case in India today, even if India is not a clean slate when it comes to industry, needs to be addressed, since under more favorable business conditions, such labor would have the opportunities to migrate to urban areas for better jobs. But as we will see, the challenge for development is unprecedented, with an agricultural sector that stubbornly keeps large numbers of people tied to the land, while industrial expansion seems to have stalled at a low level of average income.

The everyday understanding of business is relatively straightforward. It refers to commercial activity, in which money and profit-making are involved. A business also indicates a corporation or a family enterprise that carries out money-making activities, or, as in the case of Indian agriculture, subsistence living, by organizing production and family labor, and buying and selling goods and services to its various customers. Customers can be individuals, other business enterprises, the government, or society at large. With few exceptions, in the modern capitalist world, the pursuit of profits is driven by individual entrepreneurial or corporate financial interests.

[1] See also Sen (2006). There is another issue that complicates the use of well-defined frameworks. Because India is a large federated political and economic system, different states or regions exhibit different degrees of administrative and competitive capabilities. The regional variation is an important caveat to the national narratives. However, to characterize each region as being a different type of capitalism (Sinha 2005) reduces the heuristic power of understanding contemporary capitalism as a global system with national and regional traits that cannot be assumed to be structurally independent of global capitalism. The China example mentioned earlier with reference to India suggests how the space for Indian business has been restricted even in the domestic market in the context of labor surplus. This is further elaborated in Chapter 6.

Capitalist businesses, by structural necessity, must recoup their investment with some profits. By structural necessity, I mean that owners of capital have no option other than to invest their capital in profitable ventures. No business would ever consciously embrace loss-making ventures or keep its capital under a mattress, unless hoarding for some immediate rainy-day expense or for some unscrupulous reason. Commercial pursuits are also known as capital accumulation, which, when successful, result in more capital and wealth generation than the amount one started the accumulation process with. Borrowed capital is integral to commercial pursuits.

Profits, or an economic surplus that is above and beyond all the expenses incurred in carrying out that business activity, are the primary motivation of business. Growing economic surplus gives rise to an expanding economy, which is a principal characteristic of dynamic capitalism. Marx suggested that there are two principal ways of extracting economic surplus: by making workers work long hours and by using modern technologies. This extraction of economic surplus is a result of exploitation, meaning labor is not compensated for the value it creates, but rather by some market or contractual arrangement, which by definition will have to be less than the value created if a profit is to be made. The higher the exploitation, the greater is the economic surplus, meaning the gap between the value created by the worker and the value paid to the worker for creating that value. Individuals can decide not to be exploited, but that would mean suffering from the indignities of unemployment and poverty.

Household agriculture is heterogeneous in terms of size and the type of labor used. Such households can work for themselves and hire themselves out to other families' agricultural or nonagricultural activities or hire in workers from other families. Both forms of hiring generally involve wage payments. The household production for the market or under contract from another business (or corporate) entity is mostly based on self-exploitation, meaning they are independently self-driven to produce. No one is ordering them to do so. They are their own masters or victims. Not surprisingly, the British economist Joan Robinson averred that under capitalism "...the misery of being exploited by capitalists is nothing compared to the misery of not being exploited at all" (Robinson 1962: 46). Exploitation in its raw, physical, or technical sense indicates that one party is benefiting more than the other. In a labor-surplus economy, businesses can bargain down wages to the point where even with employment, incomes are barely adequate to escape the scourge of poverty. Likewise, agricultural productivity (value of output or physical output per worker) under self-exploitation can be so low that the marketable surplus barely yields a subsistence income.

Profits mean exploitation, but it also means government revenues. Depending on the enforcement capacity of the state or government, some of the profits will be taxed to meet the expenses of running the country, such as the provisioning of public goods and services, including infrastructure, defense, and food distribution to the very poor, just to name a few. These are the very things that economic development, if managed well, is expected to offer to society. Thus, businesses through commercial activities can generate economic surplus by exploiting workers, but also contribute to employment and tax revenues. Of course, state capacity to collect taxes can be influenced by various factors, including but not limited to bureaucratic capacity that rests on well-trained staff, well-designed tax policies to raise revenues for public spending on economic development, and the curtailment of widespread tax evasion and capital flight. High taxes and politically motivated, arbitrary use of the tax authorities to penalize individuals and businesses could encourage tax evasion, illicit business transactions, kickbacks, and other forms of corruption, and discourage investments (D'Costa 2023). More importantly, large businesses with their organized oligopolistic power could lobby the state to reduce corporate and individual income taxes, thereby contributing to the disparity in incomes and wealth and reducing spending for social infrastructure and programs.

2.3 Business, State, and Economic Development

India is a mixed economy. The two central themes in this book are the relationship of business with economic development and the actual results of this relationship in India. To put it differently, it examines in what ways businesses broadly contribute to the material changes in the quality of life, and under what conditions. Answering these questions requires us to identify the various aspects of economic development, on the one hand, and to confirm, on the other, that businesses, through their private pursuit of commercial interests, generate those developmental outcomes. This idea may seem obvious or trivial. However, developmental outcomes are not due to some altruistic design of business—no matter how well-intentioned—but rather are products of its self-serving accumulation strategies that are often mediated by the state and other social institutions. Schematically, Figure 2.1 presents the interconnections between the actors and possible outcomes.

To explore further the dynamic relationship between business and economic development in India, I address four interrelated questions in a broad-brushstrokes fashion. They revolve around a) what businesses do; b) how they

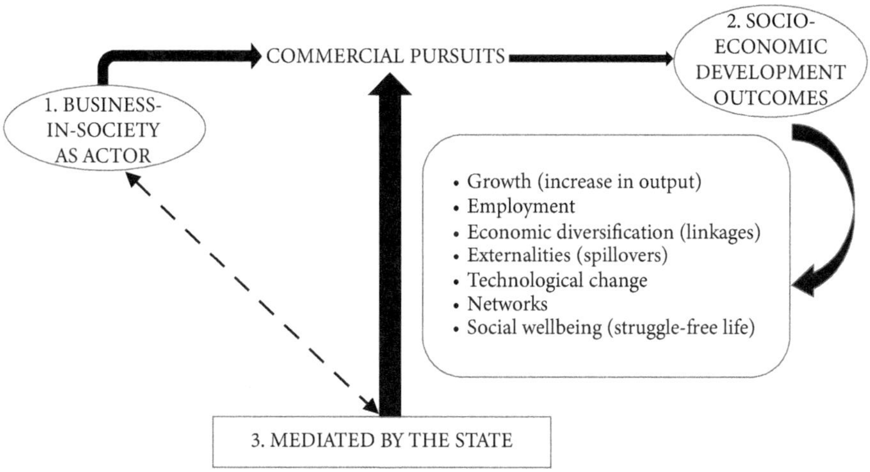

Figure 2.1 Relationship Between Business and Economic Development
Source: Compiled by the author

might contribute to economic development directly; c) how they contribute indirectly through the mediating role of the state or government (not the same thing but used interchangeably) and its many arms; and d) what the tangible results of economic development could be.

If the principal purpose of all business is to maximally generate profits through commercial activities, we can expect that the greater the profits, the greater the economic surplus for the firm or organization, equivalent to an amount over and above all expenses incurred in the commercial activity. This surplus is the extra value generated after subtracting all the input costs in the production process, including wages of workers and a reasonable payoff to the business owner or capitalist for having taken the risk of deploying its capital and coordinating production. Using raw materials, energy, fixed assets such as buildings, machines, and tools, either of their own or belonging to their employer, along with technology or know-how, workers produce a certain economic value during a typical workday. Since we live in societies that are increasingly based on market relations, economic value or price is determined by the market forces of supply and demand, forces that could also be influenced by noneconomic factors such as the role of the government, weather conditions, and warfare.

Labor surplus is a common legacy in developing countries, meaning there are far too many people engaged in low-wage, insecure jobs or looking for better work than what the economy currently offers. Millions of people are looking for work to improve their economic standing because they may be unemployed, underemployed due to labor abundance, stuck in low-income jobs, or misemployed due to the mismatch between skills and job requirements demanded by the prevailing structure of the economy. In countries such as India, where a large share of the population is engaged in small-scale farming or running a tiny family business in the "unorganized" sector and employing mostly "informal" workers, it is not easy to account for the economic surplus since family labor working on the family farm or owner-operated enterprise may not be paid wages.[2] In an "unorganized" household agriculture or nonagricultural enterprise that relies on family labor, it makes little sense to pay individual family members since the economic unit is the family. Members pool their earnings for their common survival. The surplus in this case would be the amount of output (food grains, for example) or a stream of revenues accrued over a day, several days, or months that could be spent for family subsistence and meeting debt obligations. If they worked elsewhere part of the time, they would earn wages that are likely to be low for the simple reason that there is an abundance of unskilled workers. The growth in the workforce is assumed to remain positive and exceeds the number of new jobs available, thereby always leaving an employment deficit.

In earlier eras, small European countries could expel their surplus labor, leading to large-scale international migration of the poor. Today, for labor surplus economies, this is not politically possible or practical. Witness the ferocious overall sentiment against allowing migrants to enter with anti-migrant raids in the United States, the United Kingdom, and other wealthy countries in the twenty-first century. Hence, economic development at a minimum needs to make a dent in the labor surplus by creating jobs, especially decent jobs as defined by the UN International Labor Organization (ILO 2025). This also means that businesses, while pursuing their commercial interests, must also meet the litmus test of employment creation as part of their contribution to economic development. Otherwise, high growth cornered by the wealthy to become wealthier flies in the face of societal development expectations.

Economic surplus is generated through work or by the number of hours worked. Work may vary from a few hours to the official eight hours (or more with overtime pay), enforced or mediated typically in a formal corporate setting. Economic surplus is also created by unregistered businesses

[2] The government of India defines the unorganized (or informal) sector, including agriculture, as consisting "... of all unincorporated private enterprises owned by individuals or households engaged in the sale and production of goods and services operated on a proprietary or partnership basis and with less than ten total workers" (Government of India, National Commission on Enterprises in the Unorganised Sector 2007: 15).

in sectors that are unregulated with little state oversight. Regulation of business is dependent on what the business is and whether it is registered or not. Household agriculture is a business, but it is not registered and therefore not subject to government regulations such as state-mandated codes for hiring and other labor practices. Unregistered businesses are generally part of the vast, unregulated informal sector, producing low-value economic output. This is the sector that generates the most employment, but it tends to be low-paid, insecure, precarious, and outside the bounds of formal labor regulation.

In our discussion of business activities, we are omitting but not denying the economic significance of illegal and criminally culpable economic activities such as the use of slave labor, the narcotics trade, money laundering, and prostitution. These are part of an underground "black" market, tied to the legal formal and informal markets through various economic transactions such as purchases, sales, consumption, and loans. For example, in India, a female worker employed in a stone quarry breaking rocks with a simple hammer may work informally for a variable number of hours to produce low-value stone chips. Wages paid are likely to be what the employer gets away with, which is possibly below the minimum rate since state enforcement could be weak or the power of such employers unusually strong in quarrying regions. What is far worse is that this worker could be bonded, meaning working to pay off a family debt to the employer, even if she herself did not incur this debt.

An automobile factory worker, on the other hand, is expected to work in eight-hour shifts, earning a regular monthly salary, plus some non-salary monetary or nonmonetary benefits. The market value produced by an automobile worker is likely to be high compared to stone breaking, mainly because of the larger investment needed in complex machinery and technologies, and specific skills needed for automobile manufacturing. But in either activity, at the end of the day, the cost of production, after all expenses have been accounted for, is generally expected to be less than the economic value produced. It is under this condition: Profits or economic surplus = Market value – Cost of production.

Surplus can be increased by a combination of long hours of work (by men, women, and children) and by the application of technologies in production. Long hours mean beyond the typical eight hours a day of work or a combination of long hours with technologies that increase the efficiency of producing more output per unit of time. Now, if the farmer and her family do not consume all the crops over the year and instead sell the surplus in the market, the revenues earned could be reinvested in farming and purchasing agricultural implements, nonagricultural goods, and services. This is the virtuous cycle. However, as we will see in Chapter 4, subsistence farmers have become more reliant on markets for both sales and purchases. Low output and non-remunerative prices for agricultural products have transformed many small farmers into net buyers of grain from the market. Consequently, they remain vulnerable to price movements and thus their ability to fend for themselves in rural or urban labor markets. They become indebted, sometimes dispossessed of their land, and ultimately, some may become destitute under such dire conditions. This is the vicious cycle.

Similarly, a corporation could set aside its profits (retained earnings) and reinvest them along with some borrowed capital to initiate a new cycle of commercial ventures for business growth and profits. This is the typical cycle of capital accumulation. The worst-case scenario is when the business fails, in which case there are regulatory processes to govern the exit of firms without massive disruption, which is not the case for household agriculture or small informal enterprises. In any case, successful investment activities are likely to expand the economic surplus (marketable) in the agricultural as well as nonagricultural sectors and benefit individual farmers, the corporation (including family members, business partners, and shareholders), and society through the earnings and spending in the economic system.

Economic development will result, provided the surplus is productively reinvested to create good, sustainable jobs through diversification and not consumed or frittered away by unproductive "vanity" projects. Note the conditional statement that has *provided* in it. The growth in economic surplus is brought about by the combination of the number of hours worked, referred to as absolute surplus, and technologies and other support services used, referred to as relative surplus. Both ultimately drive the growth of economic surplus and thus economic development. It also means diversifying economic activities away from backbreaking manual work, as in stone quarries, by relying on more mechanized machinery, and paying a more just wage that allows adequate consumption of basic goods and services. This mandates a shift away from agriculture to manufacturing to create better-paying jobs, adopting new technologies to enhance efficiency and diversification into novel markets, and offering more value-added goods and services.

It is evident that the initial investment for surplus generation in one activity can lead to other related profit-oriented investments in other sectors through spillover effects, which could multiply to generate more investments, jobs, and innovations. For example, the building of a port by the government or a private party could encourage necessary imports such as modern cranes and machinery for efficient manufacturing at home and exporting abroad, and encourage marine and port-related services. This chain of events thereby raises the overall level of economic activity and surplus creation. However, it is not so clear-cut that a shift from manufacturing to services in itself guarantees higher value economic output since there are many low-value services in labor-abundant economies. Economic development would depend on both the quality and value of output, but crucially also on the volume of jobs created that would begin to exhaust surplus labor and progressively raise the material quality of life for the average citizen.

These desirable outcomes of profit-making business activities constitute the nuts and bolts of economic development. The ongoing process of surplus creation is called capital accumulation. The higher the rate of capital accumulation, the faster the pace of business expansion and its effects on economic development. However, if the share of economic surplus cumulatively accrues more to owners of business (or capital) relative to workers in each cycle of production, we can expect worsening income distribution over time even with economic development. In other words, is market exchange based on the profit motive adequate to generate economic development? Business-driven economic development does not address how the economic surplus will be distributed other than through the arms-length trickle-down dynamics. It cannot be assumed away since the structural imperative of maximizing profits goes against the grain of redistribution. In principle, it is the state (or government) that is responsible for the welfare of its citizens by implementing distributive measures and thus, at least in theory, is interested in economic development for both political accountability and legitimacy. Progressive taxes on the wealthy and transfer payments, in addition to social support schemes in favor of the poor and disadvantaged, are some of the ways of ensuring distributive justice.

This role suggests that the capitalist economic system must be regulated and directed in a way that not only promotes business as one of the leading institutions undergirding economic expansion but that it also meets the material needs of society. But in a hands-off deregulatory environment, untrammeled business prosperity may exacerbate business influence over the state, and possibly even lead to state capture. In fact, the mixed economy of India has increasingly veered toward pro-business policies (see Kohli 2009), which does not portend well for sharing the economic surplus in an egalitarian manner.

On top of this, international economic integration or globalization has added greater opportunities for many businesses. Business growth in the context of surplus labor is latently inegalitarian unless countervailed by state redistributive measures. While some workers in specific sectors have also witnessed increasing employment, most others with limited skills and education are on the defensive due to the pressures of international competition, technological change, and weakened pro-poor policies. It needs to be said that businesses will be unable to orchestrate their commercial activities in an orderly and predictable way without a supportive state and its attendant institutions. These provide the necessary rules, regulations, and norms to govern the economy as a whole. It also suggests that by failing to address the income needs of the people, the economy will remain constrained by weak demand for goods and services, which may undermine the very foundations of future markets for business growth. The paradox of capitalism is that the system can lead to massive accumulation, but at the margin, without a mechanism for supporting adequate demand, accumulation itself will be undermined.

While businesses are engaged in generating economic surplus by leveraging the different inputs in the production process, including labor time, the transformation of the economic surplus into a self-reinforcing productive investment cycle is not completely in the hands of businesses. State policy and supporting government institutions often influence the prices and stability of supply for many of the inputs that businesses use, such as the price of electricity, governance of labor management relations, the extent of infrastructure investment by public authorities, and subsidies for research and development (R&D), and so on that determine the incentive structures for business. In most societies, at least in theory, the state or the government is responsible for the collective well-being of its citizens. Thus, the state inducing and guiding the cycles of productive investments by business will be critical to ensuring economic development.

The government and political leaders in charge may prioritize spending tax revenues that they collect from citizens and businesses. For a poor society, there could be multiple, conflicting needs, and the government will have to politically negotiate its priorities, including the volume of spending, the timing of spending, and the ability to work with various nongovernmental partners to deliver those public goods and services. In other words, through policy design and the incentive structure, the state or the government, along with its numerous institutions, could direct the spending of tax resources for economic development. This transformation is, of course, not automatic as there are competing interests, such as politically powerful landlords who want to maintain their grip on rural workers by not paying minimum wages or demand subsidized water and electricity from the government for their agricultural operations, while industrialists want better educated and skilled workers, urban infrastructure, and cheap loans and subsidies for undertaking investments.

Economic development is thus not an assured outcome based on profit strategies of businesses, certainly not in a society where the demand for material progress for the average citizen is high, but in reality, actual outcomes are quite low precisely because commercial interests are different from state and societal goals. Therefore, the state is expected to be an important stakeholder to ensure that the country's economy and business engagements benefit society. Efforts could be directed toward education and employment opportunities for women and other historically disadvantaged communities, better health, improved and diversified skills for the workforce, the encouragement of innovation, higher agricultural productivity, export growth and diversification, employment security, less conflictual labor-management relations, and so on. Governments, assuming that they are not internally disorganized and fragmented or captured by particular business interests, could undertake transformational social change even as businesses pursue their long-term commercial ventures and their quest for profits.

For many reasons, the actual impact of business on economic development need not be so rosy. For example, manufacturing industries such as iron and steel or paper and pulp not conforming to certain environmental standards could contribute negatively to air and water quality, even as they generate jobs and output. By not investing adequately in R&D, firms and industries could limit their innovative capabilities or their ability to reduce their carbon footprint, and thus their contribution to the quality of life and future expansion of the economy. To meet emission standards, expensive and inconvenient steps must be taken and the government could assist in meeting desirable emission standards. Furthermore, if businesses got too close to the government and obtained unfair advantages over their rivals, often dubbed "cronyism," their commercial activities could be directed toward enriching themselves and their supporters within the government rather than fostering a healthy state-business partnership and contributing to the larger society (see Chapter 6). Such unfairness resulting from the rapacious pursuit of profits and the incapacity of the government to rein in businesses that attempt to take advantage of the state could undermine tax governance and public budgets. The long-term implications of cronyism are declining investments (Nagaraj 2025: 8), reduced social benefits, possible political instability, and widening economic and social inequality (see D'Costa 2023).

We need to acknowledge that businesses do not always meet the socially expected desirable economic development outcomes, even if it appears to be doing so. For example, businesses undertake the commercial activities of their own volition with objectives that are of direct interest to them, such as the profitability of the enterprise, eliminating a rival firm, or installing new equipment to compete with rival firms. These actions and strategies of business can have beneficial or deleterious effects on the economy and society. For instance, the absence of an effective rival firm could undermine competition and subject society to higher prices. Alternatively, the absence of large firms in certain industries could fragment the sector to the point of undermining economies of scale, that is, producing less by using the same inputs, and raising unit prices. If businesses could be managed in a way that there is enough competition to prevent unusually high excess profits (also referred to as "rent-seeking") or large enough firms to allow economies of scale, this would be a positive for society. Likewise, if the government ensured better compliance with pollution standards and local environmental laws, then no doubt the society would be better off.[3] The choices a government faces in enticing businesses to produce desirable public benefits are difficult since it must also avoid jeopardizing the project of private profit wholesale (metaphorically, by not killing the "golden goose" of capitalism). If the government is effectively captured by business and other vested interests, lasting economic development benefits will not accrue to society; in fact, the result may be outright injustice and social corrosion.

Now, if the government is able to enforce emission laws, the costs for business will rise, but investments in new technologies and infrastructure will have a favorable impact by not only creating new jobs in green technologies and products but also contributing to public welfare with cleaner air and reduced incidence of respiratory diseases. There is another possibility when the economic development impact "appears" to be highly positive, but on closer inspection, it might hide some developmental distortions. For example, there is no doubt that the Indian IT industry has contributed massively to the economy in a number of different ways: export growth and earnings of foreign exchange, promotion of high skills and high productivity, assimilation of best industry practices and business professionalism, tertiary technical education, and urban development, to name a few. Yet, there are areas where the contribution of the sector is questionable such as siphoning off students and technical professionals from other fields, foreclosing alternative opportunities such as manufacturing to diversify the economy and employ more people, and driving up incomes and wealth for a select few, pushing up

[3] Rent-seeking activities refer to those business operations where profits can be easily earned either because the business has monopoly control or a captive market, which are sometimes granted by the state to specific businesses to ensure certain productive activities are initiated when jump-starting an economy. It is akin to a landlord earning rents from agricultural tenants using the land (or tenants in residing in a rental housing) with the landlord having to do very little productive work (say through investments) to keep earning rents.

real estate values thereby making housing unaffordable for many low-income communities, and worsening inequality (D'Costa 2003a, 2006).

Offsetting some of the negative effects mentioned above of an otherwise successful IT sector in India, the state could foster housing development and community infrastructure for the poor and low-income groups. It could also offer broad incentives for vocational and science and technology education for those less fortunate to gain entry into higher education. Fortunately, most states try to address some of these challenges, although they may not be able to do it effectively due to inadequate funds or lack of coherent institutional strategies. In addition to the state, there are also informal institutions that determine moral codes or ethical concerns that could tame the fundamental force of profit-making and commercial gains by not allowing "unfair" prices or mobilizing social outrage against environmental damage to reinstate the customary expectations of clean air and water. The point is that the business-society relationship is filtered through a system of institutions in which the state could play a significant mediating and coordinating role. It either encourages those business activities that have a wider positive social impact or dissuades those behaviors that secure only the narrow interests of business. Moral codes and customary laws could also work to temper business interests and shape economic development favored by society. It is obvious that the entire burden of economic development in a capitalist setting cannot be shouldered by the state, but it can influence business activities to meet some of the goals of economic development.

In this mediating role, we are, of course, making a huge assumption that the state is indeed responsive to societal needs, such as improving the material quality of life of its citizens. We also need to make the assumption that the state is able to effectively govern business without unnecessary hindrance to its pursuit of profits and other commercial goals. The real world informs us that states, in many instances, may not care that much about how their citizens live, unless pushed by political expediency, or even if it did care, a state may not possess the instrumental and bureaucratic capacity to alter the behavior of business to generate a large-scale transformation of the economy. It is not unusual to witness lofty goals announced by states that often go unmet because of their inability to politically and economically marshal the necessary financial, managerial, and administrative resources and obtain support from key constituencies.

Neither the state nor business is independent of society. The state must also offer purposeful direction to business activities to promote economic development. Often, the wealthy, the politically well-connected, and successful businesses wield disproportionate influence on the state, with individuals within the state, such as politicians and bureaucrats, along with third-party intermediaries and businesses complicit in extracting rents. Illicit transactions between commercial enterprises and the agents of the state in a *quid pro quo* arrangement, and outright abuse of laws that are supposed to safeguard public interest from private theft, such as back-room lobbying, kickbacks, and bribery, become part of the cozy state business partnership. But in a democracy, the weaker voices of the poor cannot be completely ignored due to electoral imperatives. Therefore, the challenge is how to align business interests with economic development goals, or to put it differently, how to minimize the divergence between the interests and the goals of business and the state, so that ordinary citizens can experience real options of economic and social mobility through decent jobs.

Based on this elaborate discussion of the interactions between business, state, and society and the expected difference between what the state is expected to do and can actually do, we arrived at a relatively simple three-actor social arrangement (see earlier Figure 2.1) where businesses pursue their commercial interests, the society expects some tangible economic benefits from business growth and diversification, and the state, along with other supporting institutions, plays both promotional and mediating roles to ensure that business contributes to economic development in the interest of the wider society. The difficulty with this three-actor system is that businesses, the state, and society do not magically appear on the scene to pursue, mediate, and conduct their respective activities in a social vacuum. Each carries its own unwanted historical baggage, which tends to linger on due to processes that reinforce some aspects of that baggage. The tug of the past can be in conflict with the pull of the present and the future. Thus, modern Indian businesses that may superficially look similar to businesses from the West might actually operate differently, placing greater value on family ownership rather than maximizing shareholders' dividends. As a consequence, economic power could be concentrated among a few families that could be leveraged to influence government policies. Similarly, a modern state, inclined to change the *status quo* in favor of economic development for the poor, women, and other disadvantaged groups, may be hamstrung by upper caste and patriarchal dominance and resistance to giving up their social status and economic influence.

The lesson to draw about the prospects for economic development through the self-serving interests of business is that favorable social outcomes are not guaranteed either because the state is not driven by that purpose or the state is pushed and pulled in different directions by the larger society, which is typical in a free-wheeling democratic society. Their interests are not necessarily all aligned, and they could have conflicting agendas. Under such circumstances, there may not be economic development as an explicit outcome of state-mediated business activities, but rather a result that is more of an afterthought of business activities.

2.4 Business Diversification Key to Economic Development

As I have discussed, for businesses to be more effective from a development stance, it is the state-business-society triangular relations that collectively and interactively determine the economic development process and outcomes. The state has a far greater responsibility toward the welfare of its citizens and residents than businesses do. Businesses, especially big players, who are more organized and cohesive in their narrow pursuit of profits, also have a responsibility since they are not independent of society and the state. To function, businesses rely on state-provided physical and social infrastructures such as electricity and education systems. Households ensure that their children become productive workers, while society acts as a market and supports businesses through their consumption. A weakness in any of these links will render the business ineffective and make the state's economic development goals elusive. Businesses have a responsibility as well to work with the state's developmental goals of creating plentiful jobs and ensuring redistributive policies. Runaway business profits in the absence of job creation will likely result in skewed income and wealth distribution, limited markets, and a corresponding increase in the undue political power of very large businesses. Hence, what businesses do in the pursuit of their commercial self-interest must be directed by sound state policies and checked by societal demands to generate not just the desirable goals of economic growth, which they may be good at, but also to harness commercial energies to create employment and rising incomes more or less equitably.

To achieve these goals, production diversification, both in its extensive and intensive form are crucial. This means creating higher-paying jobs in different sectors and shedding low-productivity agricultural and urban-based services jobs. Increasing productivity can come about from increased investment, education, skill development, new technologies, and organizational change. This means increasing opportunities for business as well. Extensive production entails more of similar output (also known as scaling up), while intensive production involves differentiated output (wider variety) that is also of increasing unit value. For example, textile manufacturing or leather processing represent extensive production. They are labor-intensive, face low barriers to entry, and rely mostly on unskilled and semi-skilled workers. The price of clothing or leather goods is generally affordable for most people. Both activities could be scaled up should demand conditions be favorable. Furthermore, the economy could diversify from textile production to leather processing, which would be a form of horizontal diversification. This change would be part of economic development, but not necessarily of the intensive kind, unless the market value of leather goods is considerably higher than that of garments due to the specialized equipment used.

On the other hand, manufacturing machines to process and make textiles from yarn to fabrics on a large scale or producing petrochemicals to make synthetic yarn for textiles, as exemplified by India's Reliance Textiles (a company discussed in Chapter 3), represents vertical or backward integration and intensive production. The manufacture of both machines and petrochemicals requires large investments and skilled workers and technical professionals. The establishment of an elaborate transportation network to deliver oil-based products to a range of industrial customers, fashion designers, and marketing professionals for garments are good examples of forward linkages for the two sectors. The value added by services diversification, such as trucks and drivers for the transportation of oil products, may not represent intensive production. However, the movement away from informal, low-wage non-tradable service workers, such as drivers for oil transportation, to formal, well-paid designers, marketing professionals, and software engineers in the downstream sector of textiles indicates diversification of not just the services sector but also the intensification of the textile sector. The growing diversity of economic activities contributes to the increasing sophistication of both industry and services, which is presumed to generate two critical outcomes: employment and income.

The formation of forward and backward linkages, as illustrated in Figure 2.2, are examples of integration and diversification in both vertical and horizontal directions. It signals the movement from extensive (textiles and leather) to intensive forms of production (machinery and marketing), adding more economic value per unit of output. All of these business activities—from textile manufacturing, machinery, petrochemicals, synthetic yarn, and trucking and delivery services—will create a variety of jobs with different skill requirements. Qualitatively speaking, intensive diversification is likely to encourage more skilled-based employment, producing more economic value per worker and thus, higher wages or salaries than the unskilled jobs under

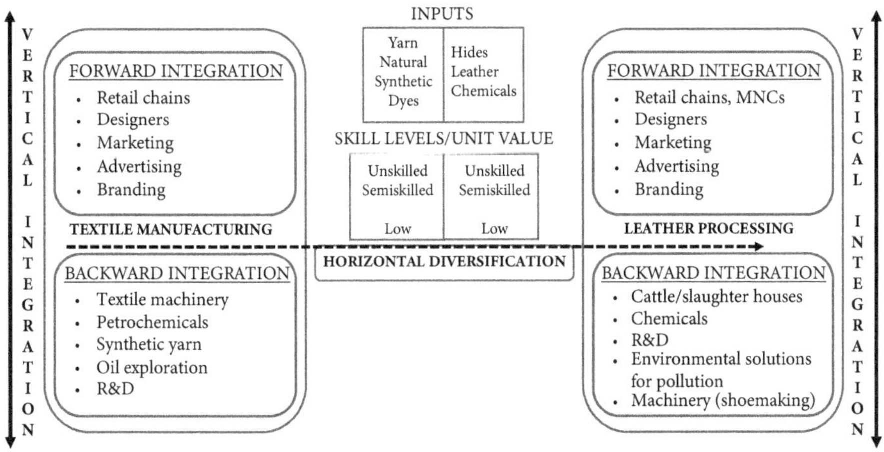

Figure 2.2 Business Diversification and Economic Development
Source: Compiled by the author

extensive forms of production. However, in both types of production, following the logic of economic expansion and diversification, a virtuous cycle of higher industrial output cascading throughout the economy could lead to employment, skill development, and organizational learning opportunities.

With entrepreneurial initiatives, one can expect the increased application of different and newer production technologies, including the employment of unskilled workers in support services. These effects in the wider economy that are external to the original firm undertaking increased production and diversification are known as (positive) externalities or spillovers. There can also be negative externalities with increased industrial output, such as pollution. Hence, output growth per se may not indicate development.

2.5 Looking Back at Business and Economic Development in India

So, how should we assess the contribution of business to economic development in India? First, it is important to recognize that there is a commercial history that predates India's independence from the British in 1947. This history can be roughly divided into pre-colonial and colonial commercial history, in which certain types of Indian businesses, mainly merchants or traders (*baniyas*), thrived. They hailed from particular ethnic communities and castes. Second, the colonial experience suggests that Indian traders and other commercial businesses were mostly subordinate to British business interests because colonial policy pretty much dictated trade policy, whether international trade or inland trade between the hinterland and port cities. It was around the early twentieth century when some Indian mercantilist families, who as incipient capitalists, entered particular manufacturing sectors. Jamshed Tata was one such entrepreneur who founded Asia's first integrated steel mill in 1907. The nationalist movement that aimed to free India from its colonial yoke offered business opportunities to local capitalists in addition to the commercial opportunities thrown open by the demand for war materiel during the two World Wars by the British army, in India and abroad. Already, the Indian political leaders had come to an understanding with rising Indian business houses (or large family businesses) in industry that in an independent India, the state and business would have to work together for the development of the country.

The combination of pre-independence commercial opportunities and the post-independence anticipated role of Indian business in national development cemented a specific form of state-business partnership and shaped the economic development trajectory for the next few decades. The 1944 Bombay Plan, introduced in Chapter 1, was an informal understanding between India's political leaders and leading business groups. The agreement laid out a division of labor whereby the state in the post-independence era would be overwhelmingly present in heavy industry and infrastructure (the commanding heights of the economy) while private business would find its profit opportunities mostly in consumer goods. The basic economic development principle behind this logic is that heavy industry is very capital-intensive. Indian businesses did not have the money or the patience to wait for profits at some uncertain future date, and without key industrial and infrastructural inputs, most other items could not be manufactured. Thus, railroads and steel making (under the state) could contribute to real estate, refrigerators, and automobiles (under the private commercial sector). There were some exceptions to this division of labor; for example, Tata's existing steel mill remained private, but all new steel-making capacity was brought under state ownership (D'Costa 1999). Thus, leading business groups who were part of the nationalist movement internalized the strong *swadeshi* sentiment of "self-reliance," clearly expecting that the Indian market, once free of colonial control, would now be rightfully available to Indian commercial enterprises. The implication of this was that economic development would be a national affair and the state would underwrite Indian businesses with key industrial inputs and protect them from foreign competition, while Indian capitalists, through their commercial pursuits, were expected to contribute to domestic economic transformation.

In hindsight, such an approach to economic development has been perceived as shortsighted mainly because of the overreach of the state in economic matters. However, the successful industrialization of the Soviet Union, the dominance of Keynesian ideas in tackling the economy from the demand side, and the developmentalist ideas that industrialization (as reflected in the rising standard of living in advanced capitalist economies) were all perceived as the path to transform an agrarian economy into an industrial one. Under Jawaharlal Nehru, India's first Prime Minister (1947–1964), both the Indian state and big business operated under his modernist drive with the expectation that rapid and dynamic industrialization would wipe out the vestiges of India's miserable colonial economic and feudal social past. Industrialization, as experienced in the advanced capitalist countries, was expected to slowly dissolve the small, unorganized economic activities, be they agriculture or petty business. Unwittingly, agriculture was given short shrift in this modernist drive, at least initially, and there was no specific policy position or thinking on the vast unorganized sector, which incidentally persists even today (see Chapters 4 and 6).

As we will see, the actual Indian development experience is, of course, mixed, meaning there are pockets of success and vast swathes of failures. Indian businesses, along with the government, did contribute to economic development in terms of investment, employment, food security, industrial capacity, technical and managerial human capital, and economic diversification when compared to its recent colonial past. However, comparing India's development experience on an international basis (fair or not), India's performance, relative to some of the smaller East and Southeast Asian economies and, more recently China, has been lackluster, especially in the areas of health, education, industrialization, and the general material standards of living as reflected in the low average and median income per person.

There are many reasons for this divergence of economic performance over the roughly three-and-a-half-decade period (1950–1985), but there are two strands that stand out prominently. Unlike their Asian counterparts, Indian businesses were not internationally oriented, thus missing out on global technological developments and learning, export markets, and cost and quality competitiveness. India's non-aligned position during the Cold War effectively excluded it from new emerging sectors such as semiconductors and electronics. These were developed under the United States security umbrella and strategically allowed to be transferred to its allies in East Asia, namely, Japan, South Korea, Taiwan, and Singapore. Also, significant in India's lagging economic performance, the development of physical infrastructure was not seen as strategic for economic development, except for what was necessary for heavy industries and mining. In a resource-scarce economy, there were other pressing priorities, and export competitiveness was not one of them. Asia, on the other hand, including China later, furiously constructed physical infrastructure in alignment with internationalization and honing of global supply chains for home and foreign markets. India is now playing catch-up with infrastructure spending.

This lacuna was predictable since self-reliance, for all its ideological and political merits at the time, created a sheltered economy. This was the case in China as well until the gradual opening up in the late 1970s. However, unlike China, the post-independent Indian state was caught in a vortex of multiple social and political demands that effectively undermined its ability to govern an economy that was heavily protected by tariffs and experienced severe periodic shortages of foreign exchange (balance of payments problems). Unnecessary state controls to rein in corporate power compelled businesses to cleverly circumvent regulations through rent-seeking behavior, while the state itself was compelled to maintain political stability through a variety of subsidies and transfer payments to unhappy constituencies, leaving little for public investments (Bardhan 1984). In hindsight, missing the infrastructure bus continues to be India's Achilles' heel even today. Poor infrastructure continues to hinder Indian manufacturing investment and competitiveness, while foreign businesses, despite the attractiveness of a large, growing market, have tended to shy away from the Indian economy.

All that has rapidly changed since the Indian economy was deregulated, incrementally in the mid-1980s, and more drastically beginning in 1991. While many commentators are dismissive of India's efforts in the post-independence period, it is important to recognize that many of the seeds of the benefits of economic development today, such as a large pool of engineering and managerial talent and basic infrastructure such as electrification and irrigation, were established during the early decades following independence. Indian businesses have matured to the point that many of them can face the world economy on their own and no longer need the Indian state to coordinate investments, although politically inspired state intervention on behalf of particular businesses has not disappeared completely, and in some instances has become more ingrained.

Today, some of these older businesses, as well as several new enterprises, are global players in their own right, with firms from the IT, pharmaceutical, and auto industries visible in the global market. Other mature Indian business sectors, such as steel, international retail, textiles, and the diamond industry, operate globally through overseas headquarters but are explicitly tied to

Indian operations. The Indian economy is also structurally different today, with a declining share of agriculture in national income, paradoxically still with high levels of agricultural employment, a stagnant share of industrial output, and a rapidly growing dualistic services sector. Roughly, two-thirds of employment is in the low-wage informal sector that contributes one-third of national output. The formal sector contributes two-thirds of the output using one-third of the high-wage formal labor and is driven by internationally oriented industrial sectors and high-value services sectors such as finance, insurance, real estate, and business services (FIRE). Of these, information technology, as part of business services, is heavily export-oriented and can be considered one of India's major success stories.

In the history of modern economic development, India's place in the world economy has changed, from one of colonial incorporation to a semi-autarkic or almost self-sufficient economy, to ultimately a re-engagement with the world economy, even if somewhat tentatively when compared to other countries. This transition suggests that the relationship between business and economic development will evolve over time since Indian businesses are no longer solely anchored to the home market but are now part of the world economy. As markets, including foreign ones, increasingly govern everyday life, Indian businesses have found not only a new freedom to pursue their commercial interests in a global setting, but their contributions to economic development at home have also changed qualitatively.

Just as India has changed, so too has the world economy. Since the 1980s, the deregulation and liberalization of economies, led by the United States, the United Kingdom, and other Organisation for Economic Co-operation and Development (OECD) economies and supported by the Bretton Woods institutions of the World Bank, the International Monetary Fund (IMF), and General Agreement on Tariffs and Trade (GATT) (renamed World Trade Organization (WTO)), has intensified international economic integration. Many countries in the Global South followed suit, aligning their policies to what transnational corporations (TNCs) were already practicing, namely, the use of widespread, labor-intensive, offshore production, particularly in East and Southeast Asia. Additionally, states to attract foreign investment ensured a pliant workforce, offered a range of incentives for export-oriented investments, undertook large-scale spending on modern infrastructure, and trained their workforce.

The resulting economic development in Asian economies, first in East and Southeast Asia, and recently and notably in China and India, has lifted hundreds of millions of people above the poverty line. However, this numerical success may not translate into a comfortable existence for most Indians since jobs remain precarious and subject to the whims of export markets. Bangladesh is a case in point, where its runaway success in the ready-made garments export business came at the expense of low wages (its principal advantage), poor working conditions, and an anti-union stance (Siddiqui 2025). Also, the pandemic had devastating effects on small garment exporters that had razor-thin margins, with many operations shut down. Similarly, the Indian economy was severely hurt during the pandemic.

As I have alluded to earlier, a successful business does not necessarily mean tangible economic development for the masses unless entire economic sectors are transformed in a way that generates sustained mass employment with favorable spillover effects in other businesses in terms of economic linkages and diversification, job growth, technological upgrading and diversification, and increased output at home and for exports. In other words, for development to happen, the institutional arrangements and mechanisms that motivate investment and reinvestment of the economic surplus must get locked into a virtuous cycle with good outcomes leading to better outcomes on an ongoing basis. Only then will both the material and nonmaterial aspects of well-being be altered. These outcomes are not easy to measure and this book makes no attempt to precisely capture the economic development outcomes from business activities. It does, however, indicate some rough magnitudes of change in a qualitative way where such data are available. More importantly, it brings out the dynamic relationship between business and economic development in India, which is the main objective of this book.

In theory, then, the state can work toward ensuring that commercial activities lead to development outcomes, but in practice, it also depends on how independent the state is from powerful business and how other institutional factors, such as politics and culture, impinge on the workings of both business and the state. The big question for India today is whether recent business growth and its internationalization in an expansionary but now uncertain global economy portend the salutary effects of widespread economic development. Whether such growth will reduce poverty and inequality and foster a more educated and healthier population are some of the concerns that go hand in hand with the employment question.

2.6 Looking Ahead at Business and Economic Development in India

In the rest of the book, I discuss the relationship between Indian business and economic development through the lens of economic, industrial, and business sectors, keeping in mind some broad parameters of developmental outcomes. The discussions reveal the dynamics of these sectors and their contribution to economic development outcomes. These include, but are not limited to, output growth, employment, technological status, skill development, spillover effects and economic linkages (both vertical and horizontal), and export growth.

Of course, it is neither possible to cover all economic and business sectors nor is it feasible to document all forms of state intervention in commercial activity; hence, our understanding of the relationship between business and economic development can only be partial. Nevertheless, a wide spectrum of sectors, including the large Indian agricultural sector, has been selected to represent the base of an economy on which other sectors emerge and thrive, such as the technology and globally driven services sector (Table 2.1). Collectively, the discussion of a range of diverse sectors offers an analytical window to capture the real workings of economic development. Since we take a dynamic view of the economy, other sectors that are not intuitively innate to India but are good examples of global participation are also analyzed. We take

Table 2.1 List of Indian Business and Economic Sectors Examined

Business/Economic Sector	Dominant Ownership	Globalization
Agriculture	Household	Limited
Steel	State and private	Somewhat
Automobiles/auto components	Private	Somewhat
Machinery	Private and state	Limited
Textiles	Private	Globalized
Chemicals/petroleum	Private and state	Limited
Computers	Private	Limited
Software services/IT	Private	Globalized
Pharmaceuticals	Private	Globalized
Diamonds/jewelry	Private	Globalized
Handloom sector	Households	Somewhat
Retail sector	Households/Private	Limited
E-commerce	Private	Globalized
Digital infrastructure	State and private	Limited
Platform economy	Private	Globalized
Renewable energy	State and private	Limited

Notes: information technology (IT). Business/Economic sectors are not strictly compartmentalized as in e-commerce and modern retail. Not all of them have been discussed in detail or equally. Dominant ownership and the degree of globalization are based on the author's subjective assessment and are based on either international trade or FDI or both. They are only for indicative purposes.

Source: Author's compilation

for granted that all businesses contribute in some ways to economic development in terms of jobs, taxes, skill development, but we do not assume that these contributions are necessarily transformative at the wider societal level, unless all economic and business sectors work favorably in tandem on a large scale, reinforcing and multiplying one another's activities in an expansive and qualitatively different way. The challenge is to address the structural scourge of surplus labor, dualism in labor markets, and the persistence of the informal sector, and reverse the worsening of inequality in India.

3
State-Mediated Foundational Sectors for Development

3.1 Introduction

In this chapter, I briefly showcase some early foundational business sectors to illustrate their evolution, interactions with the government, and their contributions to some facets of economic development. The chapter is divided into five sections. Section 2 offers a quick review of the familiar post-independence industrial development effort. The goal of this section is to demonstrate the diverse range of business sectors that emerged during this period under both the state and private sectors. They have served as the foundation for limited structural transformation with emerging and new diversified sectors. They cover specific business sectors: heavy industries such as steel and automobiles (Section 3), emerging technologies such as computers and new tradable services such as software (Section 4), and reverse-engineered pharmaceuticals (Section 5). All of these sectors represent a unique blend of state mediation from outright state ownership, state–private partnership, including foreign TNCs, state promotion of the private sector, private sector crowding in the state sector, and state-mandated social policy resting on the private sector. The concluding section revisits the relationship between business and the state in economic development.

3.2 Economic Development and Structural Shifts

One key premise behind economic development is that diversification of economic activities is necessary for growth and development. This entails a movement from extensive to intensive forms of production within and between sectors. For example, textiles, which have been a bedrock for pre- and early industrialization and employment in many countries, especially India, is an extensive form of industrialization. Similarly, India's globally visible diamond sector is labor intensive, which also contributes to economic

Indian Business, Economic Development, and the Jobs Dilemma in the Twenty-first Century. Anthony P. D'Costa, Oxford University Press. © Anthony P. D'Costa (2026). DOI: 10.1093/9780198948407.003.0003

development. But both of these sectors are extensive forms of industrial activities, they tend to grow through the addition of more workers as dictated by market expansion. The limits of their markets, non-transferable skills, low impact on other business sectors, and heightened global competition suggest that they cannot be expected to be growth sectors for economic development. They need to transition to intensive forms of production that will entail diversification through investments, new technologies, products, services, and markets, increasing productivity (fewer workers producing the same value), and rising wages. These could be new fabrics designed for new applications in manufacturing, auto industry, medical, and defense sectors and more industrial applications of diamonds, albeit with its own value-adding limits. In addition, intensive growth should lead to the expansion of other activities such as supplier industries through spinoffs and multiplier effects.

In this chapter, I have chosen sectors and actors that are visible and have large-scale impact on the economy and society. They represent the intensive forms of production and can be considered as foundational sectors, which also support extensive forms of production, and include steel, automobiles, information technology (including software services), and pharmaceuticals. They are a mix of capital-, technology-, innovation-, skill-, and education-intensive sectors. The purpose here is to demonstrate why these sectors are important for economic development and how businesses, in pursuing their own commercial interests, are also able to generate outcomes that are societally beneficial. The state's role as an intermediary has been crucial, even if not always effective, in encouraging these sectors to expand and diversify and contribute to economic development.[1] Because of the evolutionary nature of business sectors, the analysis of these and other sectors by necessity must be positioned in the wider context of the shifting structure of the Indian economy.

This discussion covers mostly the post-independence, pre-economic reform period, circa 1950–1985, when the Indian state maintained its dominance over the economy. The backdrop to the discussion is the double movement of ongoing structural shifts in the Indian economy and the broader restructuring of the global economy to which Indian businesses have been subtly adapting. Soon after India's independence, under the Second Five Year

[1] The successful joint venture between the Indian government and Suzuki Motors of Japan with the initial 80%–20% equity distribution, respectively, was due to several factors that contributed to its success: small size of investment, assembly operations using imported parts and technologies, and considerable autonomy of management to run the enterprise according to Japanese industrial practices (D'Costa 2003b, 1998b). These attributes were completely different in the 100% owned public sector steel mills. The scale, technologies, production process, and ownership could not be more different than those in auto manufacturing.

Plan (1956–1961), basic industrialization was spurred by state investments. The private sector played a complementary role by focusing mostly on consumer products, albeit with some degree of diversification in heavy industry as well by some of the big family businesses such as those of the Tatas and Birlas. This post-World War II era of rapid industrialization was also the beginning and subsequent deepening of a massive shift in global manufacturing from the wealthier high-wage countries to lower-wage ones, rapidly industrializing countries in East and Southeast Asia, and later China.

The global economic shifts in the last century began with Western Europe's post-World War II reconstruction and Japan's rapid industrialization of the 1950s, followed by smaller East and Southeast Asian countries (South Korea, Taiwan, Singapore, Hong Kong, and Malaysia, among others) in the 1960s and 1970s. Due to India's large internal market and its non-aligned political stance aimed at geopolitical independence, the focus was on the domestic market. Barring some technology transfers, its industrialization was generally disconnected from this global shift. In the third quarter of the twentieth century, there was also the commencement of a global transition toward technology-driven electronics industrial production covering semiconductors, computers, and a boom in internet-based services development. In this wave, the advanced capitalist countries, including Japan under global competitive pressure, yielded production to East and Southeast Asia and China, while holding onto R&D, know-how, and design. India was still not significantly linked to these shifting supply chains in the world economy. However, it emerged as an important destination for outsourcing tradable services such as software, finance, and IT-driven business services for the wealthy markets, especially the United States.

As investments by business and government increase and economic diversification takes place, the structure of the economy begins to change. Thus, historically, in most societies undergoing economic change, the high contribution of agriculture to the national income falls drastically while the contribution of manufacturing and services rises. This has been the classical capitalist trajectory in which manufacturing as a whole becomes predominant. As Figure 3.1 shows, to a great extent, India has not been an exception. It suggests that economic development in the country has been an ongoing process since the post-independence period with a declining share of agriculture to national income and an increasing share of nonagricultural activities, both industry and services.

However, two disquieting developments in India's ongoing structural transformation are industrial stagnation (or premature deindustrialization) and a slower decline in agricultural employment relative to the economic decline

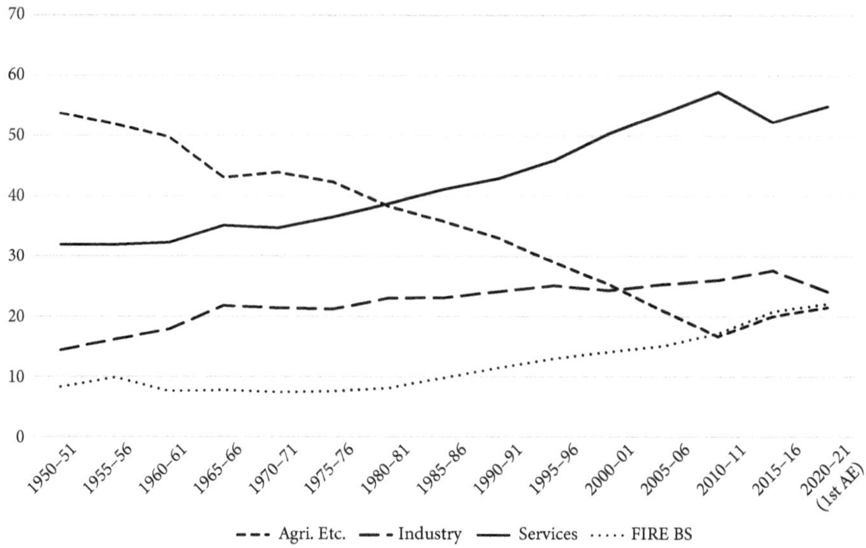

Figure 3.1 Economic Development and Structural Change in India (% Share to GDP)
Note: Due to changes in methodology and data sources, more recent GDP figures are not compatible with past series and hence, not included.
Source: Government of India, Ministry of Finance, Economic Survey, various years

in the share of agriculture to India's GDP. For example, according to the India Brand Equity Foundation (IBEF), in the fiscal year 2022, roughly 19% of India's gross value added (output value minus intermediate input costs incurred to produce the output) was from agriculture, while nearly 46% of total employment was in agriculture (IBEF Agriculture 2023). Thus, India for the most part remains an agrarian society with nearly half of the work force still making a living from land. From this, we can infer that agricultural productivity remains quite low since a lot of people produce a small part of the national income. It also suggests that rural wages/incomes on the average are low thereby making rural prosperity a necessary requirement for economic development. As we will see in the next chapter, rural India is changing, albeit gradually, moving from farm to non-farm economic activities in the countryside but not in a way that is leading to the classic form of structural change where manufacturing and services become the driver of economic expansion and diversification with significant absorption of surplus labor from the countryside.

India's recent structural change must be viewed as nested within the broader global shift in manufacturing from the rich to the rapidly industrialized countries of Asia. Instead of manufacturing driving India's growth and economic diversification, we find that it is the services sector and within it high-value services such as finance, insurance, real estate (FIRE) and business services such as IT (information technology and software services) that are driving the economy. In fact, the share of FIRE output relative to GDP has converged with the share of agriculture. Since the two sectors are highly disparate in terms of skills/education/wages/salaries/earnings, we can also anticipate worsening of wealth and income distribution (more on this in Chapter 6). This growth in services and the convergence of the economic contribution of FIRE and agriculture is somewhat anomalous when it comes to economic development trajectories. Countries on the path of structural change experience substantial declines in rural populations, increases in agricultural productivity, and expansion in industry and services. The data indicates that India does not fit this pattern, especially when compared to East Asia and China.[2]

In this global shift, the rich countries now have a very small share of agriculture, relatively low manufacturing output and employment, and a growing share of services output and employment. For example, both the United States and Japan boast a large services sector, representing nearly 77% (Statista 2022) and 73% (Statistics Bureau of Japan 2022) of their national economies, respectively. In contrast, China continues to have a large share of industry to GDP, albeit its services share is also higher as agriculture's contribution has fallen to about 8% of GDP. Curiously, India has emerged as a major offshore destination for tradable services, particularly IT services, and structurally India resembles more of a wealthy country trajectory but at a considerably lower level of income and economic development. It also remains largely agrarian. In this structural context, what has been the contribution of business to economic development outcomes and how has the state and other institutions impacted the process of change? In the rest of the chapter and beyond, we explore the evolution of Indian business and their continuing adjustments to this shifting structural reality at both the national and global levels.

3.3 Heavy Industry and the Role of the State

Jumpstarting modern economic development is no easy feat. The hard resources needed for development such as capital, technology, and skilled

[2] It is true that India has a large population and hence a large labor force. China too has a large, somewhat similar share of its workers engaged in agriculture. This might suggest that outside of the OECD economies, there are only a handful of countries that have effectively transitioned out of agriculture. But China as we know is the manufacturing workshop of the world that has absorbed hundreds of millions of people in industry, including seasonal and temporary rural migrant workers.

workers are in short supply. Soft resources such as bureaucratic capacity, adequate knowledge of technology, and organizational capabilities are also in short supply and they complement the hard ones. Furthermore, there is no single approach to initiate modern economic growth since no economy starts with a blank slate. Historical legacies such as colonial and pre-modern institutions are not conducive to modern economic development. Institutions need to be redesigned and repurposed to serve the imperatives of capitalist production geared toward increasing the quantity and variety of output while at the same time ensuring the material well-being of society.

There is a consensus that to improve the material conditions of life for all, at the minimum, critical industries need to be prioritized and fostered. These critical industries have various linkages with other key sectors of the economy and strategically fostering these linkages may not only produce a diverse range of products using different technologies but also generate employment directly and indirectly. This is aligned with the relationship between business diversification and economic development presented in Chapter 2 (see Figure 2.2). Thus, one sector's output becomes the input of another and the entire economy is expected to reach a higher level of income growth. It is with this in mind that some key industrial sectors under the state and private business, discussed below, are fostered to jumpstart economic development. In this section, two heavy industry sectors are discussed to capture their wider impact on the economy, industry, and society. The first presents the steel industry, which is followed by the auto industry.

3.1.1 The Steel Industry

It may be obvious but it is worth reiterating that steel, the fabricated metal made from iron ore and coal, serves as a critical material for manufacturing and construction, including but not limited to roads, bridges, housing, railroads, automobiles, and shipbuilding. Steel-using consumer durables and white goods such as steel almirahs (cupboards), refrigerators, washers, dryers, and kitchen appliances also constitute forward linkages of the steel industry. In low-income countries such as India, passenger cars were considered "luxury" goods and hence discouraged by the state in the early decades of industrialization. High taxes and production controls through licensing and quotas were introduced to restrain the consumption of cars. The production of buses (mass transportation) while also produced under the same regulatory regime was not controlled in the same way.

Establishing the basic backbone of the economy demanded industries that would encourage or foster other related industries and where the private sector would play an important role. Since steel production was capital-intensive with a long gestation period before earning profits, the government took on the responsibility of setting up steel and other heavy industries across the board such as machinery, coal mining, and electricity generation. The logic was that these industries would provide the critical inputs into basic manufacturing and infrastructure development. The private sector was not mature enough for such bold, risky, long-term undertakings in an erstwhile colonial economy.

In 1951, the Industries Development and Regulation Act was passed, followed by the Industrial Policy Resolution of 1956, which ensured a pre-eminent role for the public sector (Marathe 1989). Five-year plans were established, the first beginning in 1951; all commercial banks were nationalized in 1969; and regulations were enacted to monitor large domestic and foreign business houses under the Monopolies and Restrictive Trade Practices Act (MRTP) of 1970 and the Foreign Exchange Regulations Act (FERA) of 1973. Businesses therefore had to adjust to this regulatory, market-constraining environment, albeit with the silver lining that a domestic market protected behind tariff and non-tariff walls created a captive market for business, domestic or foreign.

In this regulatory environment, the overall performance of state-led businesses, including the steel industry, was lackluster.[3] There are many microeconomic and macro-political reasons for this performance. From the supply side, one of the principal reasons has been excessive bureaucratic and political control of the public sector's steel and other heavy industry enterprises. In addition, the closed nature of the Indian economy prevented technology borrowing and learning to keep up with industry innovations elsewhere. On hindsight, too hasty a leap into large-scale industrialization with different sources of technology such as the UK, Germany, and Soviet Union (D'Costa 1998a) in the absence of accumulated industrial learning handicapped the Indian state sector. The state steel sector was also weighed down by its obligations to maintain unusually large employment rolls of captive state-owned mines. Not saddled by the state sector's cumbersome obligations, it is not surprising that Tata Iron and Steel Company (TISCO) of the Tata Group, established in 1907, was the only major private sector steel business that performed better than its public sector counterparts.

[3] There were some exceptions, such as the state-owned Bharat Heavy Electricals Limited (BHEL).

The few scattered successes of both public and private firms in an environment of *dirigisme* (or state dominance of the economy) suggest that the mobilization of the internal strengths of firms was also a factor for competitiveness and growth. Thus, both TISCO and BHEL (a public sector firm) were star enterprises in their own way when it comes to their contribution to economic development. Both employed a sizeable workforce but also supported high-quality jobs. TISCO is known for its relatively harmonious labor–management relations and worker-focused human resource policies, including considerable welfare for the Jamshedpur community where the company is based. Similarly, BHEL, a public sector enterprise established in 1964 to manufacture power equipment such as boilers for thermal plants, was established to support the industrial foundation of the country. Domestically, it had no real competition. However, instead of simply leveraging its monopoly power in the protected domestic market, it also exported power equipment competitively. It was a profitable company and one of the successful public sector enterprises (Ramamurti 1987). However, similar to many other production facilities, public or private, the scale of production was small and BHEL, even with licensed capacity expansion later, could not compete with foreign manufacturers in terms of price and production capacity, especially from China.

Similar to most other industrial sectors of the time, BHEL too suffered from inadequate demand at the economy-wide level. For example, critical sectors such as agriculture were initially neglected thereby undermining the expected and developmentally critical agriculture–industry linkages, which implied that growth in agricultural income would have generated industrial demand. Unlike some countries such as Singapore, South Korea, and Japan, which reaped considerable economic benefits from such investments in national infrastructure development, India did not view infrastructure as strategic to building overall industrial capacity at that time. It is common knowledge that physical infrastructure is a major consumer of steel and other heavy industry products such as cement. Even relatively successful BHEL did not develop adequate in-house R&D capacity and instead located manufacturing in areas away from centers of innovation such as in Bengaluru (formerly Bangalore) and Roorkee.[4] In India, there were not only production capacity constraints resulting in shortages of cement but the overall demand remained constrained due to an impoverished society that did not

[4] Some manufacturing locations were of course close to markets, such as Haridwar where BHEL's turbines for generating hydroelectricity could be used in dammed rivers in the surrounding area.

have adequate income and spending power and savings to motor the economy on a sustained basis.

How then are we to assess the contribution of steel and other heavy industries to economic development? It needs to be emphasized that the public sector cannot be assessed in the same way as private enterprise because the purpose of the former is to lay the foundations of economic development and not commercial gain. That said, this is not an argument for justifying inefficiency of state enterprises, which in the Indian case was clearly driven by the ideology of the state commanding the heights of the economy, namely, heavy, capital-intensive industries that would ultimately induce other activities through economic linkages. A large, heterogeneous, fragmented country with massive backlog of development needs was an enormous governance challenge for the state. Nevertheless, state-led development from economic backwardness was not absent since many critical industries were established by both the public and private sector. The major drawback, on hindsight, was the inward-looking policies that both shielded and deprived Indian business of competition, resulting in a high-cost economy and technological backwardness due to a rapidly shifting global technological frontier.

Overall, the general level of economic output increased as the number of public sector units increased from four to 241 between 1950 and the mid-1990s. This level of state investment contributed to a higher level of employment with higher average salaries and benefits compared to other private business. Beyond this, there is no easy and precise way to gauge the economic impact over the roughly four decades since the heavy industry sector, mostly under the state, has been in existence. The steel industry directly and indirectly employs several million people today. Recent estimates suggest that nearly half a million workers are directly employed and another three and a half million jobs are in the entire supply chain (PwC 2019: 4). This level of employment is predicated on an output that has multiplied six and a half time times since the 1980s. Assuming that productivity today in the steel industry is higher than what it was in the earlier decades, we can infer that in the pre-reform period (circa 1950–1985), the industry employed far more people per unit of output, thereby meeting the two important goals of jobs and income and their effects on demand in the rest of the economy.

But we must also acknowledge that India's heavy industry production was characterized by high costs, which meant that economy-wide demand in downstream industries would have been dampened. For example, in 1992, India's five large mills produced 9.83 million tons (mt) of steel with 185,000 employees (53.1 tons per employee) compared to South Korea's steel output of 20 mt with 23,951 employees (835 tons per employee) (D'Costa 1999: 102).

Notwithstanding measurement issues, this massive divergence in labor productivity suggests not only a wide gap in technological and organizational resources in the two countries' steel industry but also a big difference in their corresponding economic impact. Since this book is about the evolutionary relationship between business and economic development in India, we will stay away from industrial policy that could have been employed by the government and thus do not engage with counterfactuals (something that did not happen and therefore cannot prove what could have been possible). Instead, I focus on the ongoing interactions between business, state, and societal goals of economic development.

If we could go by the simple physical output figures for the economy as a whole and conclude that these heavy industries have transformed the material foundation of the society to some extent, the average output per capita is unimpressive due to India's large population. However, as long as output is increasing consistently in these critical sectors and economic diversification is taking place, which it is, we can assume that businesses, both public and private, are contributing to economic development of the society directly through their investment decisions and indirectly through the multiplier effect (or positive externalities).

The state, with a limited partnership with Indian business, did alter the material foundation from India's colonial roots. From simple to complex industrial products, there has been considerable industrial deepening and diversification, encompassing mining, metallurgical, mechanical engineering, electrical, chemical, textile, and food industries. Since the 1950s, output growth virtually increased manifold in all heavy industries such as steel, machinery, transport equipment, and chemical sectors (Table 3.1). For example, between 1950–1951 and 1980–1981, several crucial industries increased their output: coal (3.7 times), finished steel (6.8 times), commercial vehicles (8.3 times), nitrogenous fertilizer (240.4 times), and man-made fiber (4.5 times). Over the next two decades, these industries expanded further, with some industries, such as man-made fiber (mainly for synthetic textiles), growing rapidly under the private sector (see Box 3.1 and Figure 3.2). However, barring a few firms, such as Reliance Industries in synthetic yarn and petrochemicals, most businesses in heavy industry were not internationally competitive.

Due to the capital intensity of these sectors with an underdeveloped user market for their products, the employment impact has been limited. Any alternate option that could have been pursued is a counterfactual and hence not relevant to the discussion. However, there were clear signs that the

Table 3.1 Expansion of Selected Indian Industries, 1950 to 2003

	Units	1950–1951	1980–1981	Change by a factor of	2002–2003	Change by a factor of
Coal	million tons	32.3	119.0	3.7	367.3	3.1
Petroleum	million tons	0.3	10.5	35.0	33.0	3.1
Finished steel	million tons	1.0	6.8	6.8	34.4	5.1
Aluminium	thousand tons	4.0	199.0	49.8	467.0	2.4
Machine tools	Rs. million	3.0	1692.0	564.0	21,794	12.9
Commercial vehicles	thousands	8.6	71.7	8.3	199.0	2.8
Agricultural tractors	thousands	na	71.0	na	192.2	2.7
Power transformers	million KVA	0.2	19.5	97.5	74.4	3.8
Nitrogenous fertilizer	thousand tons	9.0	2164.0	240.5	10,559.0	4.9
Cement	million tons	2.7	18.6	6.9	116.3	6.3
Cotton cloth	million sq.m	4215.0	8368.0	2.0	18,989.0*	2.3
Man-made fabric (synthetic yarn)	million sq.m	300.0	1350.0	4.5	13,725.0*	10.2
Electricity generated	billion KWH	5.1	110.8	21.7	480.7	4.8

Notes: * for the year 1996–1997, change refers to the number of times output increased by from the previous data point.
Source: Government of India, Ministry of Finance (2004: S-31-S33) in D'Costa (2005: 51)

economy under the regulatory environment was operating poorly. Whatever efforts were mounted in the mid-1980s to streamline the economy were mostly thwarted by powerful business and political interests who were content to serve the large protected market (Kohli 1990). Only an external crisis, the first Gulf War (1990–1991), ultimately pushed the leadership to deregulate the economy to allow a new institutional foundation conducive to higher growth in a global setting.[5]

Today, the Indian steel industry is the third largest in the world, with a mix of private and public sector units. In fiscal year 2024, production of crude and finished steel was 143.6 and 138.5 metric tons, respectively (IBEF Steel 2025: 10).[6] The developmental impact of heavy industry, in addition to increasing employment, improving technology, and fostering a supplier industry, is also likely to enhance India's woefully inadequate, albeit improving physical infrastructure. From a supply chain point of view, this development is critical.

Box 3.1 A Tale of Backward (Vertical) Integration and Diversification

The promotion of economic linkages for industrial development was not confined to the state alone. Under certain circumstances, the private sector could foster such linkages even when the state was the dominant investor. The difference is the underlying motives behind the two types of enterprises. Under the state, public enterprises in principle are geared toward serving the larger society with goods and services directly or indirectly, including private business. Businesses, on the other hand, can promote similar benefits but the strategic capital accumulation motive precedes the would-be outcomes that benefit society. This implies that these beneficial outcomes are not integral to investment decisions since there could be several strategic investment options faced by the firm. It is only on hindsight that certain strategic investment decisions can be seen to dovetail with the societal impact generated through the deliberate intervention by the state.

[5] The Gulf War involving Iraq's invasion of Kuwait subsequently involved the US-led military coalition against Iraq. This resulted in a foreign exchange crisis in India as the flows of remittance income earned by Indian workers in these countries stopped. By resorting to an IMF loan to meet its external payments obligations, India had little choice other than to follow IMF's standard policy prescription of internally deregulating and externally liberalizing its economy. In any case, the ideological shift had been in motion since the 1980s (Mukherji 2013). Increasing middle class consumption also favored a deregulated and internationally engaged Indian economy (D'Costa 2013).

[6] A handful of TNCs such as Nippon Steel, Sumitomo, and ArcelorMittal (owned substantially by Laxmi and Usha Mittal and headquartered in Luxembourg) are optimistic about Indian growth, including auto industry expansion. Nippon Steel of Japan and ArcelorMittal of Luxembourg jointly acquired the debt-ridden Essar Steel, formerly owned by the Ruia family. Arcelor Mittal had several overseas plants in Vietnam, Indonesia, the US, and the Caribbean.

We have one well-known case, where a single entrepreneur, Dhirubhai Ambani, created one of the largest enterprises in the world. With strategic vision, Ambani not only expanded his enterprise, Reliance Industries, but in the process also established some critical industrial sectors beginning with synthetic textiles and culminating with oil and gas exploration. This integrated approach to economic activities was no different in terms of outcomes that the state expected through its investments, that is, sectors that could act as industrial anchors for economic development and social change. This growth took place when the Indian state still owned and controlled the heavy industries of the country. The main difference is the underlying motive: for Reliance, it was commercial strategy and for the state an economic development strategy. Reliance was confined to the organizational boundaries of the firm, even if expanding in different directions, while the state was focused on positioning critical sectors strategically in the wider economy.

As a young boy, Ambani went to Aden and worked as a gas station attendant. He returned to India in 1958 and using his Aden connections set up a spice-exporting business. In 1960, he founded Reliance Commercial with a partner and sold polyester. Subsequently, in 1966, he entered the textile business by establishing Reliance Textiles, which manufactured synthetic fabrics. Using the foreign exchange earned through spice exports, he imported nylon yarn to produce textiles. Once the polyester filament yarn was opened up to the private sector in 1980, Ambani obtained a license to produce polyester filament yarn. His connections to the relevant Indian bureaucracy as well as India's then Prime Minister Mrs. Indira Gandhi facilitated securing a production license, which was de facto a license to monopoly control. However, rather than simply exploit this privilege, he strategically built the manufacturing plant above capacity, ahead of anticipated demand. In order to further integrate backward, Ambani obtained production licenses to produce chemicals, which would be used to produce polyester fiber. By 1980, Reliance already had twenty company-owned outlets for fabrics, over 1000 franchises, and more than 20,000 retail outlets.

In 1991, along with his son Mukesh, he set up a petrochemical plant, a refinery, and a few years later the world's largest multi-feed cracker plant to produce from start to finish ethylene for ultimately polyester fiber. This is a good example of industrial upstream and downstream activities. Along with these investments, affiliated businesses such as liquified gas, logistics, and transportation were also established. A few years before his death, Reliance with its many subsidiaries spanned many other businesses but the core integrated business that began with imported synthetic yarn led to the manufacturing of synthetic textiles, the production of petrochemicals for synthetic yarn, fiber, and ultimately oil and gas exploration to further deepen industry linkages. By 2002, the Reliance Group had over 85,000 workers, revenues represented 3% of GDP, and contributed 5% of central government revenue.

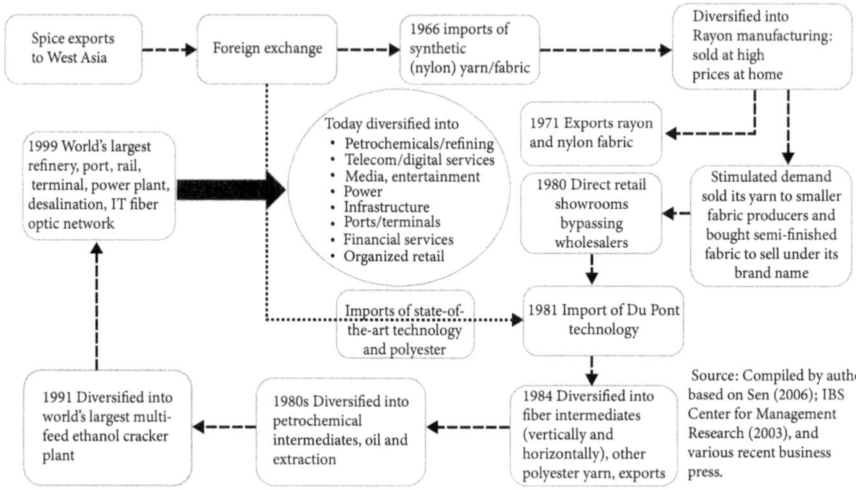

Source: Compiled by author based on Sen (2006); IBS Center for Management Research (2003), and various recent business press.

Figure 3.2 Strategic Diversification by Reliance Industries through Vertical Integration, an Abridged Version

We can infer that large-scale investments such as those by Reliance in a wide range of industrial goods induced local learning and deepened the capital and intermediate goods sectors. Over time, they also gave rise to a capable professional managerial class. Yet, the Indian economy remained slow growing. There were many reasons but the principal one was the highly restrictive regulatory environment in a protected market, which distorted the economic incentives for growth and diversification. Only a few businessmen such as Dhirubhai Ambani, with his business acumen and his personal relationship with the government, could circumvent these constraints. Added to this, or perhaps because of it, an institutional *malaise* arose from the many social and political demands on the state, which pushed the economy into a slow-growth mode. These took various forms: demands for subsidies by business sectors, rent-seeking behavior (earning excess profits in protected or monopoly sectors) by business, and outright corruption in the bureaucracy and political establishment (D'Costa 2023, Bardhan 1984). Not surprisingly, the complicity of business in currying favors from the state also undercut the well-intentioned economic priorities and development goals of the state.

3.2.1 How the Indian Private Auto Industry Became a State Success

The automobile industry is part of the heavy industry group because of the many engineering and manufacturing sectors associated with it that use the output from heavy industry such as machinery, steel, and manufactured components. However, as discussed earlier, government priorities were not in consumer products, and that included passenger cars. Instead, within the automotive sector, there was an emphasis on the production of commercial vehicles for goods transportation, buses for the public transit systems, and tractors for farming. Since the automotive industry was also bound by the same larger regulatory environment of protectionism and production quotas, making domestic markets effectively closed from foreign competition and technologies, private manufacturers were profitable in the captive market but remained far behind the international technological frontier.

The automotive industry was a high-cost, low-volume one mainly because of the lack of scale economies. Government taxes on passenger vehicles were unusually high and the queues for purchasing a vehicle were long, with waiting periods often exceeding three years. Interestingly, the development of the Indian auto industry, until the early 1980s, was independent of the global shifts taking place. The European and Japanese auto makers were making inroads into foreign markets, including the US, which was the world's largest auto producer and market. Not surprisingly, India's share of global production remained under 0.5% until 1981 (United Nations Centre on Transnational Corporations 1983:14). With the establishment of the Maruti-Suzuki joint venture in 1982, the Indian industry gradually joined the global restructuring of the auto industry.

Before 1982, there were three main manufacturers of passenger vehicles: Hindustan Motors (HM) near Kolkata (formerly Calcutta), Premier Automobiles in Mumbai (formerly Bombay), and Standard Motors in Chennai (formerly Madras). Of the three, HM's Ambassador model was far more popular than any passenger car produced by the other two manufacturers.[7] Between 1955 and 1980, HM dominated the Indian market. With the entry of foreign manufacturers, all three of India's original auto manufacturers have now ceased production (Table 3.2).

HM has been the flagship company of the C. K. Birla Group of the Birla family business house. In 1948, HM began producing the ubiquitous Ambassador car from a Morris Oxford model. HM strategy was no different from most other Indian firms, including its nearest rivals Premier Automobiles from Mumbai and Standard Motors from Chennai. These companies did not technologically upgrade their products nor introduce new models as long as output was controlled through licenses, prices were regulated, and imports of

[7] The quality of Indian manufacturing behind closed doors turned out to be inferior compared to international standards. For example, the Ambassador car has been light-heartedly referred to as having an engine the size of a coconut or that every part of the car made a noise except the horn!

Table 3.2 Passenger Car Production (Numbers) by Firms and Their Market Share (% of Total)

	HM	PAL	SMP	SAL	M&M**	MUL	TELCO	Others#	Total Number
1955	4,874	3,581	1,526	-	2,864	-	-	-	12,865
Mkt. Share	37.9	27.8	12.0	-	22.3	-	-	-	
1960	9,217	6,616	3,364	-	5,501	-	-	-	24,598
Mkt. Share	37.5	26.5	13.7	-	22.4	-	-	-	
1970	22,703	12,054	448	-	9,334	-	-	-	44,539
Mkt. Share	51.0	27.0	1.0	-	21.0	-	-	-	
1980	21,752	8,729	6	51	15,068	-	-	-	45,606
Mkt. Share	47.7	19.1	0.0	0.1	33.0	-	-	-	
1990	26,204	42,737	-	924	32,706	116,194@	265*	-	218,765
Mkt. Share	12.0	19.5	-	0.4	15.0	53.1	-	-	
1997	24,059	14,169	-	-	69,277	349,780@	6,302	22,545	486,132
Mkt. Share	5.0	2.9	-	-	14.3	72.0	1.3	4.6	
1999	23,306	12,988	-	-	69,265	393,837	70,768	83,812	654,036
Mkt. Share	3.6	2.0	-	-	10.6	60.2	10.8	12.8	

Notes: HM = Hindustan Motors, PAL = Premier Automobiles Limited, SMP = Standard Motor Products, SAL = Sipani Automobiles Limited, M&M = Mahindra and Mahindra, MUL = Maruti Udyog Limited, TELCO = Tata Engineering and Locomotive Company (now Tata Motors).
*for the year 1991,
**Jeeps/Utility Vehicles, @ includes 9238 and 6959 utility vehicles for 1990 and 1997, respectively, # includes Daewoo, General Motors, PAL-Peugeot, Mercedes-Benz, in 1999 also Hyundai and Fiat.Shares are rounded.

Source: AIAM, ACMA, various issues in D'Costa (2005: 86)

technology restricted due to a shortage of foreign exchange. They strategically favored protection, without which they certainly would have disappeared earlier. As early as the mid-1960s, HM was already quite defensive about competition that could have arisen with the introduction of small cars (Hindustan Motors Limited 1966: 83–84). HM argued that small cars in India would be inappropriate as Indians traveled together as families and would have had to carry "beddings" (typically quilts, pillows, and the like rolled up in a hold-all).

Although production of cars was discouraged by the government due to the impoverished state of the country, the stifling of auto production hurt overall industrial and economic development. Following the same logic of economic and technological linkages, greater dynamism in the auto industry would have spurred upstream manufacturing activities in the parts and components segment. The low-key production system based on in-house production as opposed to extensive subcontracting arrangements, which had increasingly become the industry practice, limited the diffusion of independent parts manufacturers, except in the case of spare parts, which were sometimes deemed "spurious" and of dubious quality by the industry. There were some spillover effects of auto manufacturing with a variety of ancillary industries sprouting around auto manufacturing centers in Pune and Mumbai, Kolkata, and Chennai. However, with small volumes of auto output and in-house production, the economic impact and competitiveness of the sector were limited by low productivity, labor-intensive production, technological backwardness, and high costs.[8] As we will see briefly in Chapter 5, it is only when output increased in the 1980s with Japanese collaborations in an increasingly deregulated environment, an entirely new kind of supplier industry linked to a major assembler emerged (Table 3.3). After 1995, the industry expansion was catalyzed by further relaxation of production regulations. It also marked the beginning of a new phase in industrialization with output and employment growth, production innovations, and exports. Such a sectoral transformation has been good for economic development but is not without its contradictions (or negative externalities) such as traffic congestion, undermining the urban quality of life, vehicle emissions, and continued dependence on imported fossil fuel (more on this in Chapter 5).

As Table 3.3 illustrates, the decadal output of the auto components industries expanded rapidly beginning in 1981–1982 when the state formed a joint venture with Suzuki Motors of Japan. India had 80% equity in the

[8] Here, labor intensity suggests that auto production in India was not automated as they were in other parts of the world. There are two implications of this: employment per unit of output would have been higher with corresponding low productivity and lack of modern technologies would have impacted the quality of vehicle assembly (see D'Costa 2027a, forthcoming).

Table 3.3 Expanding Market for the Indian Automotive Components Industry

April/March	Engine Parts	Electrical Parts	Transmission and Steering Parts	Suspension Braking Parts	Equipment	Other Parts	Total
1961–1962	80.78	6.60	9.42	36.85	8.26	36.41	178.43
1971–1972	479.44	124.66	273.26	303.80	65.82	63.64	1310.63
1981–1982	2529.98	897.03	1680.89	1150.55	231.03	290.11	6480.00
	(282.11)	(110.02)	(187.43)	(128.30)	(25.76)	(32.35)	(722.57)
1991–1992	10,491.73	2212.17	6782.52	3696.05	1116.70	1775.74	26,074.91
	(428.69)	(90.39)	(277.13)	(151.02)	(45.63)	(72.56)	(1065.41)
2001–2002	38,370.88	13,000.66	26,332.03	19,556.74	11,114.23	52,998.54	161,642.09
	(804.56)	(272.60)	(552.13)	(410.06)	(233.04)	(1111.27)	(3389.29)

Notes: US$ values are in parenthesis, based on the appropriate official exchange rates taken from Government of India, Ministry of Finance (various issues). Data is for the organized sector only and does not include the "small scale industry" sector as defined by the Government of India.

Source: Automotive Components Manufacturers Association (various issues) in D'Costa (2005:136)

partnership; Suzuki Motors had 20% equity. Curiously, the first round of limited opening up of the private auto industry in India resulted in one of the most successful public sector companies in India! The joint venture was the beginning of a major transformation of the Indian auto industry (D'Costa 2005, 1998b). Businesses in classic linkage fashion responded to the market opportunities that opened up for parts and components production. Subsequently, the growth in the automobile industry fostered a massive expansion of suppliers and many of them also became exporters. For example, from almost zero exports, India exported 28,122 vehicles in 1998–1999, which by 2002–2003 had reached 71,653 (India Today 2003). Later, the industry as a whole returned to private hands, mostly multinational companies such as Suzuki, Hyundai, General Motors (GM), Toyota, and others. Tata Motors, the only domestic company of any standing, failed to enter the passenger vehicle segment in a significant way even as it consolidated its market position in the commercial vehicle segment and in 2008 strategically acquired the high-end British auto companies Jaguar and Land Rover.

3.4 The Computer Sector

Notwithstanding the challenges facing the Indian economy, both the state and business were acutely aware of the importance of new technological breakthroughs. After all, economic development was about increasing productivity. Technologies, when combined with organizational innovations and appropriate human skills, offer the best antidote to low productivity. In the 1950s, the computer hardware industry was in its infancy. A few Western multinationals, especially from the United States such as International Business Machines (IBM) and Burroughs, dominated the global industry. However, the related upstream electronics industry was rapidly changing with new, ever-smaller transistors or semiconductors (the basic building block for all electronic products and services). This opened up opportunities for applying computers and software for rudimentary office automation, manufacturing processes, and scientific endeavors. In this transformation, electronics became ubiquitous and the design and manufacture of microchips not only became technologically complex and investment-intensive, but the labor-intensive aspects of the electronics industry, namely, assembly of parts (chips and circuit boards) were initially farmed out to low-wage countries of Southeast and East Asia such as Malaysia, Singapore, South Korea, Taiwan, and later China. Advanced capitalist countries such as the US, Japan, the Netherlands, and Germany concentrated on the knowledge-intensive aspects of the electronics industry such as design and the manufacturing of chip-making equipment. India was not a participant in this changing international division of labor mainly because of its inward-looking, self-reliant strategy, Cold War geopolitics, and a lack of domestic policies to take advantage of global technologies for economic development. Much later, having missed the manufacturing bus, India serendipitously found an opportunity to utilize its technical professionals to serve the growing software needs of multinational companies.

4.1.1 Making IT Hardware (Computers) behind Closed Doors

Unlike heavy industry, where sectoral linkages and the multiplier effects were tangible, the impact of the computer industry was more indirect. While the Indian state initially did not own any enterprises in the sector, it put in place some of the institutions, such as the Department of Electronics in 1970, and relaxed some of the restrictions on imported technologies to nurture the sector. Due to the shortage of foreign exchange, imported hardware was discouraged while the government encouraged a home-grown electronics industry using imported parts and components. From a cost point of view, this strategy did not make sense. However, the government realized the importance of this sector and introduced the 1972 Software Export Scheme (Heeks 1996: 42) to encourage exports of software to pay for the imports of hardware with foreign exchange earnings. Seeing new opportunities, large businesses such as Tata Consultancy Services (TCS) and Hindustan Computers Limited (HCL) leveraged India's growing number of technical professionals to begin exporting software services to obtain imported hardware. A handful of multinationals such as IBM (US) and International Computers Limited (ICL) (UK) were granted entry into the Indian market to supply mainframe computers. A few joint ventures between Indian and foreign multinationals such as Tata-Burroughs were also selectively permitted mainly to tap relatively abundant technical talent for software services for multinational corporations.

Similar to other sectors of the time, protection was extended to the electronics and computer hardware sectors (Sridharan 1996). In line with the import substitution industrialization (ISI) strategy, the Indian state tried to nurture a self-sufficient hardware sector (see Sarma and Krishna 2010: 29–31). However, the macroeconomic environment and geopolitical circumstances were not conducive to the promotion of a local hardware sector. Being on the wrong side of the Cold War fence, India's international participation in the global electronics and computer hardware sector was restricted. Many of these technologies were categorized as dual-use, meaning, they had both civilian and military applications. The Department of Electronics was keen to support the computer industry through import liberalization despite political opposition to large-scale imports. India's stance toward multinationals and cold India–US relations further restricted the flow of know-how. Although multinational computer companies such as IBM were already present in India beginning in 1951, these companies bundled their hardware (mainframe computers) with software, leaving little space for domestic development. Only application software specific to the foreign-made hardware was developed locally. In the end, the lack of imported know-how constrained the development of a domestic hardware sector and not surprisingly failed to prevent the imports of mainframes and later microcomputers. Local efforts were not much more than the assembly of imported components and the Indian hardware sector lacked economies of scale to be viable (Heeks 1996).

The anticipated needs for economic planning under state-led import substitution industrialization as well as the vast expected needs for technical professionals for industrialization led to the first imports of computers by the government and by state-established technical institutions of higher learning (Mistree 2019). Motivated by India's quest for a science- and technology-based industrialization, tertiary technical education was fostered (Balakrishnan 2006: 3866). The growing number of engineering graduates in a slow-growing, jobs-scarce economy contributed to software competence as technical students began working for multinational and a few domestic hardware firms (see Sharma 2009). Such policy shifts as well as changes in business strategy clearly set the precedent for training large numbers of technical professionals, which unwittingly marked the beginning of India's growing prowess in software exports.

There was another unintended impetus to generating technical professionals. In 1977, the short-lived coalition government implemented the 1973 Foreign Exchange Regulation Act (FERA), which limited foreign ownership to 40%. This compelled IBM and ICL (as well as Coca Cola) to leave India rather than dilute their equity. The exit of these computer multinationals, especially IBM, led to the creation of a public sector unit, the Computer Maintenance Corporation (CMC) and privately owned Operations Research Group (ORG) Systems. These companies were mandated to maintain IBM and other large computer systems in the country. Both CMC and ORG Systems were staffed by many former IBM engineers. In addition to these large enterprises such as CMC, ORG, Hindustan Computers Limited (HCL), and Tata-Burroughs, several small IT firms emerged as well. The big boost for software development in India came in 1984 from Citicorp Overseas Software Limited (COSL), an independent subsidiary of Citibank to export software for Citibank's worldwide computerization needs (Sharma 2009: 296). Hardware efforts by the state also included the Centre for Development of Telematics (C-DOT), a telecommunications equipment manufacturer, especially for rural telephone exchanges (D'Costa 2002).

While these state and business efforts served India's information technology needs in a limited way, the sector's growth trajectory was abruptly cut short with the economic reforms of the mid-1980s and 1991 onward that opened up the Indian market to foreign businesses. East and Southeast Asian economies such as Japan, South Korea, Taiwan, and Singapore already had a head start in the electronics industry through aggressive industrialization policies that included aggressive export drives. These strategic approaches by the different states were followed by domestic market development, including infrastructure spending and attracting foreign investment to further boost exports. Naturally, these countries could keep up with the international technological frontier and compete internationally by not restricting imports as well as having an explicit strategy of national technological learning.

The gaps in investment and technological capabilities in the electronics industry between India and those of East Asia, which was linked to foreign multinationals, were much too wide to be quickly narrowed. The huge investment, know-how, and infrastructure entry barriers for manufacturing electronics and the related hardware sector could not be justified economically. Without a commercial chip-manufacturing plant, which is critical to the electronics industry and would require at least a billion dollars in investment, the idea of a domestic electronics manufacturing industry was abandoned. For better or worse, it was also too late for India to enter the hardware sector as the availability of a relatively abundant pool of technical professionals could be quickly and profitably mobilized to serve the growing global software services market. The net effect of India's hardware policy was the creation of a handful of short-lived local and joint-venture hardware firms. Paradoxically, with a growing army of engineers generated by the Indian technical education infrastructure, these firms indirectly incubated software services firms for the US market.

4.2.1 A Giant Leap into Software Services

A slow-growing Indian economy by default generated an abundance of technical professionals as the supply of engineers, aimed to support a faltering ISI program, exceeded the demand for them. However, with the global proliferation of electronics, digital technologies, and the emergence of independent global software firms such as Microsoft, the demand for software services increased dramatically with India gradually becoming an important source for inexpensive technical professionals. One advantage India had, at least among the educated, is English-speaking capability. During the state-led industrialization phase (circa mid-1950s to early 1980s), the Indian government established several elite technical education institutes to serve industrial growth. Few of the engineers were absorbed by the nascent computer industry for hardware development since this sector could not match the scale nor competitiveness of the East Asian electronics and hardware sectors.

Given the abundant college-educated, English-speaking, middle-class technical professionals and the rapidly emerging global market opportunities in software services, Indian hardware firms such as Western India Vegetable Products Limited (Wipro, a syllabic abbreviation of the original name), Patni, Tata Consulting Services (TCS), and HCL reoriented their businesses increasingly toward software services. The technical capabilities of Indian engineers were informally confirmed by the American firm Texas Instruments in the 1980s when it successfully tapped Indian engineers on an experimental basis for a small but complex software design project. The success of Citibank's COSL also firmly set India's software trajectory. Since then, many home-grown and multinational firms such as TCS, Infosys, HCL, Mastek, Ramco, Citicorp, IBM, and Philips have made India their preferred location to develop software services, delivering them worldwide for both in-house use and third-party clients. The United States has remained India's largest software export market followed by Western Europe and other anglophone countries.

The rapid growth in the Indian software industry (see Table 3.4) can be disaggregated into two segments that have different implications for economic development. The first is information technology-enabled services (ITES), which comprises mainly back office (call center) services for various (international) clients such as telecom companies, manufacturing firms who need after-sales service, subscription-based services such as insurance, internet, TV, and mobile phone services, and banks. These services use labor-intensive jobs dependent on college-educated youth with neutralized English-speaking competency. They rely on high-quality internet infrastructure. Unlike software services, this segment of IT services generally does not rely on highly trained technical professionals. Despite the tediousness of phone- or web-based services working with a foreign language, these are relatively good jobs in a market of labor surplus and scarce employment opportunities for

Table 3.4 Growth in the Indian Software Industry

Year	Domestic Software Market ($ b)	Software Exports ($ b)	Total Market ($ b)	% Change in Software Exports	Software Exports as Share of India's Total Software Market (%)	India's Total Exports (b $)	% Change in India's Total Exports
1991–1992	0.2	0.8	1.0	-	80	25.5*	-
1995–1996	0.8	2.1	2.9	190	72	40.8**	60
2000	2.4	3.5	5.9	490	59	60.9	49
2005	10.0	18.0	28.0	375	64	160.8	164
2010	24.0	50.0	74.0	164	68	375.4	134
2015	34.0	99.0	133.0	80	74	416.8	11
2019	41.0	136.0	177.0	33	77	529.2	27
2022	49.0	199.0	248.0	31	78	779.5***	46

Notes: b = billions
% Change = year/period to year/period, as reported in the Table
*for the year 1992
**for the year 1996
***for the year 2023, from Macrotrends, https://www.macrotrends.net/global-metrics/countries/ind/india/exports, accessed August 17, 2024.*Sources*: Heeks (2010) for 1991–1992 and 1995–1996. Jalote and Natarajan (2019), Macrotrends for Total Exports, India Exports 1960–2022, https://www.macrotrends.net/countries/IND/india/exports, India Brand Equity Forum (2025). IT and BPM Industry in India, https://www.ibef.org/industry/information-technology-india (for fiscal year 2024), accessed March 18, 2025

undifferentiated, nontechnical, college-educated youth. While not always guaranteed, a steady job has long-term favorable developmental implications such as access for their children's education, better health, and higher disposable income through promotion and career development.

The second segment is IT services proper, which comprises software development for a range of large customized enterprise solutions for business and government such as supply chain management, logistics, payroll, inventory management, airlines reservations, and e-commerce. Employment in this segment is also labor-intensive but the value addition is higher than for ITES since formal technical training and skill development are necessary requirements for software development. Correspondingly, the revenues and foreign exchange earned by software service companies are also high.

From a development perspective, the rapid expansion of software exports has led to India's growing foreign exchange reserves, contributed to relatively well-paying white-collar employment directly and indirectly, and indirectly to lower-paying and less-skilled support services jobs such as domestic help, security guards, drivers, gardeners, and so on who are employed by the IT sector and the well-paid technical professionals. These support services jobs tend to fall under the informal labor market, clearly indicating the asymmetrical codependency of the formal and informal labor markets. The ripple effect of high salaries impacted other low-wage service providers in a positive way but also reproduce the stark inequality. The sector is estimated to employ a combined total of 5.4 million IT software and IT-enabled services workers (IBEF IT and BPM 2025), which is less than 1% of India's workforce. Indirectly, an estimated 15–16 million are employed in the low-wage services sector on account of the IT sector.

The ITES and software services sectors have reinforced the middle class's penchant for tertiary technical education, and quite narrowly, to information technology fields. The Indian education system has also responded to this growing demand in a virtuous cycle by quantitatively increasing enrollments in technical education. According to the All India Council for Technical Education (AICTE), there are 5868 approved engineering colleges with more than 2.5 million approved in-take of students in 2023–2024 (AICTE 2025). Leading Indian and multinational software companies such as Infosys, TCS, IBM, and Accenture recruit from the handful of elite public and private technology institutions. With significant wage arbitrage, especially for technically less demanding work, the availability of abundant workers, and the increasing scope for tradable services via modern digital communications systems, India has become the preferred destination for global outsourcing of software services.

However, there are long-term limits to employment growth if the sector continues to rely on abundant supplies of labor. Automation and international competition from China, Eastern Europe, and the Philippines, among others, pose threats to India's IT sector. Since extensive growth takes place by adding more people, which does not necessarily yield higher returns per employee, there is pressure to move toward an intensive form of growth using new technology and deeper skills. This will ensure higher revenues and greater inflows of foreign exchange earnings. The industry is trying to move in that direction but the heavy reliance on the US market, even with linkages back home, limits the economic and technological multiplier effect in the domestic market. There is also the inherent apprehension surrounding technologies such as artificial intelligence (AI) and machine learning (ML) that may have a substitution effect at the lower end of IT and IT-related jobs, while complementing higher-value-adding jobs (Halal, Kolber, and Davies 2016, Bessen 2018).[9] Another disquieting feature of the success of the Indian IT sector is enclave economies. They result from the tight linkages of particular cities such as Bengaluru, Chennai, and Hyderabad to the world economy, which are economically weakly connected to the different states and regions in the country where most of the professionals come from (D'Costa 2006). Digital India is an initiative by the government to spread the benefits of IT broadly to the society (see Chapter 5) and minimize the income and regional polarization that results from its very success.

It is obvious that the IT sector has a skill bias, which effectively excludes most Indians from joining the industry (D'Costa 2003a). Better placed middle-class students vie for the few spots in technical institutes, colleges, and universities. IT professionals are paid well compared to most other professions in the country mainly because there is an informal indexing of salaries and wages to the US market. An economic dualism is readily apparent with IT cities such as Bengaluru and Hyderabad experiencing significant gentrification and real estate inflation, while vast numbers of informal workers residing in these cities continue to struggle for a livelihood. More importantly, the hasty process of expanding Indian higher education and the clamor for technical degrees has also resulted in "surplus" professionals with the quality of such training often found to be inadequate by the industry. The National Association of Software and Services Companies (NASSCOM), the industry body with more than 90% of Indian IT firms as members, has often lamented that only a third to a quarter of technical graduates are readily employable,

[9] There is no certainty of the magnitudes of displacement of jobs on the IT/ITES sectors. However, if AI and ML are seen as new forms of automation and applications, then some jobs will disappear and others appear, including new tasks in the same job category.

resulting in considerable investment by businesses to train their workforce and thus absorb higher costs.

It would be a great omission if some of the credit for the success of the IT industry is not attributed to the Indian government. This is of course a contentious issue. What has the government done for the IT industry? This reasonable question is unlikely to lead to direct evidence of government support that contributed to the sector's success since most of the initiatives were undertaken by businesses themselves (D'Costa 2025a). However, economic activities do not take place in a social vacuum and like most such activities the effects of the past have an impact on the future in a path-dependent way. Take for example the state-led effort in import substitution industrialization, which prompted the government to establish several technology and engineering schools. These institutions became the critical supplier of technical talent initially for industry, then the hardware segment of the IT industry. Today, the global IT industry is led by many of the graduates from these Indian public educational institutions. The establishment of state-owned CMC to maintain imported computers after the departure of IBM and ICL in 1977 also incubated technical engineers for the IT services sector.

The growth of the software sector reoriented engineers away from the hardware sector. On top of this, as shown earlier, tens of thousands of students enrolled in engineering in both public and private institutions with an eye to the fast-growing IT sector. The state reinforced this growth, with state-funded Software Technology Parks, which provided a tax holiday for ten years and infrastructural support to IT businesses as long as 100% of software output was exported. Bengaluru, Hyderabad, Chennai, and the greater national capital region (NCR) of Delhi are India's leading software centers. Creating a favorable export-oriented policy environment, the Indian government together with NASSCOM (National Association of Software and Services Companies) ensured the "India" brand for IT services exports (D'Costa 2025a).

While a precise balance sheet of development benefits and costs isn't possible, it is important to remember that the IT industry is one of the best performing sectors in India and can be credited for its many contributions to economic development. It represents about 8% of India's GDP and employs over 5 million people directly, plus another 15 to 16 million people in low-wage, un- and semi-skilled service sector jobs, often in informal labor markets. The sector is a major earner of foreign exchange, to the tune of almost $193 billion in fiscal year 2023 (IBEF IT-BPM 2025: 9). Tied to the United States and other international markets, the Indian IT industry is compelled to keep up with innovations and thus improve its technological capabilities, moving toward higher-value services such as cloud computing. Although improving, the Indian IT sector is ranked at forty-six of the top 100 and is roughly a middling position in the Global Innovation Index (GII). The GII is a composite number based on around eighty indicators to broadly capture the innovation environment covering various economic, social, political, regulatory, and online activity dimensions, and the availability of knowledge workers, among others. For all the hype of the Indian IT industry, there is little visible innovation. There is every possibility the sector will continue to grow and diversify into higher value-added services, but the world is not standing still. There is growing lower-cost competition from the Philippines and Eastern Europe, especially if Indian IT salaries continue to rise in tandem with the US market. Also, India's open access could be jeopardized by unpredictable tariffs and other protectionist policies, including the possibility of tightening employment visa allocations by the United States.

3.5 The State, Pharmaceutical Sector, and Affordable Medicines

Economic development can also be seen as a means to achieving good health. It could result from increasing incomes thereby allowing people to spend some of that income on basic healthcare. However, if the society is impoverished to begin with, higher incomes will not be adequate to keep citizens free from disease and early death. Here, the role of the government is critical and the independent Indian state very early on recognized the importance of ensuring access to critical modern medicines. This access is not the same as offering adequate healthcare services but it is one facet of it. So, what did the government do that enabled India ultimately to become an affordable pharmacy to the world?

The critical policy intervention was the 1970 Indian Patent Act. By this decree, India did not recognize product patents but recognized process patents when it came to pharmaceutical products. The logic was simple although highly controversial from a capitalist property rights point of view. The government of India wanted to ensure that people of limited economic means had access to essential drugs, which morally and ethically justified the Act. Consequently, the Patent Act of 1970 legally allowed Indian pharmaceutical businesses to reverse engineer foreign-made drugs with different processes and come up with inexpensive drugs through "creative imitation" (Athreye, Kale, and Ramani 2009: 732). Major drug prices were controlled by large Western multinationals. The results were not inconsequential. Between

1970 and 2003, of the ten largest pharmaceutical companies operating in India, multinationals in 1970 had 15.1% of the market, which by 2003 had declined to 12.8% (Athreye, Kale, and Ramani 2009: 733). During the same period, the number of Indian companies in the top ten pharmaceutical companies operating in India rose from two to six.

With economic reforms, the pharmaceutical sector in 1991 was deregulated and prices were decontrolled. This introduced significant competition, restructuring, and growth of the sector. Furthermore, India thereafter joined the WTO in 1995 and in 2004 also signed onto the Trade Related Aspects of Intellectual Property Rights (TRIPS) Agreement under the WTO, which led to the dismantling of the 1970 Patent Act. However, as incomes rose in the post-reform period and income inequality worsened, there were public concerns about manufacturers raising drug prices and using active pharmaceutical ingredients (API) to market their products (see Sen 2005 for details). An API constitutes the core material of any drug that serves to produce the desired therapeutic effect in the body. Lacking significant product innovation capabilities, under the WTO regime, the industry was compelled to quickly move into generic drugs. New drug development based on R&D capacity was limited in India. The 1970 Act had given ample time for Indian manufacturers to develop generic drugs that could be competitively exported since patents on several products had expired. High drug prices in wealthy countries charged by their own TNCs also boosted the global demand for alternative, cheaper generic drugs. Almost 20% of the global generics market today is supplied by Indian companies.

This international exposure pushed Indian firms to move away from generics, which are copies of chemical drugs, to undertaking R&D for biosimilars. The latter closely resemble complex, biologically derived medical products. Today, India is the generics pharmacy to the world as well as the largest manufacturer of vaccines. Of the top fifty pharma companies in the world, sixteen are from the US, eight from Japan, three from China, France, and Germany, two from Switzerland, the UK, and Denmark, and depending on the year, there are one to three Indian companies in the list. Table 3.5 illustrates the presence of an Indian pharmaceutical company in 2024 that has made it to the top fifty global list, indicating that the sector has diversified from domestic to international markets. Although not listed, Serum Institute of India is also credited with being the world's number one vaccine producer and exporter under license, with revenues of roughly $10 billion. Who could have imagined a patent act designed to protect India's poor would also benefit the global community at a later date?

Table 3.5 Globally Ranked Indian Pharmaceutical Company in 2024

Rank	Company	Headquarters	Revenues (2024) billion dollars
1.	Merck and Company	US	64.17
2.	Pfizer	US	63.63
6.	Roche Group	Switzerland	52.45
10.	Sanofi S.A.	France	44.47
11.	Novo Nordisk	Denmark	42.11
12.	GSK PLC	UK	40.10
15.	Takeda Pharmaceutical	Japan	28.16
40.	Jazz Pharmaceuticals	Ireland	4.07
42.	Sino Biopharmaceutical	China	4.02
46.	Dr. Reddy's Labs	India	3.35

Source: Drug Discovery and Development, Pharma 50: The fifty largest pharmaceutical companies in the world, https://www.drugdiscoverytrends.com/pharma-50-the-50-largest-pharmaceutical-companies-in-the-world/, accessed July 15, 2025

The contribution of the pharmaceutical industry to economic development can be seen in two ways. The first by using a narrow lens, which is consistent with a sectoral approach, shows us the business contribution to economic development. Accordingly, the pharmaceutical sector has generated considerable revenues, employment, and exports (Indian Pharmaceutical Alliance 2019). The Indian Pharmaceutical Association (2019) reported that nearly three million jobs have been created both directly and indirectly. The total market size is about $50 billion, of which 50% was exported (IBEF Pharmaceuticals 2025). As mentioned earlier, India supplies 20% of the global generics market. Sun Pharmaceutical, Cipla, and Dr. Reddy's are major generic drug suppliers from India. These companies have been able to maintain drug prices that even the poor in India can access.[10]

Using the second, broader lens to capture the benefits of the pharmaceutical industry is a more difficult task since the benefits of public health measures, of which the pharmaceutical industry is just one component, cannot be solely attributed to the sector. For example, high doctor-patient ratio, good distribution of primary health centers in rural areas, easy access to hospitals for

[10] In 2025, one branded drug in the United States was estimated to cost $1600 for a three-month supply compared to a generic version that retailed in India for a little over a dollar. Cipla, an Indian pharmaceutical company, priced its AIDS drugs in India at 7%–11% of multinational prices. It offered to sell them to Africa through Doctors without Borders at even lower prices, at 4%–6% of what TNCs were charging (McNeil 2001). See also Organisation of Pharmaceutical Producers of India (2019).

critical services, committed preventive care regimes, and so on are all part of a complex constellation of necessary public health services. Also, the benefits of good healthcare are likely to be felt gradually in multiple ways over a long period of time in the form of higher attendance of children in school, fewer absences from work, longer lives, better employment opportunities, thus higher income, among other benefits.[11]

Assuming that good health is also good for economic development—as opposed to the more conventional view that health outcomes are a function of economic development alone—we find that India has made substantial improvements since 1990. For example, polio has been virtually eliminated, maternal and infant mortality rates have decreased from 410 to 160 deaths per 100,000 live births and from eighty to thirty-four deaths per 1000 live births, respectively. Also, life expectancy and universal immunizations have increased from fifty-eight to sixty-nine years and from 20% to 63%, respectively (Organisation of Pharmaceutical Producers of India 2019: 6–9). Similarly, the United Nations Human Development Index (HDI) which includes a health component in addition to income and education also shows improvements. Between 1970 and 2019, India's HDI score increased from 0.258 to 0.645 (United Nations Development Program (UNDP), various years) although its ranking relative to the rest of the world did not register a perceptible shift. While the effect of the availability of affordable drugs on improving HDI may be difficult to capture, increasing HDI demonstrates the general improvements in the health of the population. This confirms the long-term effects of past health-related policies which, while very inadequate, included the promotion of the pharmaceutical sector for supplying affordable drugs.

However, the lack of a universal health care system and skewed income distribution might be partly responsible for India's declining HDI rankings relative to other countries such as China that are doing better on this front. Introducing a universal health care system, a daunting task for a large country, is feasible with the right set of deliberative institutions and modern delivery logistics. With state commitments to universal health care, Indian businesses could intensify their engagement with the manufacture of higher-value drug therapies and R&D for biosimilars and affordable healthcare centers, including non-profit ones, for the public. New businesses could be also launched in healthcare delivery logistics, independently and integrally as part of the Digital India initiative (see Chapter 5). The complementary role of public and

[11] To track the flow of benefits over time is a demanding task and the causation effect is suspect since access to drugs and medical cures is only one important element of many other variables that contribute to a reliable public health service. Also, there are some pitfalls to cheap generics in a society where prescription rather than prevention has become the norm.

private sector can be expected to further boost the pharmaceutical industry in new directions and contribute to India's future economic development.

3.6 Business, State, and Economic Development Revisited

In this chapter, I briefly showcased some of the foundational business sectors that lay behind India's post-independence, state-mediated economic development. The industries covered illustrated their evolution in the specific Indian context, especially the different forms of interactions with the government and revealed in broad brush strokes their multifarious contributions as well as limitations to economic development. Heavy industries such as steel and machinery were part of India's early developmental thrust, guided very much by the idea of self-reliance that explicitly relied on the dynamics of economic linkages, multiplier effect, and the complementary roles of the state and private sector. The output from heavy industries (mostly state-owned) crowded in other related manufacturing sectors (mostly privately owned), thereby jumpstarting the economic development process, including jobs creation, technological and organizational learning, and of course, capitalist business enterprises.

Some sectors have been critical to employment but may not be high growth-oriented because of the nature of the product. These sectors provide economic and political stability because they absorb unskilled and semi-skilled labor on a large scale. The textiles and apparel, diamond, and leather industries fall into this category. They remain important for employment, provide livelihoods for millions of people, and contribute to economic diversification. However, because of abundant labor supply and fierce international competition, they do not necessarily represent more value-adding, better-paying jobs. Of course, within each of these sectors, there are different value-adding segments. For example, making footwear with international standards and high brand value or simply exporting cured hides, polishing diamonds, and marketing and retailing of diamonds directly to consumers are all different value-adding activities. Understandably, tapping final international consumer markets is not easy because of the huge marketing and branding investments needed to cater to different tastes and negotiate the rigors of global competition. Here, the state can play a promotional role in encouraging diversification through forward and backward integration of economic activities within the Indian economy as much as possible. Provision of global market information will be also critical in this effort.

Two important manufacturing sectors that did not take off during the period of state-led industrialization were the automobile industry and the computer hardware sector. The former was not a priority of the state, missing out of course on the very same concept on which other heavy industries were justified, namely, economic linkages and positive externalities. The state saw cars as luxury items and import controls gave domestic business opportunities to thrive in the sheltered market but failed to foster economic development contributions in a big way, until the arrival of Suzuki Motors and its partnership with the Indian government. Technology import restrictions justified by foreign exchange scarcity denied opportunities for industrial upgrading. However, with subsequent changes in policy, the Indian automotive sector today has been transformed into one of India's leading growth sectors (IBEF Automobiles 2025, IBEF Auto Components 2025).

The Indian computer hardware sector was not so fortunate for three reasons. First, faced with technology import restrictions, the hardware sector remained behind the international technology frontier. Second, liberalization of imports that was permitted later with foreign exchange earnings through exports was too little and too late. Third, lacking a dynamic domestic electronics sector, the hardware sector had few backward linkages, while foreign exchange scarcity pushed many hardware firms to start exporting software services. In the meantime, government initiatives in East Asia and foreign direct investment in Southeast Asia by the United States and other high-wage countries and later East Asia gradually fostered a highly developed, regionally integrated electronics sector. It began with simple product assembly using local labor and imported components to manufacturing a wide range of high-value electronics components and final products, which narrowed the scope for establishing an electronics industry in India.

Thus, in a path-dependent way, given the abundant availability of low-cost technical professionals, the Indian hardware sector unwittingly placed India on the global software map. Here, too, the Indian state played a role by first establishing a set of science and technology institutes for technical training at the tertiary education level for its industrial effort, which unwittingly was repurposed to serve the nascent software sector. Second, by providing export incentives and critical satellite communications infrastructure, the software sector began taking off. The export success of the software sector illustrates the complementarity of business and state roles, although in this case the state has followed the industry rather than leading it (D'Costa 2025a). However, because demand for software services is mostly external, economic linkages have not been very dense. The spillover effects, aside from high salaries for technical and managerial professionals, have been largely in the real estate and high-value consumer markets and in unskilled, nontechnical, labor markets such as construction, security staff, domestic help, and other non-tradable services.

This chapter also demonstrated that in addition to the direct economic benefits such as employment of both semi-skilled and highly trained technical professionals, sectoral growth, economic and industry diversification, and export revenues offered by a few sectors, the pharmaceutical industry has also served an important social purpose. With supportive state policy in making drugs affordable through its patent policy, the Indian pharmaceutical industry has served millions of patients at home and abroad. With investments in a universal healthcare program, we can expect better health for Indians and further economic development.

From a structural point of view, stating the obvious, India is an agrarian society with a large informal labor market (see Chapters 4 and 6). Hence, the global economic visibility of the IT sector, while noteworthy, cannot be a driver of transformation that will lead to a better-quality life for most. It is an illustration of an island of excellence in a sea of low productivity and largely dismal jobs. What the economy needs is a manifold replication of the performance of the IT industry across other sectors in activities that create environmentally friendly decent jobs. Then only will business success percolate down to society for genuine economic development.

Economic development of course is not an end-state and it is also not necessarily a product of industrialization alone. As this chapter has highlighted, India's success in the global software services market marks a process of economic development that is nonindustrial and at low level of per capita income. However, it also sits uncomfortably with industrial stagnation (or premature deindustrialization) and high level of agricultural employment. Thus, India remains an agrarian society with nearly half of the work force still making a living from the land. Could this status quo offer an alternative form of economic development, one that is low-key, rural, nonindustrial, and possibly nonpolluting? From the dynamics of Indian agriculture, discussed in the next chapter, the answer is a clear no if economic development means a standard of living for rural residents that at the minimum provides basic goods and services to survive and thrive.

Services by themselves, and certainly putting all the development eggs in the IT basket, cannot lift the economy (D'Costa 2003a). Manufacturing is essential, without it the services sector cannot thrive in an integrated way for a country with India's workforce. Since India's most important challenge is making a big dent in its labor surplus, while at the same time making agriculture a worthwhile livelihood for cultivators through rising agricultural incomes and thus productivity. This naturally demands massive growth in nonagricultural unskilled and semiskilled manufacturing and services jobs to absorb surplus labor from the countryside. This is where the catch is. Not enough jobs are being generated even if economic growth rates are one of the highest in the world. What then is the relationship between household-based agricultural sector and economic development and could family-owned farms diversify into scaled-up nonagricultural activities for economic development? This is the subject of the next chapter.

4
Negotiating the Curse of Surplus Labor for Development

4.1 Labor Surplus and Agrarian Transition

As we have noted, many industries jump-started by the state and accompanied by private business investments have altered the structure of the Indian economy. Heavy industries such as steel, auto, petrochemicals, and electrical machinery, along with high-technology services such as software and essential drugs, have established the basic foundations for long-term economic development. As we will see in Chapter 5, these sectors and many new lines of business continue to advance the material foundation of Indian society. However, the large population engaged in agriculture suggests that the fundamental process of reducing labor surplus continues to hold back prosperity for millions of people in the countryside and, by extension, in urban areas as well.

The principal dilemma is that the large number of people eking out a living from agriculture on increasingly smaller plots of land results in low absolute income, even if there is an inverse relationship between land size and productivity, all other factors remaining unchanged. While there are many reasons for different productivity levels, India's yields in rice and wheat have unfavorably diverged relative to China's since the 1960s (Gautam and Yu 2015). To move beyond this status quo, increasing agricultural productivity overall is central, which would release surplus labor from agriculture. The challenge is that this would require plentiful nonagricultural jobs be made available both in rural and urban areas. A further challenge is that these jobs, to be economically rewarding, must be in high-productivity sectors, suggesting continuous diversification by businesses in economic activities. We have already noted in Chapter 3 that in the process of economic development, there has been an ongoing relative decline in the contribution of agriculture to the economy. This has been accompanied by a decline in the relative share of agricultural employment, albeit much slower than the decline in the economic value of output. This suggests the continuing grip of low-productivity agriculture.

Indian Business, Economic Development, and the Jobs Dilemma in the Twenty-first Century. Anthony P. D'Costa, Oxford University Press. © Anthony P. D'Costa (2026). DOI: 10.1093/9780198948407.003.0004

The question is whether there are tendencies toward "expelling" excess workers, and could agricultural labor or owner-operated cultivators be able to find alternative sources of income outside agriculture? In other words, would it be possible to structurally transform surplus labor in the countryside into nonagricultural (or non-farm) workers in both rural and urban areas on a large scale?

Economic development at its core necessitates a transition from rural, agricultural activities to urban, nonagricultural ones. There are voices that reject this narrative and rightly so if the transition comes with huge costs, such as displacement, urban decay, loss of human dignity, pollution, and only marginal improvements in incomes and job security compared to rural precarity. However, the human compulsion to survive pushes individual households to make the best decision under their own circumstances, with urban migration as a tried and tested response by millions of rural residents. There is no reason for them not to seek better opportunities in towns and cities, especially if staying back is really not an option.

The discussion below reveals that the agrarian transition in India, if it can be labeled as such, is substantively different from the classical historical experience, namely, the transition from rural farm to urban factory. While there are some elements of this classical shift as discussed below, the shift in Indian agriculture thus far is partial and halting. Rural labor and small cultivator-owners often join the ranks of the "nonindustrial proletariat" in unorganized *rural* and urban non-farm work, mostly in services. Consequently, the transformative potential inherent in productivity-led economic diversification is weakened.

This chapter is divided into six sections. In Section 2, I provide an overview of three distinct and yet somewhat overlapping economic activities, highlighting not only the critical aspects of the process of economic development in late industrializing, labor-surplus countries such as India, but also underscoring the difficulties in transitioning to a modern, organized economy. The sectors under discussion are agriculture, the handloom (HL) sector, and the diamond industry.[1] Section 3 examines the crucial relationship between agriculture and economic development. Sections 4 and 5 go beyond agriculture to include rurally-connected HL and diamond sectors to tease out some of the implications for economic development. The final section revisits the

[1] The choice of agriculture is justified because of its sheer scale and its significant role in economic development. The HL and the diamond industry have been selected to illustrate their continuing ties to the rural economy and the difficulties in getting workers out of their informal status. Other nonagricultural sectors such as rural construction, petty services such as transportation and eating establishments could have been chosen but they are likely to yield similar challenges.

transition question to reveal some of the challenges confronted in mitigating the curse of surplus labor.

4.2 An Overview of the Agriculture, Handloom, and Diamond Sectors

In this chapter, three sectors, namely, agriculture, handloom, and diamonds, have been selected for a number of reasons. Principal among them is their economic, employment, and social significance, their capacity to absorb surplus (raw) labor, the low levels of education and training required (for agricultural work and diamond polishing), and, most importantly, the employment connections of the HL and diamond sectors to agriculture. Disparate as they may seem, these three business and economic sectors are linked to the rural economy either as a source of labor or as a sector to fall back on should nonagricultural or urban jobs disappear or not work out. All three involve mostly informal workers (what the government labels the "unorganized" sector), entailing low-wage work. However, the diamond sector in India is part of the global supply chain. A discussion of these three sectors spanning informal labor markets illustrates the challenges as well as possibilities for accommodating labor surplus. Their broadly shared and distinctive characteristics are presented in Table 4.1.

All three sectors comprise unorganized businesses to a large degree. They are not regulated in the usual ways formal businesses are (see Chapter 3, for example). They are not corporations, rather mostly family-owned or owner-operated enterprises securing low economic returns (except perhaps for large landowners, traders, and moneylenders in the countryside and the owners and traders of the diamond polishing industry). Of the three, agriculture is the most important economic activity: about half or more of India's workforce is tied to this sector for a livelihood, and as discussed below, favorable changes in this sector, such as increased incomes and productivity growth accompanied by expansion in nonagricultural activities are critical to both the welfare of the rural poor and to long-term national economic development.

The handloom (HL) sector comprises manual textile weaving by artisans located in both rural and semi-urban areas. It is a repository of craftspeople, but one that is increasingly vulnerable to fashion-conscious urban markets. Its origin, like agriculture, is pre-capitalist. It engages several million artisans across the country in weaving. There are other types of similarly pre-capitalist craftwork that include metalwork, pottery, and so on. These activities occupy a production space that is ironically threatened by economic progress itself,

Table 4.1 Three Labor-intensive Sectors in the Transition Context: Agriculture, Handloom, and Diamonds

	Agriculture Sector	Handloom Sector	Diamond Industry
Geographic spread	Rural	Rural and Urban	Urban
Factor intensity	Cheap Labor	Skilled Artisans	Cheap Labor
Income	Subsistence production, pooling of wage earnings by family members	Subsistence production, pooling of wage earnings by family members	Wage income, piece rate
Migration	Seasonal	Circular, intergenerational	Mostly permanent
Scale of production	Mostly small family-owned operations	Mostly small household units	Small, medium, and very large units
Internationalization	Limited	Limited	High
Employment dependency	Very high	Sizeable, scattered	Visible, highly concentrated

Notes: Factor intensity refers to the production factor, such as labor or capital, that is used intensively by the sector. Employment dependency refers to the high volume of workers absorbed by the sector.
Source: Author's compilation

an experience not unanticipated under capitalism as machines and technology dictate ever more spheres of livelihoods, life, and aesthetics. Unlike other sectors, diversification for the HL sector is a tricky business since it would mean yielding to new kinds of demands that could weaken the (contested) "authenticity" of their products and push them further toward their dissolution (See D'Costa 2022). Should they continue to do what they have been good at for generations and continue to suffer the indignities of precarity, or should they make the necessary adjustments to the capitalist imperatives of price competition and alternative diversified products and stay afloat?

Imitating machine-made or power loom products provides no real advantage for artisans. The handloom (HL) sector illustrates the severe difficulties in adjusting to contemporary capitalist market forces, raising the question of whether the sector should be propped up with public support to maintain jobs or to let it die a natural death, just like the steam engine. The dilemma is that millions of livelihoods are tied to this sector. As it is, many artisans and their children do not see HL production as a viable source of livelihood. But the alternatives are not that attractive either. Given the current economic context of job scarcity, sustaining the HL sector cannot be dismissed out of hand.

The diamond industry, mostly an urban activity, illustrates one facet of the economic development process, namely, the absorption of surplus rural labor in a modern nonagricultural activity in a global context. Unlike agriculture and HL, the diamond industry is deeply integrated with the world economy but does not have a large economic multiplier as in other manufacturing industries, as discussed in Chapters 3 and 5. Furthermore, almost all of the raw material, namely uncut and unpolished diamonds (or roughs), are imported. The sector relies on the abundant supplies of unskilled rural migrant workers and seemingly typifies the desirable transition from rural to urban activities that is characteristically experienced in the early stages of economic development with surplus labor. However, similar to agriculture and handloom, the diamond industry, notwithstanding its international market linkages, is labor-intensive, requiring little education and non-transferable on-the-job training. Labor in the diamond sector can be easily replenished since it is not a high-wage, education- and training-intensive sector. Hence, it cannot be expected to be a staging ground for major economic diversification, even if new branded global business *niches* and entrepreneurship are hallmarks of this rapidly expanding sector.

For the three sectors under discussion, diversification would entail moving employment from agriculture to nonagricultural activities in general, such as food processing, while existing nonagricultural activities, such as handlooms and diamond cutting and polishing, must also move up the value chain as demand increases with economic development. While the demand for HL products is uncertain, unless aggressive demand and supply-based policies are in place, the diamond industry could very well witness increasing demand with increasing income at home as well as abroad. However, the diamond business is heavily export-dependent, and without wresting control of the branded retail segment, Indian businesses will remain at the low end of the diamond value chain.

The labor-intensive diamond cutting and polishing industry, unlike both agriculture and handloom, has weaker local linkages to other sectors, other than the income-based consumption spending associated with low-wage workers. However, one area of diversification of polished diamonds is the gems and jewelry sector, which includes other stones and gold. Paradoxically, both diamond roughs and gold are imported into India. In fiscal year 2024, India's net export of gems and jewelry was $32.02 billion (IBEF Gems and Jewellery 2025). This means that the sectoral value addition for the external market was $32.02 billion. The total value generated by this sector is likely to be much higher. However, the net value, which is not insignificant, is likely to be small when shared across the sector among millions of workers and artisans. Wages are likely to be low after deducting commissions, input costs, and profits by small and large traders, corporate businesses, intermediaries, and wholesalers and retailers, both domestic and foreign. The point is that, akin to the Apple iPhone, the diamond global value chain has low-value segments and the value attributed to labor is likely to be low because of imported roughs and labor intensity of diamond cutting and polishing. Rising incomes of the large agricultural and handloom sector can act as a major source of demand for modern industrial inputs, services, and consumption goods. But the contribution of the diamond sector to India's foreign exchange reserves is more developmentally noteworthy than the value addition by local labor, since backward and forward integration of the sector are quite limited.

The handloom textile business is precariously sandwiched between premodern and modern textile weaving, with millions of livelihoods attached to it. Yielding to the forces of contemporary capitalism for economic development seems rational and pragmatic in the context of surplus labor and job deficits. Labor-intensive jobs such as handloom and diamond polishing are critical, but current market conditions limit their expansion. They are also not sufficient to absorb the ongoing buildup of people looking for work and transform rural or urban informal labor markets significantly in this era of global wage competition.

To break this stranglehold, individual businesses may apply technological, organizational, and skill-based strategies for competitiveness. However, these strategies must be multiplied many times to raise the economy-wide level of productivity with diversification and value addition. With abundant labor, this may take place only haltingly, with a few pockets of excellence and limited spillovers. Shoring up HL demand, both local and export markets, through marketing, branding, and adjustments to changing market preferences will prevent significant job losses. Diamond polishing, on the other hand, is a good way to absorb surplus labor. However, moving up the value chain for diamonds for greater retained value through diversification (thus higher wages) in a global setting isn't practical for absorbing surplus labor. While India has established the largest diamond trading hub in the world with the newest diamond bourse in Surat, Gujarat, given the absence of retail brands and direct access to high-income markets, India may have to contend with cutting and polishing lower-value (smaller) roughs for the world market for the foreseeable future.

4.3 Transforming Agriculture for Economic Development

In extending our broad understanding of economic development as one of growth and diversification, I discuss the three labor-intensive sectors introduced above to examine the nature of the transition process by which the economy shifts from an agricultural base to a nonagricultural one. This gradual transformation could be in the form of rural-based, simple manufacturing and services and large-scale industrialization with diversified urban-based services that would render agriculture increasingly insignificant over time in the national economy in terms of employment share. India has already experienced a declining share of output (to GDP) by agriculture, a sign of low productivity plaguing the sector. It is critical that redundant or surplus labor in the countryside find gainful employment in the nonagricultural or nonfarm sector at higher wage levels. If this were to be so, it would quintessentially represent the classic form of structural transformation and diversification associated with economic development.

Is such a change taking place in rural India, to what extent, and if not, why not? To put it differently, why is the process of agricultural transformation in India slow-going or incomplete? Why are so many people still reliant on agriculture, and what might be the implications for economic development as a whole? The agriculture sector is linked to the nonagricultural sector, with the former being suppliers of food, cash crops, and labor. The agricultural sector can also be an important source of demand for nonagricultural output, including services, implying that the well-being of agriculture could also translate into growth of the nonagricultural sector. However, since agriculture in India remains largely an individual or family-household enterprise, mostly small, unincorporated activities, their limited dynamism is due to a range of economic, social, technological, and policy factors. For agriculture to adequately drive structural transformation away from low-income, low-productivity agriculture to higher-income and productivity agriculture, it needs to be scaled both from the supply and demand sides. Scaling up is a triple-edged sword, if there is such a thing. First, household farming is small due to small landholding size, which is becoming even more fragmented through inheritance or coparcener laws and practices, which enable family members to have equal rights over ancestral property. Second, this fragmentation of land makes any land consolidation, with or without land reforms and scaling up, difficult. Third, scaling up is also a problem in terms of its implications, meaning, what would be the price impact of increased output if not matched by rising incomes across the board, keeping in mind that grain prices are typically inelastic. Are export markets viable? Where will the excess workers go if the rest of the economy is unable to absorb them? We briefly allude to these in the concluding chapter.

Agriculture is critical to economic development, but the role of business in agricultural development is not as clear-cut as it might seem when we examined large, visible businesses in different industries in Chapter 3. There are crucial differences between the largely unorganized agricultural and the modern corporate business sectors in India. The former, while under the influence of contemporary capitalist economic forces, for a variety of reasons, is still rooted in mostly small-scale, low-productivity household enterprises that number in the hundreds of millions. In other words, unlike formal businesses, agriculture in India is treated as an unorganized sector, family farms are owner-operated and rely on family labor, often driven by subsistence, are not registered with the government, do not (cannot) pay income taxes as incomes are too low, and are not covered by state regulations that govern and protect formal economic activities such as social security or welfare. At the economic level, small-scale production suggests low productivity and lack of investment and technology, which in turn suggests low revenues, indebtedness, precarity, and destitution. The long chain of intermediaries linking farmers to markets also introduces fragmentation, inefficiency, and waste (Gulati, Ganguly, and Wardhan 2022). The role of the state in the past has been supportive but institutionally less effective to shore up the sector in a big way. In more recent times, the state has been either indifferent or biased in favor of heavy infrastructure, industries, and tradable services. Deregulating agricultural prices has been on the government's agenda, but widespread farmer protests have stalled such efforts at the moment.

However, not all is doom and gloom, at least not at the macro level. There are segments of the agricultural sector in India (based on cropping pattern, land ownership, irrigation, and regional institutional variations) that are relatively prosperous. At the aggregate level, the agricultural sector acts as a source of both supply and demand (Saikia 2009). For example, it constitutes an important source of economic demand for urban-based nonagricultural goods and services such as farm equipment, fertilizers, and transportation, as well as consumer and producer nondurable and durable goods such as processed foods, garments, bicycles, motorcycles, TVs, tractors, and automobiles.

As can be seen from Figure 4.1, the production and consumption of industrial fertilizers have been rising in tandem with increasing output, but domestic production has not been able to keep up with demand, with the self-sufficiency ratio fluctuating over the last five-plus decades. Imports make up the difference. Increased fertilizer use for modern cultivating practices in India has been shown to be critical, along with other inputs. However, today there is controversy in the excessive use of chemical fertilizers due to soil and water contamination and other human health hazards, plus import

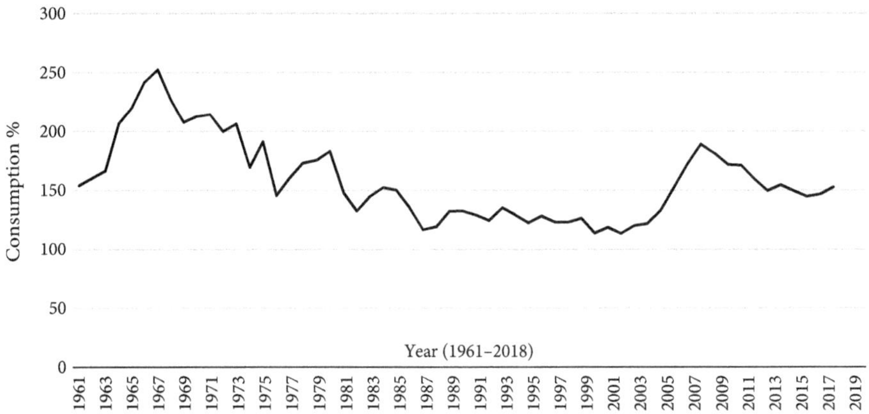

Figure 4.1 India's Fertilizer Consumption (as % of Fertilizer Production)
Source: Food and Agriculture Organization, World Bank, https://data.worldbank.org/indicator/AG.CON.FERT.PT.ZS?locations=IN

dependence.[2] This goes to show that economic development is not without its costs, but given the impoverishment of rural communities across India, foregoing fertilizer use may not be a realistic option at this time.

If agricultural productivity improves, it could be a source of savings for investment in the non-farm sector, especially for the upper landed classes. Similarly, the increasing and diversified consumption pattern of the better-off farming families and their economic engagement in non-farm rural commercial activities, such as in transportation, trade, hotels and restaurants, and construction, generate a positive spillover in the local rural economy. Education of rural children is also expected to increase as their labor on the family farm may not be needed. The increased disposable income would also allow spending more on education and health. This anticipated synergy between the rural and urban economies and within the rural economy is dependent on agricultural prices received by farmers and thus on agricultural incomes. Family labor suggests that wage costs are low, although inefficiencies associated with excessive use of chemical fertilizers and pesticides, subsidized water, transportation, waste, and reliance on intermediaries for the final sale of agricultural output may raise the final cost.

Indian agriculture at the current juncture remains in a state of crisis despite some scattered improvements (Sen and Ghosh 2017, Bardhan 2019: 189) because of low prices, poor infrastructure, the power of traders, and the state's low priority for the small cultivators. Furthermore, the evidence suggests

[2] Russia's invasion of Ukraine in 2022 has hit the global agricultural sector with high prices paid by many countries, including India for imported Ukrainian food grains and fertilizers.

that the magnitude of impact from rural non-farm activities can be limited since most of these commercial activities remain informal, implying small scale and, relatively non-innovative activities that are numerically dwarfed by the millions of struggling subsistent farmers (Binswanger-Mkhize 2013). It is evident that what the Indian planners had anticipated from heavy industrialization of the 1960s did not materialize. The expectation was that industrial development in tandem with rural productivity growth would reinforce economic development across the board, with industry absorbing surplus labor and rural India acting as a consumption sink for industrial products. There has been rural class differentiation with the growing consumption of urban-based, branded manufactured goods by wealthier farmers and petty business owners in the countryside. However, seventy-five years after independence, rural India largely continues to suffer from the scourge of surplus labor.

Rising rural income in some constituencies is consistent with uneven development, which offers opportunities for corporations, domestic or foreign, to cater to the "bottom of the pyramid" market (Prahalad and Hammond 2002). However, the growing absolute size of the rural market notwithstanding, the average level of consumption is likely to be low, as already indicated by the dynamics of Indian agriculture and the type of employment generated in the non-farm sector. Based on surveys by Kapur, Dawar, and Ahuja (2014), they found that while rural incomes were increasing faster than urban incomes and as a result rural consumption was expanding as well, the estimated $12 billion consumption by 800 million rural residents amounted to an average of only $15 per resident. Even if total consumption increased to $100 billion by 2025 (as projected by this study), the average consumption would have gone up to $125, a substantial increase no doubt, but not enough to realize what the industrial planners of the 1960s had in mind. With globalization and the pervasiveness of digital media and advertising, such consumption in rural India is expected to be highly uneven. Large landowners, households with non-farm commercial activities, moneylenders, and better-off families with migrant workers are expected to consume disproportionately more than the average rural resident and purchase urban-based branded goods. In fact, such economic and social differentiation is the hallmark of nascent capitalism, but without the prospect of further development due to the slow pace and quality of change, uneven distribution, and worsening inequality.

Since agricultural households can be considered rudimentary businesses, they will need to sell their output in the market at the going price, including any minimum price support that the government might provide. The more surplus crop beyond their subsistence needs, the higher the revenue, suggesting that increasing productivity is crucial to the material quality of life of the household. However, a massive increase in agricultural productivity could have a negative impact on the sector with declining prices due to increased supply. In general, a household's final revenue flows may exceed the cost of material inputs and wages paid, if unpaid family labor is used, or wages are earned if family labor is hired out on someone else's plot. But net revenues could also be negative if the costs of production (such as hiring labor or borrowing money from local moneylenders) exceed the revenues received based on the market price of crops.

Should the household have a negative economic surplus, meaning they don't produce enough for their subsistence, they will be net buyers of grain from the market. If they do not have savings from their own crops, they must resort to borrowing money to purchase grain from the market for their subsistence. The precariousness of small-scale, informal farming is self-evident. As most of these households operate small holdings, farm incomes are likely to be meager, compelling many rural residents under economic distress to migrate to the cities or alternatively to seek economic opportunities for non-farm work in both rural and urban areas. The lack of transferability of rural skills to an urban setting suggests they are likely to join the ranks of the unorganized, informal workers in small towns and cities (see Chapter 6). These small, unorganized businesses rely on "family labor and wage work (often concealed as self-employment) under different forms of putting out systems" (Government of India 2007: 3).

Consequently, we cannot anticipate a "Lewisian" turn whereby rural surplus labor is exhausted and wages begin to rise across the board.[3] This is a necessary condition for long-term economic development. As alluded to in Chapter 1, India is experiencing premature deindustrialization in the context of limited formal manufacturing growth and expanding service sector jobs. The implication is that low-productivity agriculture in the context of stagnating manufacturing, expanding services, and some growth in rural non-farm employment is another form of the "low equilibrium" status quo consistent with compressed capitalism, alluded to in Chapter 1. Barring the roughly 10% of workers in formal employment, the informal sector is unlikely to pull up the entire economy for sustained development. Instead, as is the case now,

[3] Arthur Lewis, from St. Lucia in the Caribbean, was awarded the Nobel Prize in Economics in 1979 along with Theodore Schultz. He had argued in a 1954 seminal paper that developing countries have unlimited supplies of labor and this labor can be deployed for urban industrialization without raising rural wages for a while until such surplus labor is exhausted. As industrial capitalists hiring such surplus labor reinvest their profits, a virtuous cycle of capital accumulation is set in motion and modern economic development is sustained (Lewis 1954). The simplicity of the model did not then and does not now quite fit reality. Nonetheless, the core idea that there must be some macro dynamics to exhaust the labor supply remains a necessary condition for economic growth and development. The big question is what will absorb the surplus labor.

India will continue to witness uneven development with pockets of globally competitive modern firms in a vast terrain of small, unorganized, and low-productivity unincorporated enterprises.

Under these conditions, rather than structural change of a transformative kind, a more subtle form of change is underway. The bulk of agriculture remains more or less the same, with small cultivators plagued by low productivity, nondiversified output, indebtedness, and declining state support. Large landowners, including some corporate entities, with greater access to capital and technology, have begun to exploit opportunities in profitable cash crops thrown open by economic deregulation, trade liberalization, and rising urban incomes over the years. Crop diversification within agriculture that caters to growing urban markets, especially through food processing sectors and modern retailing, is consistent with economic development (see Chapter 5), but by itself, it may not address the plight of the small cultivators. Related to this, class-based economic differentiation in the countryside suggests investments by wealthier farmers and moneylenders in non-farm activities in rural areas. Distressed farmers, on the other hand, are compelled to select some combination of agricultural work and non-farm employment in rural areas when available, or to seek opportunities as migrant workers in urban areas. Under all three options, the outcomes are generally informal work under both unorganized and organized sectors, with some conversion of family labor to wage labor and economic diversification. However, the informal nature of work and unorganized businesses in both rural and urban areas suggest that the transition can at best be interpreted as coping mechanisms for the desperately poor. There is some mobility of the better-off landed classes in rural areas, but not large enough to usher in a home-grown industrial diversification.

Economic growth leading to rising urban incomes also suggests market pressures to streamline and corporatize agricultural production through contract farming for large-scale retail operations and exports. Large landowners, including corporate owners of agri-business, are the new business players entering an otherwise moribund agricultural sector. The current stalemate suggests a limited form of agrarian change in the areas of non-farm economic activities on the one hand, and corporatization (or streamlining of agriculture) for modern urban retail sector development, on the other, resulting in slow-paced, long-term economic development.[4]

[4] Much of urban retail of agricultural produce, raw or processed, entails the selling and distribution of products through the widely prevalent, unorganized small sellers or petty business.

Currently, there is a five-way dynamic interaction under which the vast majority of cultivators remain mired in economic distress. The five interactions are as follows:

1. small landholders are in a status quo mode with larger landowners moving into cash crops, contract farming, and rural non-farm commercial activities;
2. urban investors are moving into the rural non-farm sector;
3. the corporate sector is strategically entering agricultural production through contract farming for urban wholesale and grocery retail chain operations;
4. an expanding rural non-farm sector is absorbing a growing share of urban-based nonagricultural output; and
5. the state is withdrawing its proactive engagement for agricultural development.

These multiple interactions are depicted in Figure 4.2. They represent agrarian distress, gradual social and class differentiation between small farmers and their wealthier counterparts, and limited economic change brought about by a receding interest of the state in small-scale agriculture. In addition, an overall state-disengagement, entry of private investments in non-farm activities in rural areas, and restructuring of agricultural production for large urban retail markets are altering the rural landscape of small landholders.

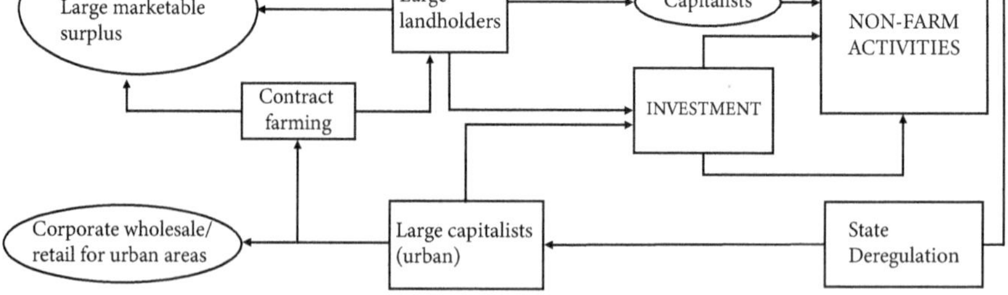

Figure 4.2 Agrarian Distress, Differentiation, and Development
Source: Author's compilation

In the context of urban-based business growth, this five-way interaction nicely captures the state of affairs in India's rural economy, notwithstanding regional variations. Under this inter-sectoral and inter-class interaction (small farmers versus large farmers and large urban-based investors), as depicted in Figure 4.2, there is economic development in the form of non-farm activities, but it is not quite the transformative kind where agricultural productivity itself becomes the engine for both extensive and intensive forms of economic production and diversification. Instead, there is partial corporatization of agriculture that caters to urban consumers through modern large-scale contract-farming-based retail business (see Chapter 5), which, for all practical purposes, should not be dismissed. However, the diversification of rural economies with non-farm activities and the formalization and organization of agricultural production on a larger-scale contract basis for urban markets are still inadequate to make a dent in the surplus labor. Most labor markets in farm and non-farm activities remain unorganized and unincorporated (see Chapter 6). Furthermore, it is not clear what impact corporatization of agriculture and modern retail chains will have on the long-term viability of small shopkeepers found throughout urban India (see Chapter 5).

The key question is how to move beyond agriculture for economic development. In other words, how to ensure that surplus labor from the countryside finds non-farm employment in both rural and urban areas. For this to occur, there must be investments in both agriculture and nonagricultural activities, which are already taking place privately by larger landowners, moneylenders, and urban investors. Investment in agriculture by family farms to improve productivity and thereby release excess labor for nonagricultural activities is difficult due to low incomes and inadequate savings. Instead, farming households are likely to undertake small measures to improve the quality of their land. At the same time, institutional mechanisms could widen the scope of productivity gains through large-scale investments in irrigation, land improvement schemes, and access to modern agricultural inputs such as farm equipment, electricity, credit, fertilizers, pesticides, and hybrid seeds. While private businesses can provide many of these inputs, the public goods nature of rural infrastructure development, electricity supply, irrigation, and land improvement calls for state investments. Furthermore, part of the rural distress can be addressed by continuing to provide price support schemes by prioritizing agriculture and reallocating state resources rather than increasingly taking a hands-off approach.

With prosperity, large landholders and moneylenders do undertake private investments in farm and non-farm activities in rural areas. This is a form of diversification undertaken by small, unorganized businesses in rural construction work, transportation, and a variety of small service businesses such as telephone booths, eating establishments, tea stalls, and other petty services. Given that rural skills and work experience are transferable mainly to labor-intensive, low-skill, off-farm work, whether in the countryside or in urban areas, many owner-operated agricultural households must supplement their meager incomes by resorting to wage income. They work on someone else's land or in non-farm activities such as (seasonal) rural and urban construction work, transportation, and a variety of petty services. There were 27.6 million *registered* construction workers in the informal sector, which was the third highest employer after agriculture (159 million) and domestic and household workers (28.4 million) (Statista 2025). The 2023 data show that the *total* (both registered and unregistered) number of workers in agriculture was 253 million, while construction had about 75 million.[5] Studies also show that remittance income flowing from migrant workers to rural households is not significant enough to alter consumption patterns, and these households are only marginally better off than those households without any migrant worker (Gnanaraj and Mohapatra 2014). Furthermore, wealthier households tend to have more migrant members than poor ones. The better-off households are likely to diversify into non-farm economic activities in the countryside or permanently migrate to cities. These non-farm economic activities, while critical for farmers at the margin, are not major drivers of growth and diversification. The implication is sobering, namely, that despite some rural transformation, the vast majority of cultivators in India have limited options to get out of their dire economic circumstances.

In the current deregulated environment, in the absence of public investments, formal credit access, and price supports, the structural impediments facing small farmers engaged with food crops are overwhelming (see Sen and Ghosh 2017). Witness the sixteen-month farmers' agitation in India that began in August 2020. They perceived the government's unilateral decisions on agricultural reforms as ones that would surreptitiously eliminate the minimum support price that they had received thus far and would allow urban-based large corporations to dominate small cultivators. Fortunately, the government backed down from its proposed reforms. However, the pre-existing structures of domination in agriculture and reforms by stealth (Jenkins 1999) are encouraging large businesses to encourage large-scale

[5] Labour Bureau India; Reserve Bank of India; Statista, "Number of People Employed Across Major Sectors in India in Financial Year 2023," FY 2023, https://www-statista-com.eu1.proxy.openathens.net/statistics/1283990/india-sector-wise-employment/, accessed July 27, 2025.

contract farming for growing urban markets (see Chapter 5 on modern retailing). This is no doubt a normal course of change under capitalism and not necessarily a bad development since it is a form of diversification. But the problem is how small cultivators, who number in the millions, should cope in the meantime when faced with competition from larger corporate agribusiness. Do they have an outlet for alternative sources of employment? That is the question that will continue to dog the Indian agricultural sector for the foreseeable future.

4.4 Holding-on or Letting-go of the Handloom Sector

The cottage industry or the artisanal craft sector has been a permanent fixture of rural India for a long time. Different regions in the country have different craft industries, often tied to the local economy and culture. Such village crafts have become part of the modern economy, but often in a subordinate way. Today, they must compete with cheaper products made with modern methods of production, adjust to changing tastes and fashion, or simply abandon the business for urban employment. The total artisanal sector is estimated to employ nearly seven million artisans (Government of India, Ministry of Textiles 2019: 199). Given the challenging conditions faced by the agricultural sector in finding decent urban employment, this section briefly examines the HL weaving sector to explore whether this form of non-farm employment could continue to complement the rural economy.

Handloom refers to the manual production (weaving) of cloth using a loom (a device) without the use of electricity. It is a labor-intensive sub-sector of the crafts industry (or the textile sector) engaged with small-scale production. It mainly uses cotton and silk yarn rather than wool or synthetic yarn. Four states—Assam, West Bengal, Manipur, and Tamil Nadu—account for more than two-thirds of India's weaving households. West Bengal, after Assam, has the largest number of weavers and handlooms. These two states together comprise 60% of weavers and handlooms (Government of India, Ministry of Textiles 2015: 25, Chakraborty and Sen 2015: 3). West Bengal stands out with the highest number of looms and weaving households serving the commercial market (Bhattacharya and Sen 2018: 7). Nationally there were 2.8 million looms, of which 87% were rural-based with women—both part- and full-time—representing three quarters of the total number of weavers (Government of India, Ministry of Textiles 2019: 17 and Table 7).

At the national level, India's HL production has been erratic. While the share of total HL fabric production over the decade of 2006–2007 to

2016–2017 has remained between 16–17% (Government of India, Ministry of Textiles 2015, Export-Import Bank of India 2018: 22), year-to-year growth rates have fluctuated considerably. Handloom (HL) exports declined from \$370.2 million in 2013–2014 to \$353.9 million in 2017–2018 (Export-Import Bank of India 2018: 30). The Handloom Surveys of India show that the number of individuals in weaving and related activities fell 35% over a 14-year period, from 6.6 million in 1995-1996 to 4.3 million in 2009-2011 (Government of India, Ministry of Textiles, Note on Handloom Sector 2015: 2) leading to considerable economic distress (Bhowmik 2019). Two-thirds of the weavers still earn less than INR 5000 per month, approximately \$0.25 above the international poverty line of \$1.90 per day.

Except for the pockets of specialized products with successful commercial marketing at home and abroad, the HL weaving sector is experiencing considerable challenges. Handloom weaving families have been hit hard by increasing capital intensity of production and automation in the form of power looms, the competition from cheaper, machine-made products, and changing demand due to changing consumer preferences from traditional woven garments to modern fashions made with synthetic yarns. Of course, capitalist economic development suggests that new types of business and employment opportunities are expected to appear with the disappearance of old businesses and economic activities such as handloom weaving. For example, successful HL owners have moved into more lucrative, modern, capital-intensive power loom businesses (Roy 1998: 899, Roy n.d., 132), while weavers from specific regions of West Bengal have turned to wage work in power loom units (Bhattacharya and Sen 2018). Both cases represent advancements in technology, higher productivity employment, possibly more consumer choice, and proletarianization of artisans, all important hallmarks of capitalist economic development. The irony, however, is that with economic development, the HL sector remains just as precarious as the agricultural sector. It is not decimated, but artisans have to continuously respond and adjust to economic distress by migrating to cities for alternative employment in non-farm activities, including construction. However, the loss of HL jobs not only does away with the craft of weaving but could very well, in the absence of alternative options, add to the roster of surplus labor.

Given the rural base of the HL sector, their links to agriculture cannot be ignored. Except for those households that rely completely on weaving, some members of a weaving household work on their family plot or work as wage labor either on someone else's land or are engaged in non-farm rural activities, outside the HL sector. Since handloom weaving is a family enterprise (an unorganized business in regulatory terms, though sometimes organized under cooperatives), wage income is likely to contribute to total household income. This is a form of risk diversification by the weaving family, but it cannot be seen as economic diversification since the goal implied by the process of economic development is to reduce surplus labor in the countryside. The reverse process of agricultural workers joining the HL weaving sector is rare since weaving is a specialized artisanal craft, and the incomes earned in HL weaving are unpredictable. Therefore, the HL sector cannot be seen as attractive for agricultural households.

Low profit margins and the declining number of weavers are signs of precarity. Both the rising cost of inputs and shifting markets due to changing technology and consumer preferences have squeezed the sector. Often victims of usurious rates of interest (Bhaduri 1983), indebted weavers under distress could be forced to transfer undervalued assets such as looms or land to local moneylenders (Khasnabis and Nag 2001: 4839). Competition from power loom units owned by local moneylenders tends to hasten the transformation of HL weavers into wage labor and contributes to deskilling (see Khasnabis and Nag 2001, Bhattacharya and Sen 2018: 19).

The paradox is that economic development demands more non-farm employment, but here we have a situation of a reverse process whereby weavers could join the ranks as agricultural wage labor should financial distress become unmanageable. When desperate weavers and some of their cultivating family members migrate to urban areas seeking non-farm employment, the outcome is quite consistent with economic diversification and development. However, the choice of urban work for highly specialized weavers abandoning their craft is limited to the informal sector with limited opportunities for advancement such as security guards and drivers (Government of West Bengal 2017: 9). At the same time, as a survival coping mechanism, weavers often move back and forth between rural and urban areas and between weaving and non-weaving informal economic activities to stabilize household earnings (Mamidipudi, Syamasundari, and Bijker 2012), which in a generalized context has been characterized as "the vicious cycle of the interaction between small-scale production in agriculture and industry" (Basole and Basu 2011: 15). The children of weavers, however, are increasingly less interested in their parents' craft for a livelihood, implying indeterminate livelihood diversification.

The rural-based HL sector is an example of non-farm activity, albeit one that is not completely independent of the farm economy. The crisis of the HL sector compels a back-and-forth movement of workers between rural and urban economic activities to stabilize earnings. However, such mobility does not portend a linear progression of permanently "expelling" surplus workers from the countryside. It suggests that HL is here to stay as a sector of small family enterprises in the rural economy that is adjusting to the imperatives of contemporary tastes and fashions. There are various government policies to shore up the sector, which is critical if jobs are to be protected in a context of limited employment. There are also efforts to create upscale "demand" through marketing and branding (D'Costa 2022). Some HL products enter the global value chain of transnational corporations for their global retail operations. But these volumes are small, and markets are not guaranteed. The dilemma is stark: either adjust to market preferences and lose its traditional identity of artisanal craft, or not change and face the onslaught of competition from power loom products. In either case, its precarity limits its contribution to employment and economic diversification in the rural economy characterized by surplus labor.

4.5 Diamonds Are Not Forever

In this third and final business sector, I examine the Indian diamond industry. Unlike both agriculture and the handloom sector, it is highly internationalized and integrated in global value chains (see Figure 4.3). The diamond industry can be broken down broadly into three value-adding segments: upstream activities, the middle market, and downstream activities. Upstream mainly involves mining, which entails exploration and logistics for securing and sorting diamond roughs. India has not been a major source of diamonds for over a century. Russia, Canada, Botswana, Australia, and South Africa are key mining regions. Overlapping with mining is the role of Antwerp in Belgium, which acts as the leading diamond trading center, especially for higher-value diamonds. The second segment, which is the most important for India and relevant to the discussion of non-farm activities introduced earlier, is cutting, polishing, and diamond jewelry manufacturing. India occupies a pre-eminent position in this segment due to abundant labor with experience in the traditional jewelry business and low wages. Indian traders also dominate the industry in acquiring roughs through auctions. In fact, Antwerp, a longtime center for Jewish diamond merchants, is being gradually replaced by ethnic Gujarati traders from India. China has a small share in this segment. The final segment in the value chain is retail sales of diamond jewelry, where marketing and branding play a big role. This segment is generally dominated by the final markets in the United States, China, Europe, the Middle East, and India.

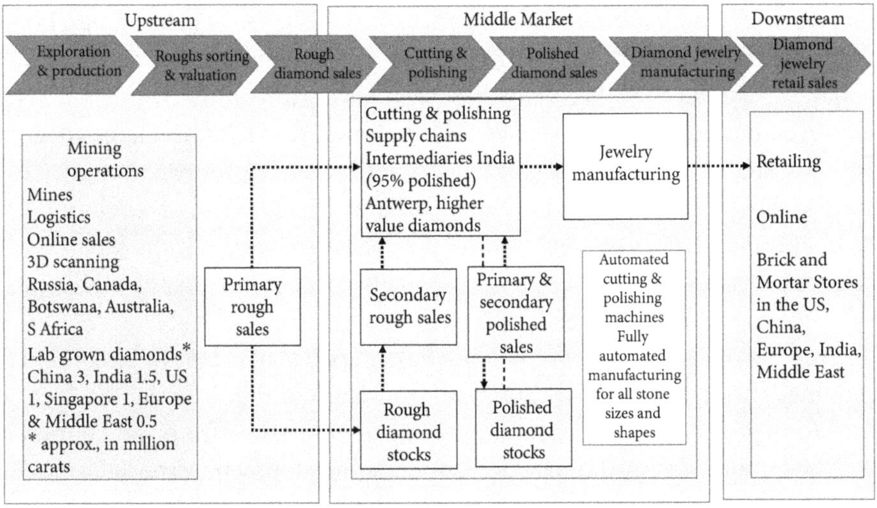

Figure 4.3 Indian Diamond Industry in Global Value Chains
Source: Compiled by author using Bain and Company and Antwerp World Diamond Center (2021, 2013: p. 37), IBEF Power 2022, and the business press

While India is no longer a producer of diamonds (roughs), it is the world's largest destination for cutting and polishing imported rough diamonds. Almost 90% of the world's diamonds are processed by over 6000 enterprises of various sizes in India, employing roughly 5 million people, with over half a million in the city of Surat alone in the state of Gujarat.[6] Earlier optimistic employment predictions of over eight million diamond workers by 2022 (IBEF Gems and Jewellery 2021: 3) do not seem to have materialized. India's exports of cut and polished diamonds are substantial. In the 2011 fiscal year, exports were valued at $28.2 billion, which fell to $23.8 billion in fiscal year 2019 (Statista 2021). Although the pandemic hit both demand and supply of cut and polished diamonds, the industry is still a sizeable contributor to India's GDP, export revenues, and employment. These are all the classic indicators of economic development, quintessentially illustrating expanding business, economic diversification away from agriculture to nonagricultural economic activity, and one of the few sectors of successful integration in global value chains. Productivity as measured by revenues per worker in the diamond industry is inferred to be greater than in agriculture, considering

[6] Precise figures for the number of diamond-cutting and polishing units as well as total employment are hard to come by because most of the units are unregistered while the jobs are informal, trust-based arrangements between employers and workers who are mostly from the same social (caste) background (Rao and von Glinow 2012).

that workers are migrating from villages to join this trade in urban areas. Furthermore, the establishment of the world's largest diamond bourse in Surat, Gujarat, suggests that the sector has been successful in the world market. However, it is common knowledge that the low cost of labor is a huge advantage for the sector, suggesting, on the one hand, its absorptive capacity of surplus labor from rural and urban areas, and on the other, an evolution of diversification away from agriculture. It remains to be seen if the sector will continue to add low-wage workers and whether it could further diversify into more value-adding activities.[7]

Since the diamond industry fits the characteristics of expanding economic activities through diversification away from agriculture, how robust is this transformation? As a first step, absorbing surplus labor from the countryside is an advance on the path to economic development, especially when incomes are anticipated to be higher. Rural migrants, with a concentration of Saurashtrians in Surat as well as from other states, comprise the principal workforce (Rao and Bhatnagar 2009: 2), and their numbers are growing in the industry.[8] Many small firms are located away from diamond processing hubs such as Surat in nearby villages and small towns. Evidence also suggests that many former diamond workers (or *karigars*) have moved up professionally to become diamond business owners (Engelshoven 1999: 357). This is, of course, the classic form of capitalist development where entrepreneurship accompanies business dynamism and social differentiation generally. This kind of entrepreneurship may be taking place in other newer dynamic sectors, such as in manufacturing and digitalization and digitalization and the platform economy (DPE), such as e-commerce for business and consumer commercial transactions (see Chapter 5). Whether entrepreneurship in diamond and other newer sectors are harbingers of economic diversification and better jobs remains to be seen.

The diamond industry itself is still largely unorganized and caters to foreign markets. Between 60% and 70% of workers are temporary and are on-contract, suggesting that these workers are outside the regulatory framework and thus vulnerable to changes in market conditions. The cutting and polishing of diamonds is labor-intensive, involving long hours of back-breaking work. Despite certain specializations, the work is mostly unskilled, requiring a few months of on-the-job training for which there are no wage payments.

[7] As alluded to in Chapter 7, if high US tariffs against India's exports persist, the diamond sector could face new employment challenges.

[8] Saurashtrians are an ethno-linguistic community from Gujarat, many of whom have migrated to southern Indian states.

Given that the sector is dominated by a particular social caste group, non-member trainees are often charged a fee for training. Most of these workers are barely literate. Intuitively, we know by parsing the global value chain that the labor-intensive segment of cutting, bruting (shaping a diamond by using another diamond), and polishing, while profitable for the owners, generates the least value due to low piece-rate or low wage rates. Workers are paid a piece rate by the stone (rough), by the type of cuts made, and by the quality of the roughs (Engelshoven 1999: 363, Richman 2009: 34). A worker aiming to earn more must work faster but with precision. Since most firms are small, with fifty or fewer workers, and only a handful of diamond enterprises employ a large workforce (4000–5000 workers) (Hirway 2009: 9), the industry structure determines who will receive the larger, better-quality roughs. In small enterprises, workers are likely to receive smaller, lower-quality roughs, thus making higher earnings difficult. Working conditions, though improving, are still quite harsh in the diamond industry (Miklian 2013).

There are other disquieting features of this sector that reduce the developmental impact of the industry in India. The industry is heavily reliant on the global supply of roughs (controlled by foreign firms or locations such as De Beers in London (currently under financial duress) and Antwerp in Belgium) and on global demand dominated by major international jewelry markets such as the United States, China, and Europe. There is a high degree of external dependence on both the supply and demand sides of the global value chain. However, with few barriers to entry and the relatively unskilled nature of cutting and polishing, the diamond industry could anticipate competition from other Asian countries such as China and Thailand, as evident by India's declining export figures. More importantly, the primordial link of diamond workers to rural India has not been completely severed. When global supply and demand conditions change, considerable adjustments are imposed on the industry, and it is the rural economy that bears the brunt of these adjustments by absorbing urban informal workers. What this implies is that the rural economy continues to be a reservoir of surplus labor, as the three telling episodic upheavals presented below testify.

The 1994 bubonic plague in Surat compelled about 60% of its residents, including diamond industry workers, to leave the city and head home to their villages. Following the 2008 Global Financial Crisis, a steep decline in export demand forced several hundred thousand diamond workers to return to their villages as the manufacturing units were shut down. The recent 2020 nationwide lockdown during the COVID-19 pandemic caused massive disruptions in the lives of migrant workers in manufacturing as a whole and not just in the diamond sector. Millions of workers and their families traversed long distances to return to their villages and small towns. In each of these episodic swings, there was a reverse mass migration, suggesting that labor-intensive, urban non-farm activities are not necessarily stable and permanent, nor a source of robust diversification with rising productivity that would lift the entire economy on a sustainable basis. The main reason is that rural India still acts as a buffer for millions of insecure urban workers, signaling the incomplete, "ongoing" transition out of agriculture and thus the limits to wider economic development.

There are two levels of obvious but unstated development implications of the diamond industry, namely, inequality, a theme picked up in Chapter 6, in the discussion of new technologies. The diamond industry's global value chain at the first level illustrates the pronounced inequality between the Global North and South on the one hand and at the second level, inequality within the Global South. In the North, the monopoly control of roughs, market power of merchants and traders (also in the South), and high-end retailers carry far greater market clout than the South, with its abundant unskilled workers. Within the Global South, as in India, wealth inequality between workers and diamond factory owners, traders, and merchants is getting wider, even if there is some mobility of workers to higher-paying diamond cutting and polishing jobs and ultimately ownership of a few of small diamond operations. Added to this, the consumption of diamond jewelry in India is itself highly inegalitarian since the cutters and polishers of diamonds are generally excluded from this type of market due to low earnings.

With limited supplies of naturally occurring diamonds, businesses are diversifying into lab-grown diamonds (LGD).[9] China has the largest estimated market of 3 million carats (mcts), followed by India's 1.5 mcts; Creative Technologies, New Diamond Era, and Diamond Elements are leading firms. The United States and Singapore have 1 mcts each. This development may not impact the cutting and polishing industry. In fact, it may enhance it, provided such LGDs complement a growing market for the real thing, with an expanding Indian middle class. However, the industry is also subject to other technological changes, such as automation, precisely for those cutting and polishing operations in which Indian workers excel. Fully automated manufacturing for all stone sizes and shapes is also on the commercial horizon.

If we follow Joan Robinson's dictum that "The misery of being exploited by capitalists is nothing compared to the misery of not being exploited at all"

[9] See Money (2025) for the negative impact on Botswana's diamond industry.

(Yelvington 2019: 401, also Chapter 2), meaning any job is better than none at all, then the diamond industry, along with several other labor-intensive sectors, is indeed a success story. At the minimum, it provides a livelihood by addressing an important existential question of coping and survival of people who otherwise cannot make an adequate living out of agriculture. If the diamond industry, along with other labor-intensive sectors such as textiles, leather, footwear, and handloom are multiplied manyfold, theoretically at least, it points to the possibility of near exhaustion of surplus labor. This outcome not only raises the prospects for wages to rise but also pushes diamond and other business owners to invest in more machinery and automation or simply diversify into other, more profitable commercial activities, including expanded exports of a wide range of goods and services.

This, in theory, is the classic economic development process where increasing incomes accompanying qualitative changes in industry and other economic activities initiate structural transformation. This is the desirable process of economic development. But as the production landscape of the diamond industry illustrates, the entrepot nature of cutting and polishing imported roughs for exports has limited economic linkages. Hence, under the surplus labor condition, the future growth of the diamond sector is likely to remain extensive with a quantitative increase in both the number of workers and volume of output, but not an intensive form of growth where wages steadily increase as productivity rises and there is a gradual shift of workers away from the diamond sector to other higher value-adding activities. Given the very specific, non-transferable type of skill in the diamond industry, the opportunity for better alternatives is likely to be narrow.

One can imagine that laboratory-grown diamonds, the manufacturing and exporting of programmable machines for automation, and the retailing of finished jewelry at home and abroad would create a global value chain where more economic value could be added to the economy. Manufacturing machines, if part of a wider industrial effort, could mitigate premature deindustrialization and add an *intensive* dimension to the growth of the diamond industry. Some labor displacement can be expected, but as long as there are other similar or better-paying sectors that diamond sector workers could move into, the engine of development will have been initiated. However, while the particular juncture India finds itself in today allows specific businesses to expand globally, as in the diamond sector, the expansion itself drives a wedge between business growth and diversification on the one hand, and decent job creation on the other. In Chapter 6, I address why this is the case by linking the problem partly to the curse of surplus labor but also to the changing nature of business strategies under globalization that exacerbates inequality and limits employment growth in the formal sector.

4.6 What's Next with the Incomplete Agrarian Transition?

In this chapter, I have highlighted the importance of the agricultural sector to economic development. The idea is simple: to improve the standard of living, promote economic growth, and diversify the economy. India is still an agrarian society with almost half the workforce engaged in agriculture, even as the economic value of agriculture to national income has steadily fallen, industrial change has plateaued, and the residual category of services has been on the upswing with plenty of low-wage informal jobs. The task at hand is twofold. First, increase agricultural productivity to reduce the number of people dependent on low-income agriculture. Second, ensure continuous economic diversification that will create non-farm work. This classic form of agrarian transition does not fit the Indian case well, or at least not yet.

As the discussion in this chapter showed, agriculture in India is largely unorganized, characterized by low productivity and entails a precarious form of livelihood for many farmers. While there has been some diversification out of agriculture in rural areas in simple services such as commercial retail and wholesale trade, transportation, hotels and restaurants, and construction, most of these jobs are informal. Economic diversification is also revealed by rural migrants taking up nonagricultural jobs in urban areas. However, given the difficulty of transferring rural skills in an urban setting, here too employment is of the precarious, menial, informal kind. Those jobs that require certain skills, such as in the artisanal handloom weaving sector, work is informal and without a safety net, and is subject to the vagaries of customer demand for handmade fabrics. In fact, economic progress itself is a threat to this sector due to the progressive onslaught of machine-made products. Letting the handloom sector go would have been a pragmatic choice if there were other newer, emerging sectors picking up the slack. But with millions of craftspeople dependent on this sector without alternative options suggests that the sector needs to be sustained in some form. Similarly, in the diamond industry, a few months of training in polishing and cutting does not lead to high-paying jobs for most, although these wages are likely to be higher than the average agricultural income. As we will see in Chapter 6, even those jobs that demand production skills, such as automobile and components manufacturing, are increasingly based on insecure hiring arrangements, a clear reflection of labor market conditions that have swept much of the world.

What is evident is that informal workers in the farm and non-farm sector circulate between agriculture and nonagricultural jobs in rural and urban areas, demonstrating that agrarian transition is an incomplete or ongoing process. The diamond industry confirms this: during major crises such as the bubonic plague of 1994, the global financial crisis of 2008, and the COVID-19 pandemic of 2020, workers were compelled to return to their villages. This was a response not only to the health hazards posed in the city of Surat in Gujarat state, but also to find alternatives to earning a livelihood that was lost due to lockdowns during the pandemic and the fall in global demand for diamonds during the financial crisis. This reverse form of migration back to rural areas also implies that the agricultural economy can act as a buffer in times of crises and defers the much-anticipated agrarian transition indefinitely.

The contemporary experience of Indian agriculture shows a stalemate in its transition. On the one hand, the persistence of the small cultivator coexists with the limited prosperity of farming and non-farming (money lending) households. On the other hand, the diversification initiated by prosperous rural households offers a narrow avenue to supplement the incomes of those unable to make a living out of agricultural work alone, be it owner-operated or as wage workers on farms. The small farmers are typically engaged in basic staples, while the prosperous households are increasingly present in profitable cash crops, supplying to large contractors who, in turn, supply to organized retail chains in urban areas. Many of these prosperous households also invest in various petty non-farm commercial activities in the countryside. The ensuing class distinctions in the countryside, within rural and urban areas and between them are part of the ongoing uneven capitalist economic development. This process is also integral to worsening inequality in the wider Indian context (discussed in Chapter 6).

Excluded from the economic development process in rural areas, many rural residents, out of desperation, are seeking informal employment opportunities in urban areas. While there is increasing demand for urban products and services by the rural economy, a necessary interconnected dynamic for economic development, it is mostly confined to the higher-income rural households. On closer inspection, the average consumption of urban goods by the rural economy on a per capita basis is not significant. The state, which in the past has played an important role in rural development, has become more passive. Aside from the political difficulties of carrying out land reforms today for the landless and small farmers, the fragmentation of land holdings makes the consolidation and redistribution of land impractical, unless, of course, high prices are offered or land acquired by coercion and trickery. Small farmers under favorable terms may find contract farming attractive, but as price takers with limited bargaining power, negotiating with larger corporate entities may not be easy. Furthermore, specializing in one crop may take away the risk insurance that diversified crops might offer. In this context, the absence of state investment programs in irrigation, land improvements, and price supports to increase productivity and rural incomes will no doubt reduce the expected benefits of externalities and multiplier effects on non-farm employment.

The state's direct employment programs in rural areas, such as the Mahatma Gandhi National Rural Employment Guarantee Act (MNREGA), are laudable for targeting the rural poor. The National Rural Employment Guarantee Act provides 100 days of guaranteed rural employment to anyone from a rural household willing to undertake manual work for local governments. However, since the program is implemented at the local state level, the results are mixed, with some states doing better than others (see Lakha 2019). This employment program is not aimed at creating agricultural entrepreneurs and capitalists but rather providing a stopgap measure to ensure a minimum income for rural residents to avoid more drastic consequences of poverty, malnutrition, and precarity.

One of the unintended consequences of this program, should it be sustained successfully, could be emerging labor shortages in the countryside, which could raise rural wages and spur a productivity-enhancing process in agriculture and in other related sectors. Businesses faced with a tightening labor supply and thus rising labor costs will be compelled to undertake continuous upgrading and diversification of their commercial activities. But experience shows that the MNREGA program is most utilized by rural residents outside of sowing and harvest seasons, suggesting that there is not enough work to be found in the countryside. To reiterate, close to half the Indian population remains tied to low-productivity agriculture and whatever non-farm work is available in the countryside are also low-paying informal jobs. Small-time business entrepreneurs and service providers are emerging in the countryside while urban-based investors are scouting commercial opportunities in rural areas. But the agrarian transition remains hobbled by surplus labor. The economic development process underway appears to reproduce small-scale, low-value production units. The persistence of unorganized, informal workers also seems to be a permanent feature of the economic landscape in India, unless new labor-absorbing business sectors emerge on a large scale.

5
Reinvention and Diversification of Business for Economic Development

5.1 Reinvention and Diversification of Business

The dynamics of the Indian agricultural sector, as discussed in the previous chapter, does not seem to follow the classical pattern of economic development, namely, the disappearance of surplus labor from the countryside by their absorption in nonagricultural rural and urban economic activities. A high proportion of workers relative to the workforce continue to earn a livelihood from agriculture. The obvious question is what other business possibilities exist to raise employment and output that would begin to make some dent in, if not completely absorb, surplus labor. In Chapter 3, we noted that critical manufacturing industries that are the backbone of a modern economy are not huge job creators. These sectors are needed more for what they produce and how they contribute to a wider ecosystem of manufacturing and industrial infrastructure. Employment is a byproduct of such critical investments, not large enough or a good fit for India's vast unskilled labor pool, but nevertheless necessary for a modern economy.

There is also the critical question of efficiency or productivity. One cannot simply add workers to the payroll, as was often the practice in earlier public-sector, heavy-industry units. There are some minimum technological, economic, and social criteria by which jobs are created for a given investment. Of course, India's technological trajectory did not follow the international frontier. Hence, it is understandable that labor being cheap and markets being insulated from foreign competition, more workers could be added on economic and political grounds with a choice of technology that was less capital-intensive (see D'Costa 1999: 103–104, Nayar 1990). It needs to be reiterated that both employment and output growth are crucial outcomes of economic development and social well-being. However, recent experience suggests that employment growth has not kept up with output growth (Sharma and Mehta 2024: 39, D'Costa 2017, 2019). This decoupling of output from employment suggests jobless growth, a subject taken up briefly in the next chapter.

Indian Business, Economic Development, and the Jobs Dilemma in the Twenty-first Century. Anthony P. D'Costa, Oxford University Press. © Anthony P. D'Costa (2026). DOI: 10.1093/9780198948407.003.0005

If agricultural links to urban industries are weak due to the low incomes in the countryside, does it mean that the nonagricultural sectors, namely manufacturing and services—could sufficiently lift the overall economy toward higher value economic output and generate better-paid jobs? Given that the Indian economy, since the early 1990s, has moved away from its state-commandeered economy, has business-led commercial dynamism in both agricultural and nonagricultural sectors taken advantage of new technologies and growing domestic and world markets? This is precisely what many East and Southeast Asian countries have done continuously since the 1960s, when transitioning from labor, capital, and technology to knowledge-intensive manufacturing and services.[1]

These are interesting but difficult questions to address in great detail in this introductory book. A quick response to the possibility for India to transition to a higher value, diversified economy, is that the world is a different place from the 1960s when many of the Asian economies launched their labor-absorbing, export-oriented industrialization efforts. Much has changed in terms of not only what is produced but also how it is produced, by whom, and where it is sold in the world market. The finely tuned, long supply chains across the world economy established by manufacturers, suppliers, importers, and exporters represent a complex evolution in the international division of labor. India, for the most part, was not an active participant in these value chains until very recently.

Could existing business and economic sectors be modernized and new ones established for economic diversification and development? Could this enhance productivity and efficiency for long-term sustainable development and create new jobs? In this chapter, we explore how the traditional agricultural sector is being extended and modernized for tighter linkages with urban markets and assess new types of activities that are contributing to labor-intensive jobs as well as economic diversification through digital technologies and energy transition. This chapter examines the extent to which Indian businesses today are participating in new markets, at home and abroad, transforming old business sectors in new ways, applying new technologies, and contributing to new types of employment. Here, a quick recap of four selected business sectors is presented to indicate the challenges of job creation despite

[1] There are many other dimensions to East Asia's economic trajectory since the 1960s, few of which can be found in India at that time. Suffice to say these countries were relatively small compared to India, some of them had effective land reforms that ultimately avoided deep inequalities in society, a capable state in carrying out narrowly focused effective industrial policy, tapped into external markets while regulating imports, emphasized universal education for all, and remained under the tutelage of American protection during the Cold War.

economic and business diversification. These are automobiles, IT, pharmaceuticals, and gems and jewelry. Moving forward, this chapter also briefly analyzes three relatively new types of sectors to highlight the growth prospects and the limits to resolving the surplus labor problem. These are food-related retail businesses; the energy sector, which also overlaps with the transition to electric vehicles (EVs); and digitalization and the platform economy (DPE).

The chapter is divided into six sections. In Section 2, a quick review of four previously examined sectors is provided for their contributions to economic development and their limits to job creation. In Section 3, the Indian food retail sector that is linked to agriculture is discussed in terms of new organizational and supply chain models. Section 4 presents a new approach to contemporary economic development, namely, the DPE. It offers digital infrastructures for new types of businesses and services, including public services, and new prospects for mass employment. Section 5 explores India's energy transition from fossil fuels to renewable energies. Aside from addressing climate change, to which India is a major contributor and could become even more so with economic growth and rising consumption, large swathes of India's population are particularly vulnerable to climate disruptions, such as coastal flooding, rising water levels, water scarcity, and rising temperatures.[2] These problems, while not wholly resolvable given the global nature of expanding material consumption, need to be abated for no other reason than ensuring a sustainable human environment. At the same time, there are good business, technological, and employment opportunities in the process of energy transition. The final section concludes with some implications of the reinvention and diversification of business and economic sectors on employment prospects.

5.2 A Recap of the Economic Impact of Selected Business Sectors

This section quickly reviews the automobile, information technology (IT), gems and jewelry, including diamonds, and pharmaceutical sectors.

[2] Whether climate mitigation through various international, national, and private bodies, including green-friendly business practices, will solve the problem is unclear. What is known is that climate change is real and hence demands a human response. It should be also pointed out that on a per capita basis India's emission of greenhouse gases (GHGs) is low compared to major energy consumers such as the United States and China. However, the Earth's carrying capacity is dependent less on relative contribution of GHGs, which is a way to allocate national responsibilities for GHGs, and instead the carrying capacity is influenced more by the absolute quantum of GHGs emitted into the atmosphere. Within this broader problem, specific communities around the world, including those in India are unequally impacted by climate change without being contributors to it as the poor have very low levels of consumption.

These sectors broadly represent high-value manufacturing and services, labor-intensive exports, and innovation- and education-embodied manufacturing and services. They indicate the possibilities of the variety of employment possibilities. Other sectors, both public and private, older and newer, were discussed as well, such as steel, agriculture, and the handloom sectors. Here, references that were made to modern retail as extensions of the diversification of agriculture in the last chapter are elaborated. In addition, new sectors such as e-commerce-based delivery services (the digitalization and the platform economy (DPE)-based gig economy), digital infrastructure for financial inclusion, and the energy transition are discussed in this chapter as part of India's ongoing economic diversification and implications for employment growth.

In Table 5.1, I present some sectoral contributions to economic development in terms of output, employment, and exports. The significance of exports to economic development is the generation of foreign exchange, which in turn supports critical imports such as oil, components and supplies, and technologies that support overall economic activities, employment generation, and skill development, among other things. Exports are a sign of international competitiveness, but the workers behind those exports should also benefit so that the inequality that is already quite worrisome is not exacerbated (see the next chapter). Since export markets are competitive, there is a tendency to hold down wages and leverage the surplus labor situation to keep wages from rising, unless matched by rising productivity and increasing (external) market share. But the success of many export-oriented sectors suggests that the owners of capital are rewarded at a much higher level compared to the workers who actually produce economic value, such as that exemplified by the diamond sector.[3] Economic diversification will be critical for those low-wage export services, such as diamond cutting and polishing, even though the sector could absorb more workers at low wages. There are, of course, market limits to this expansion as already indicated, which could be made worse by the uncertainty of American tariffs, discussed in Chapter 7 (Tirodkar 2025).

The combined output of the four sectors is not trivial. The automobile industry, due to its capital intensity and skill requirements, generates the highest output of the four sectors, mostly for the domestic market. On the face of it, the IT software and the diamond sectors, with relatively low barriers to entry, are both export-driven and produce more economic value per

[3] The software sector exhibits more widespread benefits for the people who work in it, although it too is a reflection of inequality at the societal level in terms of access to technical education and uneven regional development.

Table 5.1 Economic Impact of Selected Business Sectors

Industry	Output (US$ billions)	Employment (millions)	Exports (US$ billions)
Automobiles	251.40[a]	9.49[b]	13.64[c]
Information Technology[d]	186.89[e]	4.47[f]	149.10[e]
Gems and Jewelry, including Diamonds	74.89[g]	5.00[h]	29.07[i]
Pharmaceuticals	38.78[j]	2.70[k]	19.05[j]

Notes:
[a]Value of components, 2026 projection, upper range $282.8 b (IBEF Auto Components 2025).
[b]2022 projection (includes OEMs and components), Consortium of Training and Placement Officers of Tamil Nadu, https://cotpot.in/human-resource-and-skill-requirements-in-the-auto-and-auto-components-sector/, accessed November 8, 2024.
[c]2020–2021, vehicles other than railway or tramway rolling stocks, parts, accessories (Government of India, Ministry of Commerce and Industry 2022).
[d]Unless otherwise stated, IT data from NASSCOM (2022). "Facts and Figures," https://nasscom.in/knowledge-centre/facts-figures, accessed March 21, 2023.
[e]NASSCOM (2022). In 2019, the domestic market size was $37.79 billion, and exports (IT services, BPM, ER&D, and Software products) were $149.1 billion.
[f]Direct employment and an estimated 12 million indirect employment (Ministry of Electronics and IT).
[g]3% of GDP.
[h]IBEF Gems and Jewellery (2025), direct employment in the diamond sector is estimated at 1.3 million (Economic Times, December 6, 2024), https://economictimes.indiatimes.com/industry/cons-products/fashion-/-cosmetics-/-jewellery/diamond-sector-facing-challenges-during-last-three-years-due-to-reduced-demand/articleshow/116040586.cms?from=mdr, accessed March 23, 2025.
[i]Net exports, 63% are cut and polished diamonds
[j]Government of India, Ministry of Chemicals and Fertilizers, Department of Pharmaceuticals (2021), Annual Report 2021–2022, p. 3, https://pharmaceuticals.gov.in/sites/default/files/English%20Annual%20Report%202021-22%20%281%29.pdf, accessed September 22, 2024.
[k]Indian Pharmaceutical Alliance (2019: 7).
Sources: "Indian diamond industry in 2020 and 2021," Analytics, 11 January, https://www.rough-polished.com/en/analytics/119913.html, accessed January 7, 2022
India Brand Equity Foundation (IBEF) (2025). Automobile Industry in India Report, https://www.ibef.org/industry/india-automobiles.aspx, accessed March 29, 2022
Human resource and skill requirements in the Auto and Auto components sector—NSDC Consortium of Training and Placement Officers of Tamil Nadu, https://cotpot.in/human-resource-and-skill-requirements-in-the-auto-and-auto-components-sector/Ministry of Electronics and Information Technology, https://www.meity.gov.in/content/employment#:~:text=Direct%20employment%20in%20the%20IT, to%20be%20over%2012.0%20million, accessed January 19, 2022

worker compared to other labor-intensive sectors. Information technology (IT) software is not subject to high capital requirements but relies on technical professionals and the diamond sector relies on an abundant and available supply of low- to medium-skill workers. It is understandable that the IT industry generates high overall revenues since the sector demands large numbers of college-trained, mostly technical professionals, with demand for software services arising mainly in the wealthy economies. The diamond industry, on the other hand, as we have seen in Chapter 4, employs non-transferable skilled workers, and it also imports nearly 100% of the diamond roughs or about \$18 billion (21% of global imports) and \$55 billion in gold imports. Hence, the net local economic value added per worker is substantially deflated, as it should be, given the complete reliance on imported diamond roughs (and gold for jewelry) for exports. The strength of this sector is also its weakness, namely, the availability of abundant semi-skilled, low-wage labor with limited opportunities for better-paying jobs.

Of the four sectors under consideration, the pharmaceutical industry has the least employment and output value. However, it exports nearly 50% of its output, much of it in generic drugs. Past government patent policy that encouraged reverse engineering based on process patents fostered the manufacturing capability and competitiveness of the Indian pharmaceutical sector for the large, low-income domestic market. With the expiry of many patents and the imposition of World Trade Organization (WTO) mandates, the industry has had to focus its energy on exports of generic drugs and on developing other businesses. These include active pharmaceutical ingredients (APIs), contract manufacturing and R&D vaccine production, and innovative products and processes entailing biologics (use of living organisms), and biosimilars (approved for commercial production of a product that is similar to the original biologic, after meeting regulatory and intellectual property conditions). However, India has become heavily dependent on China for APIs, importing about 70% of its requirements (BioSpectrurm 2024). It is cheaper to import APIs than manufacture them at home.

Similar to the auto and IT sectors, the pharmaceutical industry contributes to economic development through output, employment, innovation, and exports. Incidentally, the value created by the pharmaceutical sector exceeds that generated by automobiles, implying its international competitiveness. India remains the "pharmacy to the world" with the largest vaccine producer, Serum Institute of India, based in Pune, and many globally oriented Indian firms such as Sun Pharma (merged with Ranbaxy), Cipla, Biocon, and Dr. Reddy's. At the same time, importing Chinese APIs on a large scale suggests that the sector is yielding manufacturing capabilities in a critical input. Related to this, there are some interesting business breakthroughs in basic healthcare. For example, Aravind Eyecare in the state of Tamil Nadu provides free eyecare to the poor, which is subsidized by wealthier patients who are charged on a sliding scale (Saldinger 2018). Simultaneously, the coexistence of a growing and lucrative private health care sector, with some enterprises matching world-class standards, reflects the highly dualistic, unequal, and overall underdeveloped system. Paradoxically, while the Indian pharmaceutical companies are not known for developing new drug therapies and are now dependent on Chinese APIs, these sectoral and business accomplishments contribute substantially to social well-being, domestically and globally, by producing affordable critical drugs.

Roughly twenty-two million people are directly employed in these four sectors. This is not a small number, five million short of Australia's population, or nearly four times Singapore's population. However, the share of such employment in India's workforce is around 4.5%. The differential wages and salaries within and between these sectors, with the highly internationalized IT sector commanding the highest salaries, the average value added per worker is considerably lower than in countries with higher productivity rates. Economists argue that India's low productivity is one of the reasons for lower incomes, which in turn is the consequence of a lower level of economic development to begin with. Improving productivity requires disrupting this catch-22 situation.

Both the state and the private sector must make investments on the supply side: investing in physical infrastructure, upgrading antiquated factory equipment and technologies, training and reskilling workers in a wide range of occupations, and fostering new types of economic activities and reinventing others. However, this is not sufficient. It must be matched by the demand side as well. How can workers be productive if much of their time is spent in back-breaking work under harsh conditions, they remain undernourished and fall ill frequently, and could be laid off easily? What is critical is adequate income and employment security. Whether businesses should provide such conditions is not a rhetorical question but one that must be tackled if the jobs dilemma is to be resolved in some meaningful way and the built-in inequities addressed. Increasing productivity can be a double-edged sword. Labor displacement under increasing productivity in the urban manufacturing and services sector must be matched by plenty of investment in productive, physical, social, and educational infrastructures. However, knowing what we know about India's agricultural sector, productivity is necessary, but it can only be sufficient if the labor surplus so released can find alternative employment opportunities in non-farm activities in rural and urban areas.

Recent developments are not encouraging. India has been regressing when it comes to agriculture. With economic development, instead of continuing the decreasing trend in the share of agricultural employment to total employment, it has reversed recently.[4] Agricultural employment has actually increased due to the triple shocks of demonetization in 2016, the chaotic implementation in 2017 of a uniform goods and services tax

[4] Bharadwaj (1985: 23) in a related context terms "muted" or "truncated" capitalist relations in the countryside.

(GST) or value-added tax (VAT) at state borders, and the impact of a muddled government response to the pandemic of 2020–2021. The absolute size of the agricultural workforce had declined from 343 million in 2004–2005 to 337 million in 2009–2010 (Thomas 2012: 39, 41). However, more recently agriculture employment has increased,[5] from 42.5% in 2018–2019 to 46.1% in 2023–2024 (according to the PLFS 2024 data). This is unusual by any historical standard, where capitalist development generally leads to shedding agricultural workers, not adding them.

The informal sector, which includes medium-, small-, and micro-sized enterprises (MSMEs), relies on cash transactions, which have been hit hard by demonetization and GST, especially if they operated on credit (GST must be paid in advance). The impact of the pandemic was even more disastrous, with millions of urban workers returning to their villages on foot and whatever other modes of transport were available after the national lockdown. The pandemic cut off the earnings of urban informal workers and remittance income for their rural dependents in the countryside. All three "episodes" had and continue to have severe lingering effects on the cash flow of the poor, daily wage workers, remittance income from urban to rural areas, and small businesses, especially in the informal sector.[6] As a desperate coping mechanism, laid-off workers, as indicated earlier by the diamond sector, and petty business owners returned to the countryside, suggesting that low-productivity agriculture still remains a fallback option in India. Agricultural distress has compelled workers to seek non-farm employment in both rural and urban areas. However, since the pandemic began, even the rural non-farm sector has begun to show signs of stress, thereby foreclosing some of the possible economic diversification options. It is conceivable that this rural reversal is a temporary phenomenon, but thus far, given all the other attendant undercurrents mentioned above, this stalemate might become ossified.

5.3 Transforming Agriculture with Modern Indian Retail?

Given the near-unlimited supplies of labor, it is not unusual to find that the Indian food retail sector is highly fragmented and dominated by small-scale, often family-owned, informal, mom-and-pop type of neighborhood stores.

[5] Of course, a stable rural life that generates a decent livelihood is an acceptable way of life. However, because the rural economy is subject to the volatility of market forces with ever more people working on small plots of land, it does not promise a struggle-free existence. This does not account for the environmental pressures that also result from more intensive use of land and water.

[6] See Chodorow-Reich, Gopinath, Mishra, and Narayanan (2018) on the impact of demonetization. While demonetization increased digital payments, as also acknowledged in Chapter 5 in this book, these authors find the effects to be temporary, ignoring the lingering long-term effects of demonetization that wiped out many small businesses.

These are known as *kiranas*. They sell fresh and packaged food items, grains, toiletries, and other low-value consumer goods. Their supply chain is erratic, mediated by layers of intermediaries, and lacks modern storage and transportation, which often results in considerable spoilage. These basic features are not uncommon in other low-income countries. However, with economic development, there has been a transformation of the informal retail sector to more formal, larger corporate entities in a number of late-developing countries. In India too, a similar, if slow-paced, change is taking place. The convenience of shopping at larger stores for middle-class households who are also experiencing rising incomes, the entry of women into the professional workforce, and the demonstration effects of western-style consumption patterns all contribute to the gradual entry of organized retail in India. The new retail segment offers large volumes of a wider range of goods, including grocery items, apparel, and other fast-moving consumer goods (FMCG). They also entail long value chains in the agri-food sector under which different types of actors, such as aggregators, intermediaries, transporters, and wholesalers, are involved (Barrett, Reardon, Swinnen, and Zilberman 2019).

One of the hallmarks of economic development is increasing productivity or efficiency. Compared to the *kiranas*, organized retail tends to be more efficient as measured in terms of revenues per employee, revenues per square foot, or total profits of the store. To achieve higher productivity, it is evident that the small-scale *kiranas* will have to be transformed into their organized, formal form. This calls for both state and private business investments in infrastructure, real estate, technology, and skill development. Expansion of the modern retail sector as a whole implies that employment at various levels will also increase. The expected knock-on effects (or spillovers) are likely to be a more robust supply chain, including regulatory links for quality and health safety, all the way back to agriculture when sourcing fresh produce and grains.

It may seem obvious that the transformation of the retail sector into a large-scale, modern, organized business with regular employees, governed by applicable laws, when no longer confined to catering to the needs of neighborhoods but the wider urban clientele, is an indication of expanded output, diversification, and employment. What is not so clear, especially in the context of labor surplus, is the impact of large-scale retail business on employment. Roughly, there are 15 million *kiranas* (Pathak and Kandathil 2020) with a conservative estimate of another 15 million informal jobs associated with these *kiranas* or 6% of the total workforce, assuming 493 million people in the workforce. There are three ways to unpack this employment issue. The first is the immediate dislocation and job displacement that results from large-scale retail. The second is the longer-term adjustment of the economic and social system to their presence, and subsequently to the ubiquity of organized retail stores across the country that is largely informally organized. The longer-term impact could be the large-scale disappearance of *kiranas* and many of the associated informal jobs, but also the growth of new jobs in the corporate retail sector. The third, and most likely outcome, is the coexistence of both types of retail formats—*kiranas* and organized retail—for the foreseeable future, although the precise nature of the mix is anyone's guess. In fact, with some integration, digitally connected *kiranas* could result in hybrid retail formats that retain the small size but also use modern technologies for their operations. However, there is another parallel development that could work against the growth of modern retail and modernized *kiranas*, namely, the rise of "quick commerce" preferred by urban consumers. This is similar to a platform-based delivery business, discussed later in this chapter, which may add more employment in the form of self-employed, independent contractors under a digital platform (Parthasarathy et al. 2025).

It is theoretically possible for the *kiranas* to hold their own with the various advantages that they offer to their neighborhoods, often with low-income clientele, such as credit, small volume purchases, home delivery, and, for some, a certain degree of social connection as opposed to the impersonal organized retail sector. Alternatively, large-scale retail, through its efficiency, size, and fewer middlemen in the supply chain, could offer lower prices by eliminating high transaction costs due to multiple layers of intermediaries (Pingali, Aiyer, Abraham, and Rahman 2019) for standardized goods. Large-scale retail could also become the dominant player in the retail sector, impacting competition in local markets.

Under all three possible outcomes, there are likely to be second and third-order externalities of various degrees, meaning that the entry of DPE into organized retail transactions (discussed in the next section), entailing increasing productivity, could spur investments in a number of related activities. As Figure 5.1 illustrates, these include horizontal and vertical integration of the supply chain, beginning with cultivation by small and large contract farmers and cooperatives; agricultural logistics; processing; infrastructure development and real estate; transportation and storage; development of a cold chain; and distribution channels for domestic and export markets.

Significant business opportunities are expected to open up in the entire ecosystem, from agriculture production to final markets, including supermarket chains. Many of these retail businesses are morphing into e-commerce

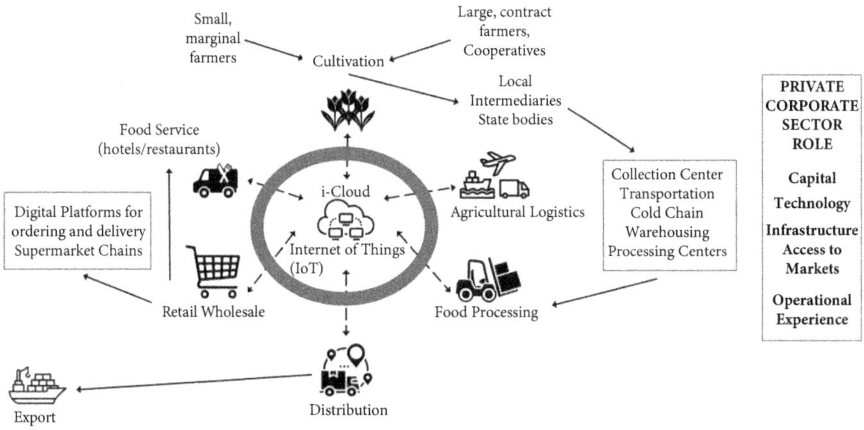

Figure 5.1 Economic Development Impact of Modern Agriculture and Food Ecosystem
Source: Compiled by author based on Deloitte (2018: 5), Pingali et al. (2019: 195), and Bain & Company and Centre for Innovation, Incubation and Entrepreneurship (2017: 9)

models that are integrated by information and communications technologies (ICT) such as cloud computing and Internet of Things (IoT). These upstream activities are likely to be complemented by downstream activities, such as technology development, marketing, branding, advertising, and exports. The expected contribution of the corporate private sector in this ongoing restructuring of the agri-food ecosystem are capital investment, technology development and its transfer, physical and digital infrastructure, market access, and operational expertise (Bain & Company and Centre for Innovation, Incubation, and Entrepreneurship 2017: 9). Output growth is expected to increase rural employment in off-farm activities and for specialized professionals related to digital technologies. They could leverage their technological capabilities and global market reach, thereby contributing to exports, foreign exchange, and employment. However, large-scale production and related automation by corporate retail, whether by domestic or multinational firms, are likely to dislodge initially some of the urban-based, *kiranas* in high-impact zones. Consequently both owners of *kiranas* and their informal low-wage service employees can be expected to be hit.

With expected multilayered, multisectoral, intertemporal employment effects of organized retail, it is difficult to anticipate a priori what the *net* contribution of total jobs would be under such a business sector transformation. Available information suggests that the displacement effect on *kiranas* may not be immediate and deep since they still enjoy locational and social advantages. Thus, both *kirana* and corporate types of businesses could coexist, but jobs created in the expanding capital- and information-intensive organized retail sector will be accompanied by some job losses in the *kirana* sector. Increased urbanization, a growing middle class, and lifestyle changes toward convenient processed foods are some of the drivers behind corporate retail. At the economy-wide level, we can also expect secondary employment effects in both rural and urban areas with expanded agricultural output. These include infrastructure, IT, related transportation, and supply chain logistics brought about by contract farming.

However, studies show that small cultivators have a more difficult time favorably participating in modern food supply chains due to lower volumes of marketable surplus, indebtedness, and incomplete market information (Singh 2020). Nevertheless, the weak agricultural links to urban industries due to the low incomes in the countryside could be somewhat offset by the growth in contract farming of larger scale, supplying directly to organized retail outlets. If such practices proliferate, some farming groups in the countryside will experience higher output and income growth, while some of the mass of undifferentiated urban youth will find low-wage formal and informal jobs. In this way, the modern retail sector could link nonagricultural activities with agriculture through sourcing and value-adding supply chains.

Is this then the beginning of the end of surplus labor? Possibly not, certainly not in the medium term. Even if foreign companies make large investments in contract farming and organized retail with a massive export thrust, additional employment generated in rural and urban areas could be countervailed by imports of technology and know-how and industrial inputs, thereby dampening the employment benefits of local manufacturing. To put India's labor surplus in its proper context, it is instructive to consider China's massive developmental gains from labor-intensive manufactured exports. Deemed the workshop of the world, China has introduced seismic shifts in its economic structure in favor of manufacturing, technologically leapfrogged in a number of economic spheres, and instigated a historically unprecedented migration of 250 million rural residents to urban areas between 1982 and 2017 (National Bureau of Statistics, UN Population Fund, and UNICEF 2018). In the process, China has also drastically reduced its poverty rate, from 88.9% in 1999 to 15.8% 2019, based on a $5.50 per capita income per day (World Bank in Macrotrends 2022). However, even with large-scale migration, not all of it permanent, and massive industrialization, China still has nearly a quarter of its workforce, roughly 200 million, in agriculture.

With nearly 50% of India's workforce in agriculture and a stagnating industry, it is doubtful that labor surplus is anywhere near exhaustion since there are not enough decent labor-absorbing manufacturing and service jobs to make a dent. Counterintuitively, increasing productivity to increase overall incomes seems to be counterproductive from a jobs point of view, unless, of course, the spillover effects of productivity growth continue to generate and sustain new economic activities on a larger scale. However, we can expect continued growth in output, employment, and innovations in various business sectors as the Indian economy continues to diversify its output. We can also anticipate India to be characterized by a mix of globally visible, highly innovative businesses that will coexist with the vast low-income, precarious informal sector of laboring classes (a subject we return to in the next chapter).

5.4 Digitalization and the Platform Economy

Digitalization and the platform economy (DPE) embody technologies that are mostly software-driven and rely heavily on ICT for interconnectivity, especially the Internet, artificial intelligence (AI), and the emergent Industry 4.0 innovations. IBM defines Industry 4.0 as "smart manufacturing, [which is] the realization of the digital transformation of the field, delivering real-time decision making, enhanced productivity, flexibility and agility" (IBM 2022). While DPE is not the same thing, it does share a common digital infrastructure, namely, the Internet. Digitalization is a sweeping kind of innovation that has become ubiquitous in the overall economy and society.[7] It leverages and applies already digitized data that also includes the conversion of non-digitized objects. Examples include digitizing paper documents as well as rapidly transmitting digitized information, say for supply chain management for car production by means of computers, associated hardware, and software. They are all linked to the Internet so that businesses can coordinate and manage elaborate just-in-time supply systems. Such applications open up the possibilities for establishing inter-firm networks for business purposes and government services delivery within and across agriculture, manufacturing, and services, both commercial and public.

Digitalization can also be seen as a form of automation, which, by reducing human labor and input, increases productivity, enhances ease of use, saves time, increases market reach, and reduces transaction costs at the organizational and economy-wide levels. Businesses and government departments, as part of e-governance, are digitalizing their in-house processes and external

[7] The term "digital transformation" refers to the great advances in computing powers and analytical techniques, as well as communication and vision/sensing technologies that combine to create a new world of 5G-enabled constant connectivity, autonomous systems and robotics, blockchain, artificial intelligence and machine learning (AI/ML), data mining, and governance through "the cloud." (Schaede and Shimizu 2022: 1).

transactions, whether business-to-business and consumers or government-to-government and citizens, to facilitate the seamless exchange of information for commercial transactions and the delivery of public services.

The platform economy (PE) relies on online infrastructure such as reliable internet, connected to various electronic hardware devices, websites, digital portals, and mobile apps that act as intermediaries via algorithms (akin to a middleman or a real estate agent) to bring buyers and suppliers together (Kenney, Bearson, and Zysman 2021: 1451–1452, Cioffi, Kenney, and Zysman 2022).[8] Platforms have the added characteristic of massive network effects, that is, the overall community benefits as more users are involved. Classic contemporary examples are Amazon (the United States and India), Flipkart (India), Facebook (global), WhatsApp (global), Alibaba (China), Rakuten (Japan), Big Bazaar (India); food delivery services such as Swiggy and Zomato (India); ride sharing companies such as Uber (global, India), and Ola (India); and new payment systems such as Paytm and Razorpay (India), to name a few. All of these platforms are service portals and are backed by real producers and service providers. Platform economies (PEs) are large-scale digital marketplaces where commercial transactions, the exchange of information on products and services, as well as the digital airing of views and opinions, take place. There are a few entry barriers for participants (buyers and sellers). However, for platform owners, depending on the scale of operations, substantial investments may be required in the digital-technical sphere. There are, of course, smaller platforms and apps on smartphones for a wide variety of everyday activities, such as online banking and entertainment.

The retail sector discussed earlier in this chapter is very much part of this DPE-led transformation. Most of the services, including retail, are characterized by low-wage, labor-intensive tasks. However, DPE, with its infrastructural and technological thrust are changing economic production and services delivery toward higher value-added services. The growth spurt in the Indian DPE sector has been due to higher pay, albeit the evidence is not clear-cut, the diffusion of the internet, smart phones, high incidence of two-wheeler ownership, and the availability of venture capital (Parthasarathy et al. 2025: 576).[9] With DPE, many other services are being altered through the "servicification of manufacturing" (Matthess and Kunkel 2020: 2) and the

[8] An algorithm is a set of instructions or rules for a computer to undertake calculations and solve numerical problems.

[9] In one study reported by Parthasarathy et al. (2025: 582), only 51.5% of the sample of 1318 workers earned the legal minimum wage (after deducting work-related costs) and 76.3% of those had to work longer than 48 hours to earn just the minimum wage.

scaling up of volume and quality of transactions conducted by hitherto small-scale, low-wage, and low-tech businesses. This is a global trend, and India is no exception. While family-owned neighborhood *kiranas* are expected to coexist for some time with the formal, corporate segment of retail business, a recent survey shows that modern retail, based on digital platforms, is integrating *kiranas* by having orders and processing done online, while the merchandise for delivery gets picked up from the *kirana* (Kathuria, Kedia, and Bagchi 2021: 16). This is reflective of the inexpensive, gradual, and halting modernization of the *kiranas* through DPE.

Digitalization and the platform economy (DPE) have a lineage, namely the IT industry, in which India excels when it comes to software services exports (see Chapter 3). The organic links between the Indian IT sector and Silicon Valley in the United States, in terms of exports, technical professionals, networking, venture capitalists, entrepreneurs, and CEOs of Indian heritage in large US technology firms such as Microsoft and Google are well-known. Indian IT firms have adopted American best industry practices and reinforced India as a global outsourcing destination (see D'Costa 2025a). Global technology firms with IT and software needs have taken an avid resource-based interest in India. The relatively abundant technical professionals have contributed to captive intra-firm software exports by transnational firms and inter-firm exports by independent Indian firms for foreign clients.

At the same time, the Indian state, riding on the success of this commercial sector, has recognized the importance of digital infrastructure and networks to foster bureaucratic reforms and enhance efficiency in the delivery of government services. Already, the state with its Software Technology Parks of India (STPI) had experience with satellite links that were made available to the export-oriented software business firms. Similarly, its digitalization of public services had an early start with the computerized reservation system for the Indian Railways, which is one of the world's largest employers—with 1.2 million workers—and rail networks in the world. While the idea that productivity increases through digitalization is taken for granted today, there was a time when economist Robert Solow remarked that one could see computers everywhere except in the (US) productivity statistics. He suggested that efficiency gains with digital technologies were not readily apparent. Yet by the 1990s, digital technology-led retail, transportation, wholesale, and manufacturing sectors witnessed considerable productivity increases (Krishnan, Mischke, and Remes 2018).

The productivity increase was possible by unprecedented innovations in semiconductor technologies, which, according to Moore's Law, the number of transistors that could be packed into an integrated semiconductor doubled every two years, indicating the exponential growth in digital information processing and computational capacity, and thus, the manageability of millions of online transactions. Consistent with high-technology *services exports* and the anticipated developmental benefits of digitalization, in 2015, the government launched its Digital India initiative. The inbound onslaught of AI in the market and workplaces has considerable implications for digital technologies, subjecting India's workers of different skill levels and certain occupations vulnerable to displacement, but also employing more technical professionals at other levels and for new tasks in existing sectors. AI also requires the manufacturing of powerful computing chips and the availability of a massive amount of electricity for powering AI data centers, neither of which India is capable of now, nor in the foreseeable future.[10]

A long-standing developmental goal of the Indian government has been to reduce poverty. While poverty rates have fallen since the 1980s, how much it has fallen is based on what yardstick is used. Whatever the figure, it is highly contested. Nevertheless, the international poverty line of $1.90 per day is considered to be an inadequate benchmark, while India's own standard based on consumption expenditures (related to caloric intake and other basic needs) is also hopelessly insufficient. The government had stopped publishing poverty figures after 2011–2012 and recently, in 2024, released new figures based on surveys of consumption expenditure (Bhalla and Bhasin 2024). India's poverty rate has fallen substantially using the low 2011 yardstick of purchasing power parity (PPP) $1.9 per capita per day. But using a higher income/expenditure yardstick, India's poverty is expected to be high. This is despite the plethora of pro-poor policies enacted by recent governments. Different estimates of the poverty rate vary from 2% to 26.4% depending on the income standard and survey design used (Himanshu, Lanjouw, and Schirmer 2025: 34), or roughly 28 million to 369.6 million people.[11] The upper-level estimate is closer to the estimate of over 25% of India's population being under the poverty line as reported by Sethu, Abhinav Surya, and Ruthu (2024) and also closer to the 25% estimate using PPP $3.2 per capita per day income (Bhalla and Bhasin 2024).

[10] There could be limited opportunities in chip design activities. But lacking an ecosystem for this type of high-technology manufacturing it is unlikely that India will be an important player. This is briefly alluded to in the concluding chapter. The energy needs are massive because of the computational needs by which AI is trained using massive data sets. The data is stored in servers that are housed in large data centers, which consume significant energy for both processing data and for cooling the processors. If the energy sources are fossil-fuel based, the implications for GHG emissions are dire.

[11] India's poverty rate is notoriously difficult to measure. It is made worse by not collecting the data for comparisons and estimating the direction of change, changing definitions and survey methodologies, changing the composition of the basket of goods and services included in consumer expenditures by households as a proxy for poverty, including daily caloric intake, and so on (Himanshu, Lanjouw, and Schirmer 2025, Jose and Hussain 2025). What ought to be appropriate income standards for rural and urban areas are also in dispute.

One recent anti-poverty program is the Jan-Dhan (People's Wealth) scheme, which is to ensure that every citizen has a bank account in the formal financial system. However, a unique identity is necessary to open a bank account and receive direct government income support and other welfare transfers. In 2009, the government began working on a unique biometric identity card (Aadhaar card) for every citizen. While serious data breaches and privacy concerns were raised with this project, the Aadhaar card, over time, has become the *de facto* identity card to receive a whole range of government services and even mobile phone connections, which are provided by the private sector (Khera 2018). Notwithstanding the controversies of making the card mandatory, which disadvantages the elderly and the less educated, the project has ultimately digitally linked the poor with the formal Jan-Dhan program of financial inclusion and poverty reduction, as well as the formal banking system. At the same time, the reckless demonetization of 2016, which created havoc among the people of India—especially those in the informal sector—also accelerated the digitalization process. In this digital transformation, private telecommunications companies such as Jio and Airtel brought down the cost of wireless connectivity, while the availability of cheap (Chinese-made) smartphones further facilitated digital financial transactions between the government and the individual. The Aadhaar card effectively became the Know Your Customer (KYC) tool to provide a service that required an identity, which could also be digitally authenticated anywhere in the country.[12]

It is in this digital infrastructural context that the rise of the PE and gig workers becomes relevant. Aside from the Jan-Dhan, Aadhaar, and Mobile connectivity (JAM), the government—through the National Payments Corporation of India (NPCI), under the Reserve Bank of India and the Ministry of Finance—established the Unified Payments Interface (UPI) (see Figure 5.2). Together, JAM and UPI have created a foundational digital infrastructure. They link citizens with the government and financial institutions via the financial system and inexpensive mobile and internet connectivity. Thus far, over 600 commercial and cooperative banks and digital payment companies are linked via UPI. The government of India also has its own phone application, Bharat Interface for Money (BHIM), linked to UPI for digital payments. This digital infrastructure also crowds in the private sector to innovate in ICT and create new business platforms for commercial services through digitalization, such as online payment systems, e-commerce,

[12] The World Bank estimates that the Aadhaar KYC brought down the onboarding costs (the costs associated with verifying background for say bank or utility accounts) from $23 to $0.15, allowing poor customers to open such accounts (Vir and Sanghi 2021).

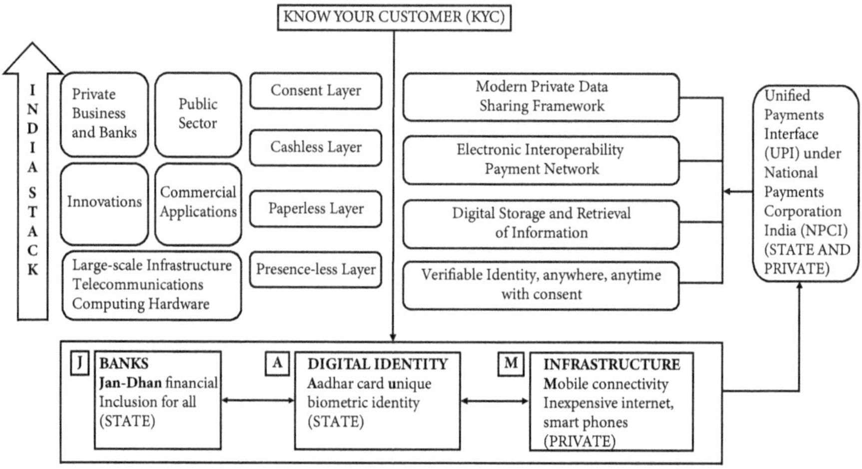

Figure 5.2 India's Digital Developmental Infrastructure
Source: Adapted from Vir and Sanghi (2021), Credit Suisse (2021), and the business press

and platform-based mobility and ride-sharing services. In addition to the highly skilled work required to set up the digital infrastructure and the business platforms, millions of unskilled and semi-skilled workers are mobilized, especially in various delivery and other on-demand and task-based services that are typical of a gig economy.

The National Institution for Transforming India (NITI) reports that there were about 7.7 million gig workers in 2020–2021, which is expected to increase to 23.5 million by 2029–2030 or 4% of the workforce (NITI Aayog 2022: xvii).[13] Gig jobs are on-demand, task-based work, and the large informal sector already caters to this kind of service demand. Platform jobs are a subset of gig work except that they use digital technologies as an intermediate interface. Platforms bring both customers and sellers together on the digital platform in various business sectors to generate value directly and foster the wider ecosystem (Kenney, Bearson, and Zysman 2021: 1452–1454).

If a platform firm emerges as market dominant through competitive advantage, then this winning firm is expected to create other winners in the emerging support sectors. This outcome is akin to the externalities associated with large-scale industrial investment, except that the multiplier effect with platform economies is unlikely to be as large as in manufacturing. Nevertheless, DPE contributes to productivity growth through

[13] Other projections estimate up to 90 million "gigable" jobs over the long term (Michael and Susan Dell Foundation and Boston Consulting Global 2021: 10). This is an unrealistically large, long-term projection. There was no mention when long term might end as far as this projection is considered.

increased labor participation (Banik and Padalkar 2021: 21). Many of the low-wage service segments such as passenger mobility, delivery services, professional home services, domestic work, gardening, elder care, simple mechanical work, and home care are being organized and scaled up under the PE (Michael and Susan Dell Foundation and Boston Consulting Global 2021) and to some extent formalizing some of the informal jobs. This could also entail inclusion under the tax net, but workers could benefit from the regulatory umbrella of workplace protection, safety, and social security.

Another offshoot of digitalization and PE has been the rise of startups, including several branded unicorns, that is, well-known companies that began with an infusion of $1 billion or more of investment. A startup is a new business, not yet off the ground and not necessarily platform based. But with low entry barriers, many recent startups—initiated with investment sourced from venture capitalists (including foreign capital), personal and family loans, and crowdsourcing—tend to be platform-based. Startups signal entrepreneurship that investors are willing to fund high-risk, high-payoff projects. Based on market capitalization, their value is often disproportionately high relative to the actual size of the business. Owners and shareholders benefit substantially after selling off the business. In fact, one of the motivations to found start-ups is to nurture and prime them to their financial peak and sell them, not necessarily to hold on to them for further growth. The implication is that owners and shareholders of such DPE-types of business tend to become wealthy very quickly, thereby also exacerbating the wealth gap (see Chapter 6).

Recently, many of these startups in India have become unicorns, meaning they are rare since they have reached a valuation of $1 billion or more. Between 1990 and 2000, 15% of India's unicorns were established, which increased to 35% and 31% in 2000–2010 and 2010–2020, respectively. This growth reflects a bullish market and an ecosystem of digitally driven enterprises. As of 2025, there were 122 unicorns with a total valuation of over $363 billion (Team Inc42 2025). Most of the unicorns are concentrated in Bengaluru, Mumbai, and the National Capital Region (NCR) of Delhi, all major locations for the IT and software services. The stamp of Silicon Valley is unmistakably evident, where successful entrepreneurs and venture capitalists, many of Indian heritage, have spawned technology firms both in the United States and India.

Of the one hundred unicorns listed by Credit Suisse (2021), the vast majority were platform firms. The sectoral distribution of these unicorns is presented in Table 5.2. Finance (or fintech, as labeled by the industry) has

Table 5.2 Distribution of Unicorns in India by Sector and Valuation

Sector	Share of Unicorns of Total (%)	Share of Valuation of Total (%)
Finance	13	17
Discretionary	10	7
IT/Technology	12	5
E-commerce	10	14
Mobility	3	3
Education	4	7
Software as a service (SaaS)	12	8
Health	9	15

Source: Credit Suisse (2021: X)

had the largest number of unicorns (13%) and the largest valuation (17%). However, while IT and software as a service (SaaS) had a similar share in the number of firms, their valuation has been uncharacteristically lower. This contrasts substantially with the e-commerce sector, with 10% of the unicorns and 14% of the valuation. This sector has become the battleground of large global and domestic firms such as Amazon, Flipkart, Reliance, and Future Retail because of the huge market potential.

Given this brief background of digitalization in India, what can we say about the relationship between Indian business and economic development that is mediated by the state? There are two main sets of development implications: on the economic front and on the social front. The key expected benefits are increased productivity and reduced transaction costs and time at the immediate business level, as well as financial inclusion in the government's anti-poverty programs and convenience of digital delivery of public services. There are other spinoffs, such as businesses that are also leveraging the internet, the Aadhaar card, and the UPI. They are directly and indirectly contributing to a wider ecosystem of technology institutions of developers, sellers, buyers, and users, and implicitly contributing to the government goals of e-literacy and access to services. By attracting large investments in digital startups and unicorns, businesses and entrepreneurs are signaling a favorable business environment for new commercial ventures, innovations, and economic growth.

Digital and platform economies can be seen as changing the relationship between business and economic development in five areas. The first is that digital infrastructure is anticipated to have a direct impact on the poor, namely, a reduction in poverty through financial inclusion, empowerment of citizens through digital literacy, and increased efficiency in the delivery of public services. Of course, the mere introduction of digital infrastructure and technology without institutional and policy reforms in favor of the disadvantaged is likely to be ameliorative rather than transformational. Nevertheless, under the National e-governance Plan, the digitalization of critical services such as agricultural and nonagricultural land records, health and education, passport applications, police and courts records and processes, and administration of commercial taxes is a step in the right direction. Second, in this digital context, businesses have also been active in utilizing the digital infrastructure for their commercial pursuits, including platform-based digital marketplaces such as e-commerce, mobility, and telecommunications services, and innovation opportunities.

Third, similar to the transition in the retail sector, platforms are disrupting the ways in which business and consumer services are delivered. Aside from the efficiency in business transactions, transparency, expansion, and diversification of offerings to far-flung markets, they are also altering labor markets. Increasingly, urban youth are relying on platform-based labor demand for employment opportunities. The profusion of platform-based marketplaces in India is illustrated by the different types of services offered and their approximate scale of operations (see Box 5.1).

Box 5.1 Variety and Scale of Selected Digital Platforms in India, Circa 2024

- PayTM (digital payments system) with over 300 million individual and small business users in India and 8 million in Japan using a modified and relabeled PayTM system.
- Zomato (food delivery platform) with over 1.5 million delivery partners (not all work at the same time, all the time) and 647 million orders in fiscal year 2023.
- Nykaa (e-commerce for beauty products), FINO Payments Bank (finance, microcredit) with services to 40 financial institutions and a network of 80,000 agents reaching out to 85 million customers.
- PolicyBazaar (insurance portal) with fifty million registered customers.
- CarTrade Tech (online research and discovery portal for buying and selling new and used autos).
- Ola (mobility services) with over 1.5 million driver-partners.

continued

Box 5.1 *continued*

- OYO (On Your Own) (branding and online hotel booking) claims to be the third largest hotel chain with 23,000 OYO-branded hotels and 850,000 rooms globally.
- Byju's (online technical education) with 115 million registered students and 7.5 million paid subscribers.
- Practo Technologies (healthcare, telemedicine) connecting doctors and patients, billing, appointments and offering online preventive healthcare.
- Apollo (telemedicine, online pharmacy delivery services).

Note: Many of these online e-commerce and other businesses are also unicorns.

Source: As reported in the business media through Google search, Statista, and other reports.

Fourth, DPE does create a small number of well-paying, white-collar, technical jobs, mainly back-office support and maintenance staff, programmers, debuggers, and administrators. Digital platforms, as seen in Box 5.1, also create millions of jobs, such as delivery staff for Zomato or drivers in mobility services such as Ola. One estimate shows that there are roughly three million jobs under eleven platforms (Fairwork India 2020), while seventy million jobs are estimated by 2030 (NITI Aayog 2022: 2). Other estimates suggest that ninety million jobs might become "gigable" down the road, with twenty-four million moving away from the old type of gig jobs to platform-based ones (Michael and Susan Dell Foundation and Boston Consulting Global 2021: 10), clearly suggesting both displacement and complementary effects in labor markets.

In the context of surplus labor, this is a welcome trend if the net addition of jobs is nontrivial, as opposed to workers switching from existing employment to delivery work.[14] Whether the compensation provided for these jobs is low is debatable. For example, the daily or monthly earnings of delivery partners are contested. According to Zomato's CEO, a Zomato delivery partner earns INR 28,000 a month at 8 hours work/day, minus estimated INR 5000 for fuel costs, or about $270 a month at today's exchange rates. This figure is considerably higher than the minimum wages set by different state governments for "skilled" workers (Dezan Shira and Associates

[14] In a recent study, it was shown that online workers who were part of the formal labor market (technical and nontechnical workers excluding delivery workers) had better pay-offs when undertaking such assignments even if the number of job seekers exceeded the demand (Christopher, Stanton, and Thomas 2025).

2025).[15] However, digitally based platform workers are not treated as employees but independent subcontractors or "partners." Consequently, they do not enjoy any of the safety nets and collective bargaining options that are accorded to regular, permanent employees in other workplaces (Banik and Padalkar 2021: 22). Recently, however, there have been some government initiatives to extend basic healthcare for unorganized workers to gig economy partners that would cover hospitalization costs (Sitharaman 2025).

Fifth, startups by definition are not established businesses yet, so unless the capital is monetized, the economy-wide developmental impact is unlikely to be felt widely (Credit Suisse 2021: 5). There is the real possibility that many of them will not survive the vicissitudes of capitalist market competition. Many of these start-ups are not doing well after the initial euphoria in attracting capital, including foreign investment through initial public offerings. Startups tend to be overvalued with excessive liquidity chasing unproven assets, such that the aggregator (the digital platform) becomes worth more than the hotel rooms or airline tickets it is aggregating (Ramphal 2022). Byju's, an education technology startup by Byju Raveendran, was valued at $22 billion, more than any other Edtech company in the world, which expanded rapidly with aggressive marketing tactics, only to face huge losses (Cornish, Singh, and Ruehl 2022). Wealth inequality is intrinsic to this sort of business disruption, where the return to capital is severalfold that of the return to labor (Norton 2017). Many of these startups and platform owners are literally transformed overnight into very high net worth individuals, even as their businesses remain in the red.

It is not clear at this time if platform jobs are displacing existing traditional jobs or adding new ones, although the evidence points to the latter. The gig economy is not a novelty in India. With surplus labor, people offer their services when they are in demand on an informal basis. However, the PE-based gig economy offers different types of services. This can be seen as a form of diversification of economic activities with higher earnings relative to alternative options available. However, it is also clear that "[p]latforms are not saviors, nor inherently evil; however, they are logics unto themselves" (Donner and Locke 2019: 41) with both advantages and disadvantages (Table 5.3). They increase the reach of markets for buyers and sellers, especially sellers who are on the fringes of the digital economy, such as handloom weavers and other artisans (see Chapter 4 for details) (Kathuria, Kedia, and Bagchi

[15] In Delhi the monthly minimum wages for a skilled laborer varied between INR 20,903 (US$250.39) to INR 21,215 (US$254.12) (Dezan Shira and Associates 2025). How skill is defined is problematic since the job categories and tasks performed are markedly different in PE-based services.

Table 5.3 Advantages and Disadvantages of Platform-based Gig Economy Jobs

Advantages	Disadvantages
Low entry barriers, hence, job creation	No job security
Entry of women and students	No healthcare or pension
Aggregator (or platform maker/owner) efficiently brings supply and demand	Workers treated as independent workers, terms of employment unilaterally set by platform, no collective action
Economies of scale, scope, and speed of output	Paid by piece rate
Offers better income opportunities	Monthly earnings may not be high
Geographical availability can reach international markets	Access to reliable internet and smartphones could be constrained
Platforms can create self-employment by linking small service providers such as food preparers	High-pressure jobs due to algorithmic management
Reliability of work as the platform can match workers with their skills	Performance of partners assessed by evaluation-based ratings by customers
Financial inclusion and possibly formalization	No career prospects
Diffusion of new technologies, smartphone usage	Requires IT literacy

Source: NITI Aayog (2022), Kathuria, Kedia, and Bagchi (2021)

2021: 16). Working conditions in many of these demand- and task-based services can be brutal. For example, many digital gig workers deliver food on bicycles and motorcycles, which are prone to accidents in India's congested roads, and the pressure to deliver quickly, many without breaks, to maximize total volume at the end of the business day. Earnings tend to be variable and sometimes lower than the minimum wage in the large metropolitan cities. In the recent past, there have been worker strikes due to poor pay, no social security, and high pressure to deliver on time (within 10–20 minutes) at Swiggy, the online food and grocery ordering platform. Job security is highly volatile. In 2022, thousands of employees were laid off in the digital gig economy, and while India's macroeconomic outlook is favorable, uncertainties remain on the types and volume of jobs that could be created in the medium term.

While it is hard to quantify the anticipated multiplier effects of startups and platforms, such as direct and indirect employment and increasing productivity across the board, e-commerce services with low entry barriers for workers have better prospects for creating low and medium-skilled jobs in large numbers. In fact, this is one segment where employment is growing faster than the general employment. Between 2011–2012 and 2019–2020, the employment elasticity to GDP was above one for gig workers, which was greater than the rest of the economy (NITI Aayog 2022: xvii).[16] Even MSMEs have started using some forms of digitalization, such as e-retail or third-party web-based e-commerce, to buy and sell online (Goyal, Kukreja, and Kedia 2022). As long as the volume of business continues to expand, which is dependent on disposable income growth, digitalization, and platform economies, labor markets will be impacted positively, even if some of the jobs themselves are not particularly inspiring. Under the condition of surplus labor, modern PE-based gig work is an improvement over not working at all.

5.5 Business, Development, and the Energy Transition

The relationship between energy consumption, production, and economic development appears intuitively straightforward. Without question, modern agriculture, industrial manufacturing, and almost every form of modern economic and noneconomic activities would virtually come to a standstill without electricity or power. In this context, both business and the government have an important role to play in India's economic development, not only through their investment activities in energy sources, but more importantly in diversifying such sources away from fossil fuels to clean, renewable energy.

Energy in the form of heat and electricity is generated from different types of energy sources. These include dirty renewable fuels such as biomass, including charcoal and animal waste, which are consumed especially by India's poor; non-renewable fossil fuels such as dirty coal, oil, and natural gas; clean but hazardous nuclear energy; clean hydropower, which has ecological consequences; and clean renewable non-fossil energy sources such as solar, wind, and tidal. The direct use of oil and electricity to run motors and engines generated from this diverse set of energy sources contributes to the workings of the social-economy, including households, business enterprises, and public and private transportation systems; tractors, irrigation pumps, and water supply for agriculture; modern time- and effort-saving electronic tools and gadgets, and physical comfort in times of extreme temperatures through heating and air-conditioning. The production, distribution, and consumption of electricity, with all the necessary supporting infrastructure, contribute to economic development through investments, skilled and unskilled jobs,

[16] Elasticity is the percentage change in the number of jobs when there is 1% change in the national income. Anything greater than one is welcome when there is a 1% change in income growth.

and intersectoral linkages or externalities in both upstream (such as coal mining and oil exploration) and downstream activities (such as turbine manufacturing, transportation networks, operation of the internet, and air conditioning).

Conventionally, the importance of energy in measuring economic well-being has been taken for granted. Until recently, it did not matter where the energy came from. Biomass, coal, oil, hydropower, and later natural gas and nuclear power have been typical sources of energy. In rural settings in poor countries such as India, natural biomass—including charcoal, wood, and cow dung—is still used, despite being highly polluting health hazards. They are inexpensive or freely available. But the broader link between energy consumption and standard of living has not been sidelined. Empirically, a high level of economic development positively correlates with high energy consumption per capita, indicating both a high material standard of living and a comfortable quality of life (see US Energy Information Administration 2021). A cursory observation of average income and energy consumption by country shows that wealthy, economically developed countries have higher energy consumption per capita than low-income, less economically developed countries (Table 5.4). The implication of this is that lower-income countries have plenty of room to increase their energy production and consumption to bring about economic development and raise the average standard of living.

As noted in Table 5.4, compared with the wealthy countries, India and other low-income countries are energy-poor, that is, they have low per capita consumption of power. However, consumption growth in rich countries is slowing down due to the already high level of energy consumption and attempts to cut back consumption with increasing efficiency. Climate change concerns are also reconfiguring the mix of energy sources. The United States, Germany, and Denmark had a negative change in their per capita consumption (Table 5.4). Developing countries, on the other hand, are rapidly increasing their per capita consumption of energy. Asian countries such as Bangladesh, China, India, and Indonesia stand out, albeit from a low base, while South Korea's rapid economic and industrial transformation has been accompanied by a massive increase in energy consumption. This is to be expected since economic development entails increased consumption of energy.[17] Poor economies initially could begin from simple, low-energy-intensive but

[17] Since the global recognition of climate change due to greenhouse gases (GHGs), electric vehicles (EVs) have been anticipated (see Black 2013). Burning of fossil fuels (oil, gas, coal) is the leading source for GHGs, with automobiles as a significant contributor. While India's per capita contribution of GHGs is low, economic growth, rising incomes for the middle classes, a large population, and continuing reliance on cheap coal have catapulted India to the third largest contributor of GHGs, after China and the United States.

Table 5.4 Per Capita Energy Consumption (kWh) and GDP Per Capita Income (Constant 2015 USD, Selected Countries and Regions)

Country/Region	1965 per capita kwh	2021 per capita kwh	Relative change per capita kwh (%)	GDP per capita (current prices, thousand USD)[a]	1965 GDP per capita (constant 2015 USD)[b]	2021 GDP per capita (constant 2015 USD)[b]	Relative change in GDP per capita (%)
Canada	70,768	101,691	44	57.41	31,223[e]	43,946	41
Denmark	34,914	32,089	−8	68.09	22,520	58,586	160
Europe[i]	25,308	37,497	48	34.23			
Germany	38,937	41,854	7	51.10	17,894[f]	42,527	138
US	72,295	77,574	7	76.03	22,697	61,280	170
Japan	18,523	39,094	111	39.24	9320	35,278	279
South Korea	2589	68,087	2530	34.99	1274	32,645	2462
Argentina	14,825	20,906	41	12.19	8202	12,391	51
Africa	2235	4044	81	2.18			
Asia	2826	18,909	569	8.89[c]			
Bangladesh	205[d]	2662	1250	2.36	504	1715	240
Brazil	3285	16,311	397	8.57	2787	8515	206
China	2121	30,322	1329	14.10	233	11,188	470
India	1241	7063	469	2.52	323	1961	507
Indonesia	843	8352	891	4.69	580	3856	565
South America	6252	15,836	153				

continued

Table 5.4 *continued*

Country/Region	1965 per capita kwh	2021 per capita kwh	Relative change per capita kwh (%)	GDP per capita (current prices, thousand USD)[a]	1965 GDP per capita (constant 2015 USD)[b]	2021 GDP per capita (constant 2015 USD)[b]	Relative change in GDP per capita (%)
Low-income countries	2488[g]	1250[h]	−50				
Lower-middle income countries	1000	6637	564				
Upper-middle income countries	8352	26,750	220				
High-income countries	37,614	55,945	49	54.85			

Notes:
[a]IMF,
[b]World Bank,
[c]Asia Pacific,
[d]1971,
[e]1997,
[f]1970,
[g]1980,
[h]2019,
[i]See Our World in Data for countries included.*Source*: World Bank Group (2025a) for GDP Per Capita, https://data.worldbank.org/indicator/NY.GDP.PCAP.KD, accessed November 2, 2024
Our World in Data for Energy Use Per Person, 2020, https://ourworldindata.org/energy-production-consumption, accessed November 2, 2024.

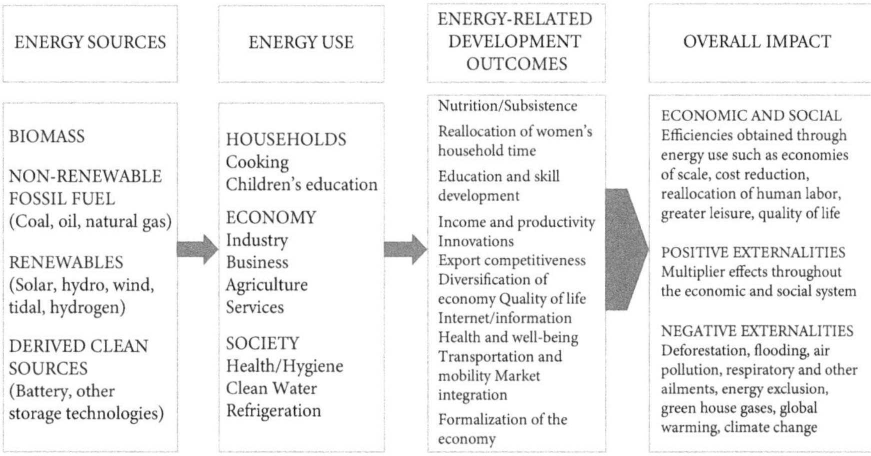

Figure 5.3 Economic and Social Development Impact of Energy Use
Source: Compiled by the author

socially impactful activities such as children doing homework, cooking meals, medical treatment in clinics and hospitals, and a reliable community water supply. They could then, as they diversify their economies, move to heavy industries, broader manufacturing, railways, residential and office towers, and the manifold increase in household appliances such as air conditioners.

As Figure 5.3 illustrates, there are various sources of energy for undertaking different activities at the household, economy, and societal levels with a range of positive and negative externalities or spillover effects. Energy requirements for basic types of activities can be roughly grouped under primary energy needs, while all other productive activities of economic development such as industrialization and jobs creation that are supported by a wide variety of energy inputs can be considered as secondary (Carley and Lawrence 2014: 18). The distinction between primary and secondary energy needs in a development context is moot since the absence of basic types of human activities due to energy poverty would hinder meaningful economic activities that are dependent on secondary energy sources. Both types of energy sources are necessary for economic development.

For a long time, energy usage has been synonymous with modern economic and social development. As Figure 5.3 illustrates, the use of electricity in social and economic life is ubiquitous. However, this interpretation today has been tempered by the awareness of the negative externalities of energy use, especially dirty biomass and fossil fuels, on the immediate quality of life and on the long-term existential questions around global warming and climate change. For countries such as India, still low on the economic development curve, moving away from fossil fuels too quickly is economically costly, practically infeasible, and temporally uncertain for development in the way we understand it, namely, raising the material and nonmaterial standards of living of the society. At the same time, not moving away soon enough to non-fossil sources could collectively add to the already high average global temperature. Such a response could also raise the specter of international political pressure to reduce India's absolute carbon footprint. This dilemma has been recently addressed by Addison and Roe (2024) by arguing that resources ought to be extracted strategically for economic development while also making the necessary energy transition to renewable sources.

The logic is quite simple, even if counterintuitive: energy transition among developing countries, such as India's shift away from coal to renewables, cannot be immediate, so why not develop mining and other extractive sectors, such as coal, in a way that generates not just revenues but also contributes to the overall productive structure of economic development? These would include, but are not limited to, infrastructure; transportation, such as rail and roads; education and skill development; and manufacturing and services, while at the same time, addressing critical developmental needs such as poverty reduction, regional imbalances, and inequality. In fact, there has to be a deliberate effort to integrate mining and energy-related infrastructure and processing of resources with the rest of the economy to create the necessary economic linkages with manufacturing and services, rather than be an enclave economy, which has been typical of resource-based extractive economies.

The implication of this strategic approach with a carefully calibrated energy transition for India is huge, namely, the opportunity to diversify the economy, create jobs, and ensure a less disruptive energy transition. More importantly, as far as business is concerned, it would mean enterprise development with a whole new startup ecosystem, as evident in the digitalization and platform economies, that can be expected to weaken economic dualism that is associated with enclave development. As Curtis and Marinescu (2022) show for the United States, many new types of jobs with higher wages, including both services and manufacturing, are created in regions with fossil fuel dependency. Thus, it is no surprise that in this energy transition, Coal India Ltd., a public sector company with the world's largest coal operations by output, is diversifying into clean energy renewables such as solar and wind while also making existing operations more efficient. Traditional private industrial firms such as Dalmia Cement and JSW Cement have launched decarbonization programs, which are consistent with the strategic integration of new clean energy technologies entailed in the energy transition. Other private businesses, such as Tata Power (solar), Suzlon (windmills), and ReNew Power (solar, windmills), Indian Biogas, and Hindustan Power (solar, windmills), have

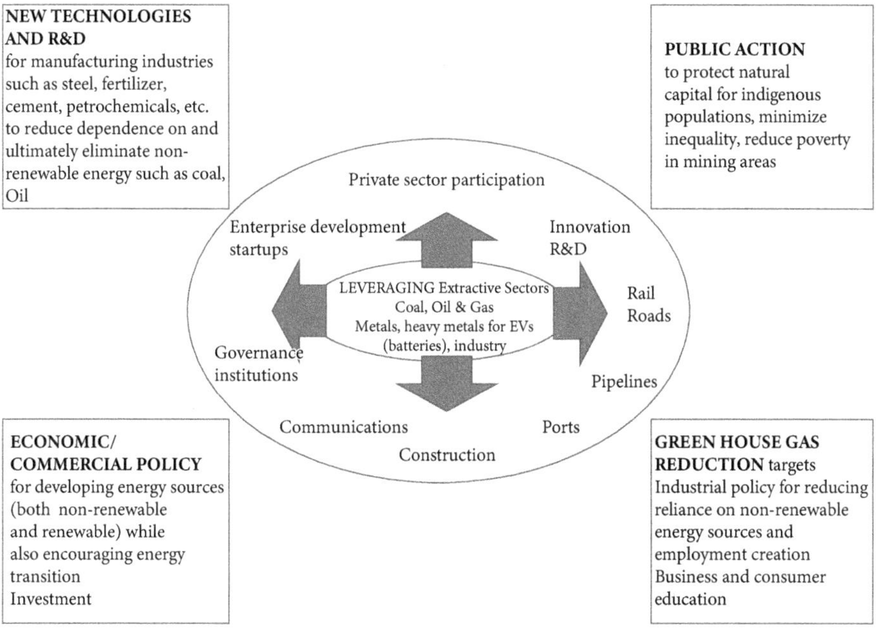

Figure 5.4 Intervention and Impact of India's Energy Transition
Source: Compiled by the author partly using Addison and Roe (2024) and the business press

begun the transition process to renewables. In this shift, the state does not take a back seat. Instead, it must actively participate in the energy transition through public action to protect natural capital for indigenous communities, pursue industrial policy intervention for economic diversification and integration of resource industries, promote R&D for renewables, and establish emission targets consistent with UN Climate Change goals (see Figure 5.4).

As of March 2022, approximately 50.6% of installed capacity for power generation from non-renewable and renewable sources was roughly shared equally by the Indian central and local state governments, while 49% was under the private sector (Government of India, Ministry of Power 2022). It must be recognized that even as late as 2010, the share of the private sector in power generation was only 10% (Bhide, Malik, and Nair 2010), thus suggesting that economic development attained with earlier state investments in the economy and in energy sources are paying off today by reinforcing India's energy infrastructure and pulling in private business in the energy sector. This crowding-in effect, resulting in the expansion in energy production and consumption, has significant economic development implications in terms of commercial opportunities, job growth, economic diversification, and various forms of economic, technological, and social spillover effects.

Currently, 59.1% of domestic power capacity depends on fossil fuels, 39.2% on renewable energy sources, including 11.7% on hydroelectric power, and 1.7% on nuclear energy (Government of India, Ministry of Power 2022). Coal and gas, with a 57.4% share of total capacity domestically, remain the largest non-renewable energy sources. It must be stressed that these statistics do not account for imports of crude oil for small-scale, backup power generation, and the massive volume of oil used for industry and transportation. In the pre-pandemic financial year of 2019–2020, India imported 227 million tons of crude oil worth $101.4 billion. In the same year, India's total merchandise exports (including re-exports of petroleum products made with imported oil) was $330.1 billion (Government of India, Ministry of Commerce and Industry 2022). India's energy dependence on imported oil cannot be overstated. Just witness the impact on India in 2026 of the US/Israel bombing of Iran, which is a major supplier of oil to India and the world economy.

India's fossil fuel dependency (or energy security), as measured by the share of oil imports to total exports (capacity to pay for imports), while lower than in previous years due to higher export capability today, still remains significant. For example, oil imports in the pre-pandemic financial year of 2018–2019 represented nearly 31% of India's export revenues. The geopolitics surrounding oil producers and buyers are well known. With Russia's invasion of Ukraine resulting in higher oil prices, India's already high oil import bill was close to $120 billion (Economic Times, April 24, 2022). In the 2023–24 fiscal year the oil import bill stood at $132.4 billion (Eximpedia 2025). Recent armed conflicts in West Asia involving Israel, Iran, and the United States have added to India's complicated oil diplomacy. Such dependence on imported oil is likely to get worse even if global oil prices stabilize and India has the capacity to pay with exports of oil and petroleum products derived from imported oil. Under anticipated increases in consumption with economic development underway, India's contribution to greenhouse gases (GHGs) will no doubt rise even further.

Two critical economic development issues that will continue to dog India are: how to conserve hard-earned foreign exchange by spending less on imported oil, and how to mitigate GHGs that result from burning coal and imported oil. In addition, in India and other developing countries, biomass such as plant matter and animal waste is still used by the poor, mostly rural households, for cooking and heating. Worldwide, about 660 million people rely on firewood for cooking, while an estimated 800,000 people, mostly women, die each year prematurely due to air pollution in the home from burning biomass (International Energy Agency 2021: 11, 28). Energy poverty leading to the widespread use of biomass is not only harmful to human health but also has wider ecological impacts, such as deforestation and flooding. Economic development is necessary to alleviate both household poverty and energy poverty simultaneously through the availability of affordable, less-polluting fuels such as natural gas and renewable sources for power.[18] However, unlike urban India, rural India is vast with little infrastructure for the effective distribution of natural gas. Furthermore, there is already a large shortfall of natural gas availability by a quarter of total demand, roughly 34 billion cubic meters, that is being met by imports (IBEF Oil and Gas 2021: 3). While importing more gas temporarily partly resolves the GHG issue, long-term energy dependency could actually become more entrenched as changing geopolitics in the Middle East illustrates

The challenges in resolving energy poverty while addressing India's economic development in the current context of climate change are knotty. While ambitious plans for increasing renewable energy sources have been launched, India remains a major producer and consumer of coal-based electricity. The catch-22 situation is apparent. Coal, oil, and natural gas are major contributors to CO_2 and GHGs that ultimately lead to global climate change. Rising temperatures accompanying income growth suggest increased demand for cooling appliances and thus greater demand for power. If coal remains cheap relative to other energy sources, the inertia to stay with coal longer will reinforce the perverse relationship between fossil fuel consumption and economic development.

The negative spillover effects, such as GHGs from pervasive usage, especially of dirty fuels and non-renewable sources, are unavoidable under the current mix of energy sources. For example, twenty-two of the thirty most polluted cities in the world are reportedly in India (Pyper 2021). Air pollution, averaging several hundred particulate matter of 2.5 micrometers (PM 2.5) in cities such as Delhi are not humanly acceptable.[19] While the causes of air pollution are many, especially during the winter months (smoke from burning post-harvest fields, dust from construction, industrial, and automobile exhaust), burning fossil fuels is not only a grave health hazard but also a major contributor to global warming. These challenges are likely to worsen as energy consumption is expected to increase among developing countries, especially in India, where economic growth is likely to drive the demand for energy growth (Figure 5.5). Barring the pandemic years, India's power generation has been on the rise. The International Energy Agency predicts that

[18] It is debatable if burning of natural gas (methane) can be considered clean because of the ecological impact of fracking by which such gas is obtained. However, for low-income households access to natural gas for cooking is far superior to burning coal or wood.

[19] Particulate matter of 35 or below of 2.5 p.m. size is considered safe.

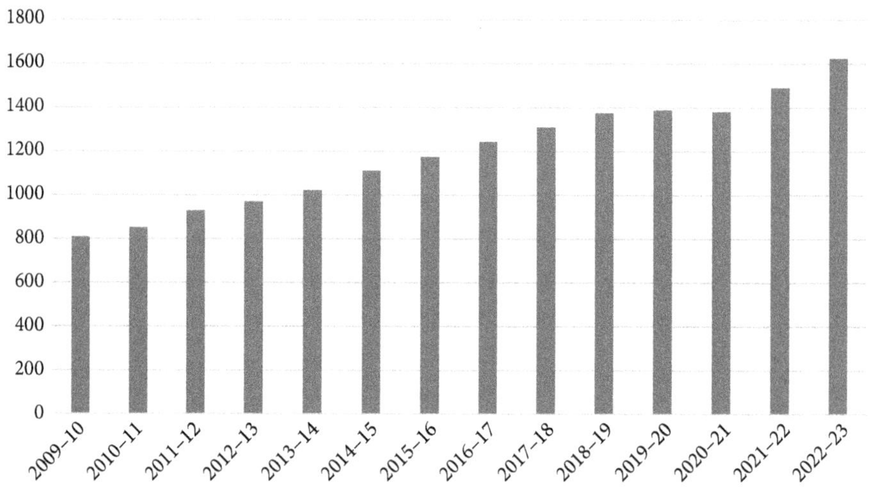

Figure 5.5 Total Energy Generation (Including Renewables) Billion Units
Source: Government of India, Ministry of Power (2022). https://powermin.gov.in/en/content/power-sector-glance-all-india, accessed May 23, 2022

due to population, urbanization, and income growth, India's GDP by 2040 will reach $8.6 trillion, anticipating an "explosive" growth in both energy consumption and diversification to solar energy (The International Energy Agency 2021: 74, 12). Short of banning fossil fuel, which is politically infeasible and counterproductive to the basic economic development aspirations underway, India's much-needed energy transition must rest on an aggressive shift by both business and the state toward renewable energy capacity as its consumption growth is expected to reach 25% of global growth by 2040 (The International Energy Agency 2021: 207).

India's fossil-fuel-based power generating capacity stood at nearly 60% of the total with coal comprising a significant 53% of total (calculated from IBEF Power 2022: 10). Given the availability of domestically mined coal with state-owned Coal India Ltd. as the largest coal mining company in the world, and India's energy-based development aspirations, coal is expected to remain an attractive source of power for the foreseeable future. For example, coal-based power capacity is estimated to increase anywhere between 62% and 116% by 2040 (calculated from IBEF Power 2022: 10). On top of this, as mentioned earlier, India relies heavily on imported oil, thereby exposing the country to the vicissitudes of global price fluctuations influenced by geopolitics, wars, and natural disasters. Therefore, just as other countries are adjusting their fossil fuel production and consumption, India, too, must embark on weaning itself away from fossil fuels and diversifying into renewable, clean energy sources. Such efforts have been initiated. Nearly 27% of installed power capacity today relies on renewable energy sources such as solar. The faster this ratio is increased by substituting fossil fuels with clean renewables, the greater will be the opportunity for both government and businesses to break the vicious energy-economic development link.

There have been some individual business efforts to tackle the vexing problem of GHGs. In 2017, Chetan Maini, the founder of Reva Electric car, formed a partnership with the SUN Group to form SUN Mobility. While the Reva itself failed in the Indian market, the principle of a green footprint was part of Maini's entrepreneurial outlook (D'Costa 2027b). The idea was to create an "interoperable energy infrastructure" with clean energy innovations, such as increasing the capacity of the battery with lithium-ion to increase the speed and driving distance of EVs.[20] By partnering with Indian Oil, a public sector company, with its nationwide network of gas stations, SUN Mobility reached out to a wider user base by initially marketing the electric car battery as a service. By separating the car and the battery, the company developed pay-as-you-go, swappable batteries for cars, e-bikes, and three-wheeler rickshaws (Ethiraj 2024).[21] Upfront costs to users were reduced since Sun Mobility owns the batteries and users pay only for the energy consumed. These small innovations by Indian businesses could go some distance in reducing India's carbon footprint.

There are at least three challenges in making the transition to electric mobility. First, battery technologies require considerable investments in R&D and access to strategic rare earth minerals from global sources. At the moment, the geopolitics of the global supply of rare earth minerals is fraught with rivalry and hostilities since they are controlled by a few countries, with China having the largest reserves (44 mt), followed by Brazil (21 mt), India (6.9 mt), Australia (5.7 mt), and Russia (3.8 mt) (Pistilli 2025). Second, while India has about 6% of global reserves of rare earth (cobalt, lithium, graphite, among others), the country remains import-dependent as it lacks refining capacities (Chakraborty 2025).[22] It will take several years before production can begin under a workable regulatory arrangement between the private sector and the government. Third, battery technology is only net-zero in appearance. If to charge the batteries or to manufacture EVs, electric power is used that is tapped from the main electrical grid, which is itself powered by fossil

[20] Sun Mobility, "Powering the Future of Mobility," https://www.sunmobility.com/about, accessed March 24, 2025.

[21] Batteries are owned by Sun Electric and users pay for the consumable (Ethiraj 2024).

[22] For example, major sources of cobalt are the Democratic Republic of Congo (220,000 metric tons), followed by Indonesia (28,000 mt), and Russia (8700 mt) (Williams 2025).

fuels, the notion of net-zero in this scenario is misleading. As shown by Buchal and Sinn (2019), the carbon footprint of a conventional diesel-powered internal combustion engine of a sedan in Germany, with a large battery-operated EV using the electrical grid to charge, yielded no CO_2 reduction after a certain distance. To realize India's energy transition, the electrical grid must be powered by non-fossil fuel sources as well.

Overcoming these challenges to reduce the carbon footprint will lead to many developmental benefits, such as reduced oil dependence, lower energy prices, less air pollution and GHGs, and increased manufacturing at home. Recently, the government announced that all new cars will be electric by 2030 and attain net zero emissions by 2070. The Faster Adoption and Manufacturing of (Hybrid &) Electric Vehicles (FAME) India scheme, launched in 2015, signals new auto-related business opportunities and the adoption of new technologies, including batteries for EVs. The aforementioned SUN Mobility is a good example. Battery technology is one area where Indian businesses, with the support of the state, could rapidly get on board with the evolving trajectory. There are other ways to introduce new technologies, reduce emissions, and create jobs. For example, Ola (the ride-sharing company) has begun manufacturing e-scooters. Auto manufacturers such as Maruti-Suzuki already produce compressed natural gas-powered vehicles and have announced production of EVs. NITI Aayog and Rocky Mountain Institute (2021) have identified a number of ecosystem enablers for electric vehicle adoption, chief among them are investments in infrastructure and financing of consumer purchases, especially from battery leasing businesses and swapping stations.

India's reliance on cheap coal makes the nearly fifty-year deadline for net-zero emissions understandably a modest pace for quitting fossil fuels and adopting alternative energy sources. However, these announcements also signal that growing energy consumption cannot be business as usual. India has almost doubled its energy consumption since 2000 (Deloitte 2018: 1) and consistently has power shortages. Thus, one can anticipate increasing energy consumption and, if unchecked by the development of renewable sources, an environmental disaster will be in the making sooner rather than later. It is therefore no surprise that India has launched ambitious programs to reduce oil dependency to 10% of demand and increase non-fossil fuel energy sources (Figure 5.6).

The inherent tension between the energy needs of a poor country that are integral to its economic development goals and the collective dilemma of global climate change is real. A more calibrated and collaborative approach

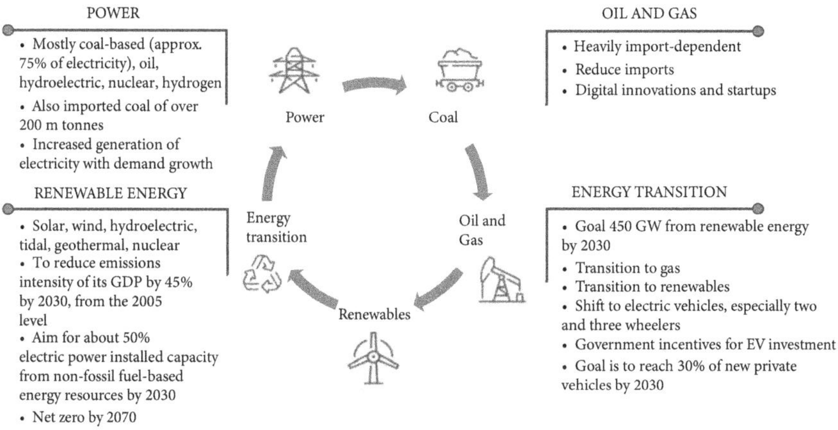

Figure 5.6 India's Energy Transition
Source: Compiled by the author from the business press

that entails state–business partnerships, international cooperation, openness to global innovations, best industry practices, and restructuring of the domestic energy sector to address both energy poverty and economic and social development will be crucial to initiate a long but necessary transition toward a green path to energy security, autonomy, and a higher quality of life. The urgency of relying on renewable energy sources implies not only bold policy initiatives by the government but also promises new lines of business opportunities in the energy sector, provided large investments are made. This is where the role of the state and its partnership with business can be creative, just as businesses, through their entrepreneurial activities, could find new opportunities and avenues to contribute to economic development in novel ways.

5.6 Conclusion

This chapter extended the examination of employment prospects and challenges in a different set of sectors. They represent economic diversification that is integral to economic development and illustrate how existing businesses can be revamped in new directions in manufacturing, services, and infrastructure. They included organized food retail and its links to e-commerce and agriculture, digital and platform economies and their links to public services, and India's energy transition to a greener economy.

The key takeaways from the chapter are:

a) These newer sectors and new business directions are critical to India's efforts to diversify the economy to generate new types of jobs and contribute to productivity across sectors.
b) Despite new linkages and opportunities due to modern retail, contract farming, and modern supply chain systems, agriculture will remain the livelihood for most Indians for the foreseeable future.
c) New retail businesses will continue to coexist with the traditional *kiranas*, but there will be some job losses due to automation and further scaling up of retail sales.
d) Digitalization enhances productivity and improves the quality of services as long as everyone is included in an accessible and transparent way. Digital literacy is critical for the effective use of such new platforms and infrastructures. The United Payments Initiative is an important innovation in this direction.
e) E-commerce and DPE infrastructure have created new types of low-wage delivery service jobs, which may be better than other informal sector jobs, especially if such jobs are to be included under the government's insurance programs for informal workers.
f) Associated digital transformation in telecommunications and wireless interconnectivity has created the foundation for other related jobs for low- and medium-skilled workers. Along with the success of the Indian IT services sector, the country is visible in startups and unicorns, which offer opportunities for entrepreneurs and high-skilled professionals.
g) India is energy poor, but with anticipated economic development, it must guard against rising GHGs to protect the well-being of its vulnerable communities and contribute to the global efforts to reduce the carbon footprint.
h) Anticipating growth and rising energy consumption, an energy transition is critical at this juncture. Some headway has been made already, but more needs to be done to not only address climate change but also contribute to employment at all skill levels.
i) India will have to balance its international partners to ensure energy and rare earth metals security, while also weaning away from imported fossil fuels and developing its own technological and institutional capacity to mine critical minerals at home.

While businesses are in the business of business anywhere, they do have a responsibility to the society in which they operate. The government can work with businesses to ensure responsible investment, facilitate decent formal employment, protect informal workers from precarity, and better share profits with workers. As will be discussed in the next chapter, the digital economy in the larger sense, for all its benefits, in a deregulated economy has also accompanied worsening inequality in much of the world. For social, ethical, and political reasons, this is unsustainable, certainly in India, where hundreds of millions of precarious workers stare in the face of growing, unprecedented billionaire opulence. In the next chapter, I address three broad questions to round out the initial discussion of the relationship of business and economic development that is mediated by the state. These are:

- What kind of possibilities exist for India in a world where manufacturing global supply chains are dominated by East Asia and China, and rich-country demand, which is now being destabilized by arbitrary US tariffs and other protectionist measures?
- How will jobs be created when businesses organize production on a large scale that limits labor-absorbing employment on a large scale?
- What kind of business–state relationship is necessary for governing the Indian economy for development and to address the monumental challenge of surplus labor?

6
Compressed Capitalism, Late Industrialization, and the Jobs Dilemma

6.1 Introduction

As the previous chapters demonstrated, Indian businesses have contributed directly to economic development through investment, employment, technology adoption, and exports, and indirectly through secondary effects in other sectors. The Indian state has also played its instrumentalist role through direct ownership and regulatory frameworks, and indirect promotion through incentives. In some sectors, India has excelled: IT and pharmaceuticals are two notably successful export-oriented sectors. The automotive industry has also witnessed considerable development. In all three, the mediating role of the state has been present, working with domestic and foreign capital. There are also successful labor-intensive export-oriented sectors, such as diamond polishing and newer sectors using digital technologies and platform economies. India's goals for an energy transition open up the possibility of not just new business opportunities and infrastructure development but also opportunities to tackle the existential threat of climate change and its impact on vulnerable communities. Modern retail and e-commerce also promise new types of labor-intensive service jobs.

These economic activities have considerable ramifications for development, especially for traditional sectors such as agriculture and artisanal handloom products. These two sectors are significant in terms of their potential for transforming the economy, contributing to millions of livelihoods, and relieving the general precarity of employment due to low agricultural productivity on the one hand, and vulnerability to new textile products becoming available and changing tastes and preferences on the other. New digital technologies have potential benefits for both of these sectors: in agriculture, digital technologies can expand output under contract farming and develop modern supply chains for grocery stores; for geographically dispersed handloom weavers and other artisans, they can reach wider national and international

Indian Business, Economic Development, and the Jobs Dilemma in the Twenty-first Century. Anthony P. D'Costa, Oxford University Press. © Anthony P. D'Costa (2026). DOI: 10.1093/9780198948407.003.0006

markets through e-commerce. To fully realize these potential benefits, the substitutive effects will have to be minimized, meaning that rather than just replacing old jobs, the new jobs will have to be either complementary or net additive. To have favorable outcomes, the foundational physical infrastructure, improvements in agricultural yields, and branding and global marketing will be needed. These strategies will advance supply-side efficiencies, business spinoffs, the sustainability of existing jobs, and the creation of new ones. New markets will also have to be created to support sectors that are vulnerable to changing markets but employ a vast number of artisans.

But there are limits to how many more jobs can be created in the various business sectors examined. Most of these sectors are capital-intensive. Recent policies designed to counter manufactured imports and address employment also tend to be capital-intensive. This is like a millstone around the late-industrialization process that locks businesses into modern technologies as part of their competitiveness in contemporary capitalism. Unless these modern industrial activities have large multiplier effects in creating plentiful jobs, they will continue to operate in a limited market characterized by worsening inequality. Labor-intensive jobs such as diamond polishing for export markets are fine as long as markets keep expanding and surplus workers are absorbed. But there are limits to markets and whether such work is transferable and can become a stepping stone for higher value-adding, better employment prospects down the road is questionable.

This chapter steps back and offers a more sober assessment and a less sanguine picture of the dilemma in job generation. This is backed up by a political economy understanding of the Indian business system as it has evolved, its relationship to the state, and the ensuing governance dysfunctionality that has left a vast number of workers and would-be job seekers in a dismal place. In Section 2, I develop a simple political economy framework to capture the lopsided development process where the economy appears to do well in terms of business growth but not in terms of employment. Section 3 provides a limited snapshot of India's labor markets and all that is not right about them. This is followed up briefly in Section 4, with a much-discussed external perception of labor inflexibility and the difficulties of doing business in India, to suggest that the ease of conducting business is more complicated than what is reported. Section 5 presents a brief discourse on worsening inequality that is integral to compressed capitalism. This in itself is an indictment of the persistence of the dualistic formal and informal labor markets and the jobs dilemma that leads to depressed overall economic demand. In Chapter 1, we saw how late industrialization imposes its own constraints on growth, notwithstanding the leapfrogging opportunities for late industrializers. India's growing dependence on imports, especially from China (presented in Section 6), confirms the significance of changing external conditions on lateness and thus India's inability to generate basic labor-absorbing manufacturing activities. Section 7 concludes the chapter.

6.2 Compressed Capitalism and the Structural Stalemate

In Chapter 1, the features of compressed capitalism were briefly presented. Without getting into an elaborate treatment (see D'Costa 2014a, 2014b, 2016a), suffice it to say that late entry into industrialization (or economic development) introduces the advantages of catch-up and the handicaps of being late. The actual development trajectory is path dependent (Arthur 1994), meaning institutional legacies, institutional efforts, and external circumstances determine the development trajectory. Lateness also implies that the state will be involved in "escaping from economic backwardness" (Gerschenkron 1962) to jumpstart the modern economy with various policy interventions. Successful East Asian countries have experienced modern, widespread economic achievements rapidly, even as latecomers, while others, such as India and Brazil, experienced these in incomplete ways due to institutional drag (Ayres 1991), policy choices, and unanticipated obstacles such as a changing external environment.

This inherited structural condition has been overcome by a handful of countries, mostly in East Asia, including China, since they began more or less independent industrial and development strategies roughly seventy-five years ago, albeit differently in each case. They calibrated their engagement with the external economy (technology imports, foreign direct investments (FDI), and exports) and pursued investment-led innovation learning approaches at home. These approaches include technology assimilation, reverse engineering, technical and universal education, research and development (R&D), and investments in infrastructure. At the same time, states used their power (democratically elected, authoritarian, or single-party states) to get their domestic house in order. There is no magic formula for how they did it, although serendipity played a part. However, the pursuit of economic growth and development clearly was favored to keep the focus on the immediate developmental goals. This can be considered the nationalist capitalist imperative by which the state assists businesses to pursue their commercial goals, and ensures that such pursuits also contribute to economic and social development goals such as productive capacity, technological learning, and employment. State capacity is a critical requirement for orchestrating industrial and economic transformation.[1]

For the sake of brevity, compressed capitalism can be conceptualized as the developmental processes and outcomes of the interactions between local institutions and external factors. In this interaction, some processes behind economic change are quickly set in motion, such as technological change, while others, such as an incomplete agrarian transition and the persistence of petty commodity producers remain stubborn. These self-employed workers with small-scales of production and reliant on family labor continue to be India's Achilles' heel. Historically, the first component behind compression is the process of primitive accumulation (PA).[2] The dispossession and usurpation of land, often violently, mark the beginning of extractive capital or the process of PA. In India, this process, begun during the colonial period, is incomplete since a large proportion of people are still tied to the land even though the share of agriculture to GDP has fallen substantially as anticipated by economic development (see Chapter 4). Instead of leading to a massive industrial proletariat (workers) emptying the countryside, as Marx predicted, the transition is truncated due to inadequate industrialization that could not draw workers away from agriculture.

For reasons specific to the time, India's industrialization and policy choices were capital-intensive and not labor-absorbing. The idea was that rapid industrialization would address rural impoverishment by luring workers into urban areas. But few industrial jobs in a slow-growing economy contributed to an ever-increasing petty commodity production (PCP), which is the second component of compressed capitalism. This is a vast, unorganized sector, which includes Indian household agriculture and all other economic activities that rely on informal labor who are outside the ambit of labor laws and social protections (see Agarwala 2019). Across the high-income and industrially successful East Asian countries, the unorganized sector has virtually disappeared with economic growth, rising incomes, and diversification. However, in more recent years, technological change, heightened international competition, and cutbacks in social protection are reintroducing informal labor market arrangements in some of these countries.

Petty commodity production (PCP) comprises a class of producers that own their tools, produce for the market, often rely on family labor, and

[1] There are many factors that played a role in East Asian development. One of them was state orchestration of business activities and economic policy. State capacity and ambition were products of society and geopolitics, which were specific to the times and place and are not in any meaningful sense replicable today.

[2] This is in the classical Marxist understanding of capitalism, that is, the alienation of peasants from their land.

remain small-scale. In the early stages of industrialization, PCP is common, but over time, with economic development, it shrinks to the point of disappearance. This is the second component of compressed capitalism. This has not happened in India, instead the informal sector as a whole has persistently remained around 90% of employment even with high economic growth. The informal sector constitutes mostly poorly paid, insecure, and precarious workers, the self-employed, itinerants, the homeless, and circulatory migrants from country to town and back again (Sanyal 2007, Samaddar 2008: 35–36). Compressed capitalism suggests that PCP will not disappear as it is reproduced by the specific conditions underlying economic development and labor absorption (see Castells and Portes 1989). Late entry to development amid changing international competition has also conditioned premature deindustrialization (Rodrik 2016), meaning, industrial growth as a share of GDP has stalled at a low per capita income.

This brings us to the third component, the advanced mature capitalist (MC) sector. This is represented by the small corporate sector running large, modern enterprises. Due to late entry into the development process, states are keen to jumpstart the economy, often at the behest of business classes. As the opening line in Chapter 1 indicated, the partnership between the state and big business (the Bombay Plan of 1944) contributed to the gradual maturity of business through protectionism, opportunities for rent-seeking activities, and a captive market at home.[3] In a global context, the MC is linked to capital accumulation at the global level (see Hoogvelt 2001), allowing Indian businesses to operate internationally while at the same time joining the global "bankable elites" by hosting foreign businesses at home and acquiring foreign assets abroad. The mature capitalist (MC) dimension is strengthened through state support, new markets, technologies, competitive pressure, and diversification strategies.

As depicted in Figure 3.1, economic development and structural change since the 1950s reflect a stagnating industrial sector but also a disproportionate increase in business-related services that include finance, mercantile trade of goods and services, real estate, and others such as IT services. Most of these sectors, unlike modern manufacturing, have relatively low entry barriers, often made lower with credit from institutional sources. The implication of the MC is that it represents a small competitive sector that tends to centralize and concentrate capital at the expense of plentiful job creation. Consequently, a vast, low-wage, PCP coexists with a small corporate sector in pockets of manufacturing excellence and in high-value tradable IT and other

[3] Rent-seeking activity was defined in Chapter 2.

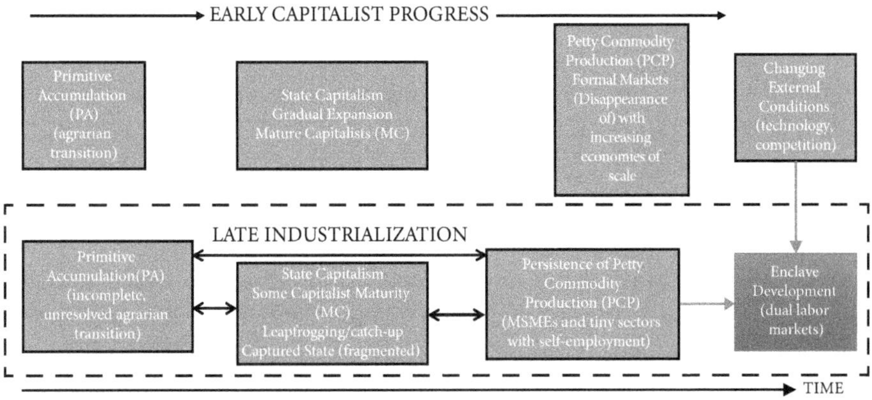

Figure 6.1 Compressed Capitalism Under Late Industrialization
Source: Compiled by the author

business services. They enjoy the fruits of capital availability, profitability, higher education, and higher wages and incomes.

The simultaneous co-existence of PA, PCP, and MC suggests that they change at different speeds. For example, narrowing the technological gaps and adopting modern industrial practices can be expected to take place relatively quickly, while agrarian transformation and weakening PCP or the disappearance of the vast unorganized sector can occur slowly (D'Costa and Chakraborty 2017). Paradoxically, a responsive state that minimizes the worst excesses of land dispossession to pre-empt political mobilization of farmers, slows down the effects of PA, namely, the separation of peasants or subsistence farmers from the land (Chatterjee 2008). While the vast PCP sector acts as a labor sink by absorbing dispossessed rural workers who cannot find decent employment in slow-growing nonagricultural rural and urban jobs (D'Costa and Chakraborty 2017), agriculture continues to remain an important fallback option. Consequently, PCP continues to be reproduced as informality remains persistent and as formal sector workers also become informalized. With a small pocket of relatively advanced MC firms mediated by the state and a low-productivity agricultural sector, India has been caught in an unusual structural stalemate. The net result is an "enclave" economy (Furtado 1976) with a severe form of economic "dualism" (Todaro and Smith 2020), which by definition suggests a highly divided economic and social order. Diagrammatically, the processes of compression are presented in Figure 6.1. The top part of Figure 6.1 refers to a stylized representation of early capitalism, while the lower half refers to late industrialization as exemplified by the Indian experience.

The important point to recognize is that the global contexts in which the three interrelated processes (PA, MC, and PCP) operate in both space and time are different. With the passage of time, economic opportunities thrown open by deregulation have been accompanied by technological, investment, and institutional constraints due to many late industrializers' inability to keep up with rapid innovations, heightened international competition, and necessary institutional adaptations to these changing conditions. These collectively have contributed to premature deindustrialization and a so-called middle-income trap (Rodrik 2016, Griffith 2011). India's contemporary manufacturing distress is due to economic deregulation since the early 1990s (Nayyar 2019: 484) in favor of big business (Mazumdar 2025) and the subsequent surge in manufactured imports, mainly from China (Nagaraj 2025: 2–3).

Slower PA ties people down to the land, but with urban alternatives not significantly better, the PCP continues to absorb people to cushion some of the economic and social fallout in rural and urban areas, while also benefiting MC through low wages. The differential rewards accruing to capital (physical and human) in MC and labor in PCP and PA make the outcomes of compressed capitalism highly unequal and, in effect, limit the size of the market. The low labor costs resulting from PA and the vast PCP disproportionately reward MC with high profits and offer a path of least resistance for business in a captive Indian market. There are a few incentives for big business to innovate. Open markets facilitate importing cheap and selling dear and discourage making cheap and selling cheap. Small businesses are content with *jugaad* and frugal engineering that offers them a livelihood, but are no match for global standards and competition.[4] If we superimpose the growing politically derived power of business over the Indian economy, the effects of compressed capitalism are further inflated.

According to Mody (2023), "India is Broken" not because of bad policies alone but also because of the monopolization of political and economic power leading to rent-seeking and corruption of public officials, politicians, and business (see also Mohanty 2022). Gradually, the dismantling of institutional and democratic norms leading to electoral autocracy in India has deflected public attention away from the welfare of and social protections for the poor, the marginalized, and others in the vast informal sector. In a path-dependent fashion, businesses have become powerful and a select few even more powerful lately due to a particular form of state patronage in a *quid pro*

[4] *Jugaad* is an "innovative fix" using simple tools, local materials, or applying existing products for new uses but mostly for the domestic market. Frugal engineering refers to creative low-cost engineering, resource-saving, effective products through simple designs and processes to cater to low-income markets. See Rajdou, Prabhu, and Ahuja (2012).

quo arrangement (for details, see D'Costa 2023). Much of the political power of the state and the commercial clout of big business are dissipated by shoring each other up for their mutual benefit in a *quid pro quo* arrangement instead of moving the multiple levers for job creation.

As a late industrializer, the Indian state created the economic space for domestic capitalists while ensuring critical intermediate inputs such as steel, coal, railroads, and power (see Chapter 3). The state–business institutional partnership allowed non-market advantages such as privileged access to the state, to resources, and thus to political influence through the industrial licensing system that was established in 1950. Witness the humble beginning of Reliance Industries that began with an import license for synthetic yarn (Chapter 3). Individuals and businesses profited (earned rents) from the artificial scarcity that arose from a highly controlled economy. Unnecessary output controls and bureaucratic regulations created a scarcity premium (prices were high, often politically manipulated in controlled rent-thick sectors where demand exceeded supply), as well as tardiness in bureaucratic paperwork (small bribes (or "speed money") were used to jump the queue for quick administrative processing). In a closed economy, privileged access to the state that dispensed production licenses contributed to rent-seeking activities such as kickbacks and bribery (see Kochanek 1974) while political stability in a raucous patronage-based system was maintained through the distribution of public funds to various proprietary groups (Bardhan 1984).

An underground economy of undeclared income and unexplained wealth thrived. Real estate absorbed large amounts of tax-avoiding "black money," including from criminal activities (D'Costa 2023).[5] Rent-thick sectors in India, beyond natural resources, included cement, infrastructure, liquor, and real estate (see Gandhi and Walton 2012, Walton 2020). They are rent-thick because production technologies are mature, while regulations encouraged informal subversion of formal rules, which offered lucrative profit opportunities for businesses and kickbacks and bribes for political elites and public officials. The potential to earn excess profits has been high in sectors such as liquor that face inelastic demand or cement where demand exceeds supply and large government projects are involved.

Contrary to expectations, the deregulation of the Indian economy increased corruption and crony capitalism (Bhattacharya and Guha Thakurta

[5] For example, the profitable real estate market attracts large investments but also acts as a conduit for recycling illicit wealth or black money. Sellers typically demand a certain percentage of the price to be paid in cash, typically black money to avoid paying capital gains tax, while buyers launder black money into a tangible, appreciating asset.

2019: 199). The corporate capitalist class had matured and differentiated itself in terms of their commercial acumen, technological knowledge, and global presence (see D'Costa 2000). They also politically adjusted to the new economic reality. As market opportunities increased and the state became more ambitious with infrastructure building, the private demand for land led to questionable land acquisitions, sometimes facilitated by the state. In an inflationary market for immovable property, the demand for both public and private infrastructure projects, factories, and real estate increased (see D'Costa and Chakraborty 2017, Jaffrelot 2019).[6] Well-connected individuals and businesses could politically manipulate credit markets and obtain easy credit through collusion, and borrowers used loans that were not invested for the declared purpose (Rajeev 2017: 221–222).

The growing structural power of business has ensured that the needs of labor are subordinated to business expansion and economic growth (Jaffrelot, Kohli, and Murali 2019: 3, Murali 2019).[7] The publicly owned State Bank of India, as well as less regulated private financial institutions, have met such credit demand under pressure from politicians and influence-peddlers.[8] It is therefore no surprise that non-performing assets (NPAs) or loans increased massively with easy credit policies (Chatterjee and McCartney 2020, 12).[9] The collective NPA ratio was 24.4% for the top four rent-seeking sectors: mining, iron and steel, aviation, and infrastructure (Rajeev 2017: 224). A number of business owners who held public office pushed for policies that favored their interests and contributed to political parties, while others sought political office to benefit from massive rent opportunities that come with winning offices (Sen, Kar, and Sahu 2018: 273–274; see also Sinha 2019: 57–67). The current ruling party introduced electoral bonds in 2017. These were scrapped in 2023 due to their unconstitutionality. Under this scheme, donors, typically businesses, could contribute any amount of campaign funds anonymously to political parties. This was an effective channel to transfer wealth without accountability from the private business sector to

[6] A 2013 government study reported that in addition to real estate, two of the main sources of black money (or untaxed income) were higher education and the mixing of kerosene available under the subsidized Public Distribution System with diesel (*The Deccan Herald*, August 18, 2014). Higher education in India is increasingly a private business that receives "capitation fees" or donations, often in black money, in exchange for preferential admission of children of benefactors.

[7] The political system has been rigged by criminals for quite some time (see Crabtree 2018, Luce 2008).

[8] The Adani group, a Gujarat-based upstart was nurtured by Narendra Modi, then chief minister of the state and now India's prime minister. It successfully obtained favorable loans from the State Bank of India for an environmentally controversial coal mining project in Australia (*The Guardian*, August 15, 2017). In 2019, the bank posted a loss of nearly $1 billion.

[9] The public sector also had large non-performing loans (NPLs) with poor farmers. Social banking begun with bank nationalization of 1969 to benefit the poor farmers in the countryside. It led to large NPLs as many of these loans were often forgiven for political ends.

political parties. The biggest beneficiary of this scheme has been the ruling party (Kaushik and Jayaram 2024).

The current Modi administration, notwithstanding the rhetoric of "maximum governance," has failed to rein in the *quid pro quo* arrangement at multiple levels that have been endemic since the 1950s. Furthermore, driven by the narrow ideology of Hindutva to politically win elections, the ruling Bharatiya Janata Party (BJP) has selectively chosen to form informal interdependent *ad hoc* relationships with a few large businesses. These include, but are not limited to, Ambani of Reliance Industries, Adani of Adani Group, and the Tata Group. Such types of relationships predate this administration, but they represent a new pecking order of oligarchic business. This is a carryover in a path-dependent way of the close relationship between Narendra Modi and some of these business groups when he served as the Chief Minister of Gujarat from 2001 to 2014 (see Jaffrelot 2021, 2019). Today, these same businesses continue to experience huge expansion in their highly profitable portfolios as the Indian market has expanded. These cover telecommunications and oil exploration for Ambani and ports and airports construction throughout the country for Adani (Bhattacharya and Guha Thakurta 2019). Paradoxically, these are also rent-thick sectors that are critical to economic development. They are capital-intensive operations, rely heavily on loans, and do not generate a lot of long-term jobs.

The insidious turn in the state–business nexus has given a freer hand to big business to pursue its profit ventures while supporting the ruling party in its quest to maintain its ideological hegemony. In this new twist, despite the structural power of (factions of) business, the fear of specific business sectors losing large government contracts and losing privileged access to the state have ensured that business and the media kowtow to the official line.[10] The threats of unannounced visits by tax officials and losing advertising revenues have also kept businesses servile. Workers as a whole, on the other hand, have been left to fend for themselves.

[10] This is not uniquely an Indian phenomenon. Such corruption and autocratic partnerships between the state and private business can be found in other autocratic countries as well, including successful East Asian economies such as South Korea of the 1960s and 1970s and more recently Russia, Hungary, and the United States. Such corporate-state partnership in its crony form is a capitalist problem. It results from the increasing monetization of all human transactions with increasingly fewer institutional checks on the rapacious profit-making appetites of business and uninhibited state power monopolized by popularly elected heads of states. In non-democratic countries this is a given, while in erstwhile democratic countries such a makeover has different drivers.

6.3 Late Industrialization and the Precarity of Employment

Representing the interests of labor has been lost in the political partnership between big corporate business and the government, each pursuing their collective interests of commerce and ideological control. Where labor is concerned, the business sector has focused on the "inflexibility" of labor, referring to the laws that govern the firing of formal workers. Formal sector employees represent only 10% of workers, while 90% of workers are confined to the highly flexible informal sector, revealing the wanton disregard for the welfare of the latter. The literature on India's dualistic labor market (formal and informal) is vast and layered. Reducing the complexities to a simple binary analysis does not capture the full picture. For the sake of analytical clarity, only a few points will be highlighted to illustrate the difficulties of creating good jobs on a large scale.

As Chapter 1 indicated, businesses can be disaggregated into organized and unorganized, formal and informal, large corporate firms and medium-, small-, and micro-sized enterprises (MSMEs), with formal and informal workers. These are not binary categories. For example, informal workers can be found in the organized sector, and increasingly so, but it is unlikely that formal workers will be found in the unorganized sector. Given the highly polarized 90–10 ratio of informal to formal, respectively, the challenge of creating decent jobs appears daunting. We began with a simple assessment of the state of affairs in India's labor markets compiled by Sen (2025). He extracts the data from the Employment Unemployment Surveys (EUS) of the Ministry of Labour and Employment and the Periodic Labour Force Surveys (PLFS) of the Ministry of Statistics and Programme Implementation. The PLFS has replaced the EUS.

Table 6.1 presents the distribution of workers by work status. There are two broad categories: self-employed and waged labor. Both self-employed and waged labor have their (small) formal and (large) informal counterparts. Within the informal sector, self-employed and wage employment have been further subdivided into upper-tier and lower-tier categories to affirm that some informal workers, especially in upper-tier wage employment, are better paid and may have some job security relative to the lower-tier workers (Sen 2025: 44–45). At the same time, many of the lower-tiered informal wage workers are casual. It should be observed that 72.96% of *total* workers fall under the lower tier of the informal sector, which means that the average job is of poor quality (not far above subsistence) and could represent fending off open unemployment. Unemployment is not a realistic choice for the poor.

Table 6.1 Distribution of Workers by Work Status (%)

Work Status		1988	1994	2000	2005	2012	2018	2022
Share of employment by work status								
Self-employed								
Formal		0.12	0.37	0.03	0.04	0.04	0.06	0.09
Informal	Upper tier	6.98	1.49	0.82	1.12	1.25	1.77	2.39
	Lower tier	47.76	49.62	48.84	51.22	47.29	47.70	49.31
Total self-employed		51.79	49.99	48.38	52.38	48.58	49.53	51.78
Wage-employed								
Formal		6.84	8.37	8.69	6.47	7.22	7.05	9.50
Informal	Upper tier	4.33	4.86	5.23	10.02	13.34	17.83	15.07
	Lower tier	33.96	35.03	36.39	31.13	30.87	25.59	23.65
Total wage-employed		48.21	50.01	51.62	47.62	51.42	50.47	48.22
Share of formal versus informal employment								
Formal		6.96	8.74	8.71	6.51	7.26	7.11	9.58
Informal	Upper tier	11.32	6.35	6.05	11.14	14.59	19.61	17.46
	Lower tier	81.72	84.91	85.24	82.35	78.15	73.29	72.96
Total of formal and informal		100.00	100.00	100.00	100.00	100.00	100.00	100.00

Source: Sen (2025: 48)

From Table 6.1, with 1988 as the base year, we can extract the following points regarding India's labor markets:

- Under self-employment, since 1988, formal workers have decreased, and so have upper-tier informal workers. However, lower-tier informal workers have increased. Overall, self-employment as a whole has remained relatively stable during this period (1988–2022), with self-employment picking up from 2005 onward. While not too much can be read into this without additional information, informal self-employment can be viewed as a coping mechanism in a tough job market. Additionally, the better jobs under informal self-employment have fallen, while lower-tier jobs have increased. Broadly, it can be inferred that the "quality" of jobs under informal self-employment is falling. In the absence of welfare support, the poor are compelled to offer their services at whatever wage the market will bear.
- Under wage employment, formal and upper-tier informal employment have gone up, while lower-tier wage employment has fallen. Again, not too much can be read into this other than to note that, most likely due to economic growth unleashed by market reforms, there has been some positive impact on jobs. After all, India's gross fixed capital formation (GFCF) or rate of investment in physical assets to produce goods and services has been on an upward trend in real terms except during the brief pandemic period (Federal Reserve Economic Data (FRED) 2025). A more disquieting feature is the virtually unchanged share of both self-employment and wage employment in the nearly twenty-five-year period. One would have hoped that such investments would lead to more wage employment relative to self-employment, ignoring the quality of jobs issue. However, counterintuitively, a recent study suggests that informal wage earnings are less than informal self-employment earnings with no mobility among the sampled workers experiencing a transition from informal to formal wage employment (Abraham and Kesar 2025: 2–3). The research team for *The State of Working India 2023* report (Azim Premji University 2023: 69) finds that there is no clear relationship between growth in non-agricultural output (industry and services, which a modern economy desires) and the growth in salaried or organized sector employment (which also an economy desires). This suggests that when there is economic growth, one could expect more informal employment but not formal employment. This is a rather discouraging inference. The share of total wage employment during the 1988–2022 period has remained virtually unchanged, suggesting that

with all the hype about economic growth, formal wage jobs are not easily forthcoming.

- Combining self and wage employment, we find that the formal sector as a whole has increased a bit along with the upper tier, whereas lower-tier informal sector jobs have gone down. This suggests that the share of formal jobs has marginally increased but remains below 10% of the total workforce in the two labor markets. With 90% of the Indian workers tied for decades to the informal sector, decades of economic (business) growth have failed to break the grip of the informal labor market by adding more formal jobs.

The jobs dilemma is real. The formal sector is changing, but not fast enough to make a difference in the size and composition of the informal sector. India's particular institutional barriers, combined with external factors, have narrowed the opportunities to create plentiful jobs. It is beyond the scope of this chapter to cover the many overlapping explanations for the persistence of the informal sector, such as capital-intensive industrialization, international competition, and not enough income growth experienced by the workers in the informal sector. Suffice it to say that the persistence of the informal (PCP) sector is that, first, there are some advantages to small enterprises remaining informal. As informal enterprises, they are unregistered and outside the tax net and reporting requirements of the government. This cost minimization strategy through tax avoidance is a reasonable business motivation to continue as informal. Extending this logic, one can surmise that should the tax burden on formal firms rise, they could strategically elect to become informal by breaking up the enterprise into more than one unit. To take another example, if government approval is necessary for firing labor with 100 or more workers, businesses can create enterprises with 99 workers or fewer under the informal sector, thereby having the flexibility to lay off workers without any permission.[11] The second, alternative explanation is that poor people do not have the luxury to be unemployed. It also means that, as informal workers, they receive no protection from the government. They are compelled to accept "low market clearing wages" (Marjit and Kar 2011: 1–13).

Third, there is a political economy interpretation of the persistence of the informal sector, namely, it is in the interest of the state to maintain the status quo since the economy is unable to generate plenty of good formal jobs. With no welfare for the poor, the informal sector acts as a labor sink or a "buffer" where people have the liberty to make the best of their circumstances

[11] This is also inconsistent with the view that labor is rigid in India.

and pre-empt social unrest (Marjit and Kar 2011: 17–34). It also subsidizes formal labor markets by depressing the general wage level and enables the overall profitability of businesses. It is, however, not a stepping stone toward waged formal work and informality does not disappear, thereby casting serious doubt on the existence of a dynamic jobs ladder (Abraham and Kesar 2025: 14).

This hands-off approach by the state is a default position of the government. But systemically, it is really a structural outcome of compressed capitalism that thwarts agrarian transition in the context of premature deindustrialization, leaving most people to fend for themselves in the mostly precarious informal labor market. This informal labor market is not divorced from the formal sector. It produces a plethora of low-cost commodities and services for enterprises belonging to the informal and the formal sectors as subcontractors. As businesses adjust to competition due to trade policy reforms, high-cost firms can be pushed out, while exports are encouraged through the flexible use of subcontracted informal labor (Marjit and Kar 2011: 1–13). This illustrates the organic relationship between the formal and informal labor markets but also demonstrates how the expansive informal labor market is reinforced over time.

In the pre-reform period between 1973–1978 and 1983–1987/1988, GDP growth increased from 3.5 to 5.3%, whereas employment growth fell from 2.82 to 1.55% (Planning Commission in Datt 1994: 421). This unequivocally illustrates that growth has become unhinged from job creation (jobless growth), with employment elasticity being less than 1.[12] In the 1990s, employment elasticity was a mere 0.2 in the large manufacturing sector compared to 0.5 in the small manufacturing sector and 1.0 in construction (Datt 1994: 421). For the post-reform period, net employment created over a period of twenty-four years, between 1981–1982 and 2004–2005 was 1.35 million or "just 0.3% of the workforce in the economy..." (Kannan and Raveendran 2009: 83). The employment elasticity from 1999–2000 to 2011–2012 fell from 0.42 to 0.05 (Abraham 2019). In the 2017–2021 period of pre-pandemic high growth, driven by construction, the employment elasticity was 1 for the nonagricultural sector. This was most likely due to falling output and an increase in agricultural employment and self-employment. Otherwise, employment elasticity has been consistently 0.6 or less for the entire 1983–2017 period (Azim Premji University 2023: 28), reaffirming that growth in India has not been a harbinger of jobs and that surplus labor is here to stay.

[12] Jobless growth has been defined as employment growth lagging substantially behind output growth or what economists would call low employment elasticity. Employment elasticity measures the percentage change in employment for 1% change in growth of output. Less than 1% increase in employment relative to 1% increase in output implies jobless growth, especially if it is substantially less than 1% and is a sustained trend over a long period. See Azim Premji University (2023: 64–70).

The substitution of labor with capital and technology, as evidenced by automation of both goods production and services, has been observed in advanced capitalist countries where wage costs are high (Ford 2015, Aronowitz and DiFazio 2010, Rifkin 1995). However, for low-income India, increasing capital intensity is also a reality due to capitalist maturity (CM). It is a product of the *quid pro quo* arrangement between big business and the state, where large investment projects can garner low-interest loans. The efficiency gains from economies of scale in large projects could translate into higher productivity activities and redundant labor in specific workplaces (see Tejani 2015). While capital-intensive production methods are necessary for productivity gains and competitiveness, under the structural stalemate, they tend to depress overall employment. Operating under the capitalist imperative of commercial profits and maximizing market shares, businesses will select the "optimum" choice of technique, given the price of capital (interest rate) and labor (wages). It would be hard to make them do anything different unless there were movements in the prices of the factors of production. However, in the real world, technologies are not on a continuum, nor are capital and labor easily substitutable. In a labor-abundant economy, the proclivity of business is to adopt labor-intensive methods, other things unchanged. But as alluded to above, for reasons of competitiveness and scale, this may not be the case. However, if the cost of capital falls due to revision of interest rates (via subsidies or market forces), businesses will certainly opt for capital-intensive projects.

Interest rates have been comparatively high in India, but recently there has been a downward movement, making long-term loans cheaper and, by default, encouraging investments in capital-intensive production methods. Simultaneously, cash-strapped MSMEs, to meet their short-term operating costs, borrow funds at much higher rates, thereby setting off a further divide between small informal and large corporate sectors.[13] A recent business report on India, indicated that the interest rate charged to small and medium enterprises was between 12–15% compared to China's 3–5% (Pai, Pagaria, Savithiri, and Trehan 2025: 50). One can only deduce that the interest rate paid by the corporate sector will be less than the MSMEs because of the former's size, ability to leverage high collateral assets, exercising market power, and tapping into *quid pro quo* informal networks. Under this scenario, there will be disproportionately less employment relative to investment and output growth.

[13] I am grateful to Pronab Sen for this insight in the larger issue of capital-intensive production in labor-abundant India.

With higher returns to capital (Piketty 2014), the slow pace of employment growth and slower wage growth relative to productivity increase is likely to depress macroeconomic demand over the long haul. When combined with state cutbacks in welfare and social protections, the entire growth model is driven by and for a narrower, wealthier market. Inequality becomes integral to this kind of growth process, as we will see below, further cramping demand. This growth focus structurally sidesteps the more urgent need for livelihood opportunities that are sought by millions of workers. Moreover, by subverting democratic norms in its pursuit of complete ideological control, the state has also politically mobilized the unemployed and the unemployable elements to police social and cultural behavior rather than searching for a workable jobs-focused policy (see Jaffrelot 2021).

6.4 Labor Inflexibility and Ease of Doing Business

One popular business perspective for the lack of job growth has been labor inflexibility, which allegedly discourages investments by domestic and foreign firms. Labor inflexibility refers to labor laws that require businesses to seek government approval before laying off workers. The notion of rigidity has been theoretically and empirically challenged (Nagaraj 2007, Thomas 2013). In reality, there are some older firms that have some "rigidity" due to legacies that protect workers but otherwise most businesses have found ways to circumvent such labor "rigidities" by resorting to hiring casual and contract workers (Bardhan 2019: 179; Chakraborty 2015, see also Chapter 1), by moving capital to other states with more lax labor regulation, increasing subcontracting by farming out work to the informal sector, and adopting capital-intensive technologies (Kapoor 2014: 17). If 90% of employment is in the unorganized sector, deregulating 10% of workers who are regulated is not a strong argument for lack of flexible labor (Kapoor 2014). Furthermore, if rigidity had been a serious issue, the country would not have witnessed a consistent increase in the GFCF during the last two decades.

According to business and other market watchers, making labor flexible is one important supply-side prescription. There are other factors that have been used by the World Bank to formulate a single index called the "Ease of Doing Business" (EDB) (see Figure 6.2).[14] Despite the many shortcomings,

[14] This index was abandoned after it was discovered that the bank leadership influenced experts to manipulate the results. There have been also questions around the methodology used in the construction of this index. Changes in rankings among countries often lead to petty claims one way or another. Interestingly, labor market regulation is mentioned as part of business institutions but it was not used in

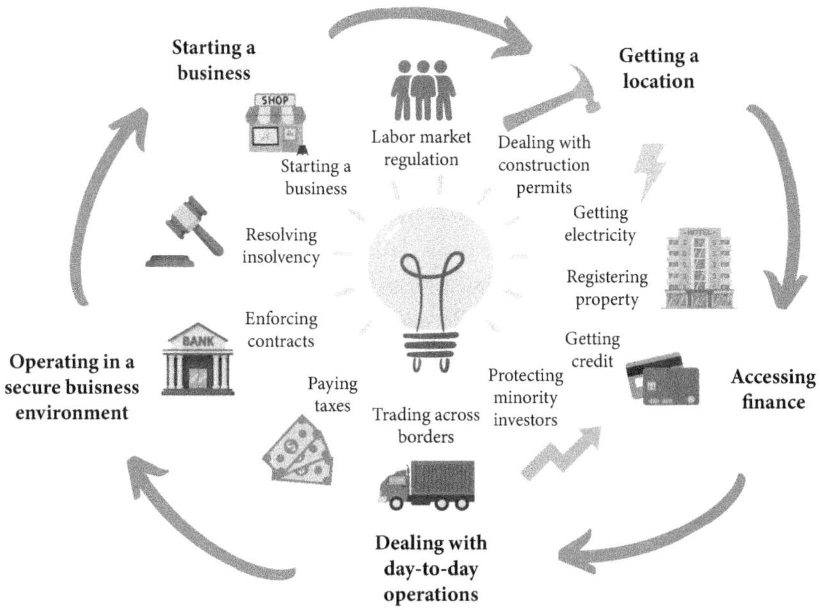

Figure 6.2 Ease of Doing Business

Source: World Bank (2019: 2). Doing Business 2019: Training for Reform. DOI: 10.1596/978-1-4648-1326-9 https://www.worldbank.org/content/dam/doingBusiness/media/Annual-Reports/English/DB2019-report_web-version.pdf

the key components that make up the composite EDB index can be used as a heuristic device to assess where the bottlenecks lie in promoting investments and creating jobs in India. As Figure 6.2 illustrates, EDB is aimed at improving the institutional environment for business. These include ease of access to credit, electricity, and construction permits; tax payments; a conducive legal and institutional environment to quickly resolve bankruptcies, enforce contracts, and facilitate trade across state borders (International Bank for Reconstruction and Development 2019: 2).

Intuitively, these supply-side factors make sense. But the practical challenges are on the ground. The "inspector Raj," meaning the bureaucratic monitoring of economic activities associated with the earlier state-led economic development approach, persists in sustaining corruption at lower levels for existing businesses.[15] There are also difficulties of starting a new business, which include the high price of land and registration fees, bribery in meeting regulatory requirements, and speed money for quick processing

the EDB index for ranking countries (International Bank for Reconstruction and Development 2019: 2). Also, the ground reality in India makes the index not particularly useful.

[15] The illegal extractive or extortionist activities through bribery and kickbacks by the police and other local public officials constitute an implicit tax on business.

of applications (Mukherjee 2025). The *quid pro quo* arrangements referred to earlier make most of these transactions bureaucratic and time-consuming. They are subject to various forms of corruption, such as kickbacks and bribery. The current government which is publicly committed to easing the business environment, has difficulties in moving forward. This is due to the three levels of government: central, state, and local. While recent central policies have been streamlined to be transparent and simplified, making it easier to start a new business, the real problem is at the state and local levels, where land, electricity, and water must be arranged. Bureaucratic procedures and processing delays are settled with speed money, bribery, etc. For existing businesses, the payoffs become operationally necessary. Paradoxically, the reach of the politically centralized administration to the lower levels of the government and its agents for governing EDB is weak. This is partly because many state-level governments are not ruled by the same political party that forms the central government and partly because the local states, including those administered by the ruling party, also have their own *quid pro quo* arrangements that involve kickbacks and bribery.

According to business, the goods and services tax (GST) is high, eroding the wage-cost advantage for construction work in India. Officials of GST may also have to be bribed to clear the goods quickly and obtain a wide range of permissions for utilities and other relevant services. Goods and services tax is also expensive for businesses, as people have to be hired to compute GST. With significant changes in some of these supply-side attributes, India's global EDB ranking moved up from 142nd in 2014 to 63rd in 2019.[16] Jumping up seventy-nine places in five years is impressive, but it seems inconsistent with little increase in FDI. While FDI inflows increased, the *net* inflow was much smaller, suggesting foreign businesses were either exiting or repatriating profits back to their home countries instead of reinvesting them in India. At the same time, the relaxation of foreign exchange availability has encouraged Indian businesses to invest abroad as the narrow Indian market becomes saturated (Ghosh 2025).

The Reserve Bank of India data shows that FDI (inflows) has been slowing down over the last few years, while also being accompanied by repatriation or disinvestment (outflows). Net foreign investment fell from \$43.96 billion in the 2020–2021 fiscal year to \$10.13 billion in 2023–2024 to just \$0.96 billion in 2025 (Reserve Bank of India 2025). Such declines have been a result of the ongoing repatriation or disinvestment: from \$18.83 billion in 2019–20

[16] Make in India https://www.makeinindia.com/eodb, accessed August 27, 2025.

to $27.04 billion, $28.61 billion, $29.35 billion, $44.47 billion, and $51.49 billion in the subsequent five years ending in 2024–2025 (Reserve Bank of India 2025). This reflects that India is not attractive for foreign investors, but it does not mean it is due to labor rigidity.

Notwithstanding the visible improvements made in infrastructure and institutional processes for starting a new business, there is a slowdown in net FDI inflows. But by focusing on the supply side factors alone, the discussion of weak effective demand is overlooked. While there is a narrow market for branded goods such as Apple iPhones and other "elitist" multinational consumer products, it is hopelessly inadequate to drive a dynamic economy.[17] Such limited market demand is a consequence of not being able to create plenty of good jobs. It also means that the sharp inequality in employment outcomes, as reflected by the persistent informal sector and a small formal sector, will further depress market growth. What is needed is investment across the board, multinational investments that will employ people at all skill levels, transfer technologies for future backward integration, and help diversify the economy. Indian businesses must rise to the occasion and not decamp or simply expand hiring in the informal sector.

6.5 Compressed Capitalism and Inequality

The foregoing analysis of formal-informal labor markets shows how inequality in India has become endemic today. Inequality is not new in India. Entrenched social hierarchies, caste discrimination, gender inequality, and the marginalization of many disadvantaged communities over the years have contributed to a highly inegalitarian society. But wealth and income distribution have not been as polarized or the differences as visible in the past as they are today, even as poverty levels have fallen and more Indians are joining the ranks of the broader middle class. What has changed, and why does it matter?

Inequality means that some people have more income and wealth than others. In an imperfect world, this is inevitable in any economic system, but for social stability and a sense of belonging to a society, a high degree of inequality is counterproductive. There is both an economic and a moral argument against inequality. If some people have far more wealth and income than others, their purchasing power will be much higher compared to the rest.

[17] There are some exceptions to the foreign investment slowdown. For example, in the "high tech" sectors such as fintech, business, finance, software, and insurance services, electric vehicles (EVs), and renewables foreign investments are being made. But these rely on limited educated technical talent, which is a form of upgrading and diversification directed toward high-revenue export markets, and tend to bypass the low to medium skilled workers.

Their lifestyle and livelihood chances will be significantly better and of higher quality than the rest. They are likely to exercise greater economic and political power in pursuing their interests than the rest, thereby undermining the workings of social justice and fairness, in effect, democracy (Domhoff 2006, Sweezy and Baran 1966). Poor people are likely to fall ill frequently, miss work, have few resources for proper medical treatment, and ultimately, the entire household may become hostage to the condition of inequality.

More importantly, from a macroeconomic point of view, the size of the economy and its growth potential will be severely constrained because the vast majority with low incomes will have limited capacity to purchase goods and services in the market. The net result is likely to be low effective demand. One estimate puts the Indian "consuming class" that drives the "narrow" corporate "branded" market at just 140 million people (or roughly 10% of the population), with an average spending of roughly $15,000 per person (Pai, Pagaria, Savithiri, and Trehan 2025: 76). Another 300 million are said to belong to the "aspirant class" with about $3000 per capita spending power but who are very price conscious. This leaves roughly one billion people outside the market of discretionary goods.

Setting aside the question of whether these two market segments together are large enough to drive dynamic growth for the economy as a whole, the sharp divide in disposable incomes suggests a highly constrained overall market. The active market transactions by a small number of people with relatively high disposable incomes limit the size of formal corporate businesses.[18] Except for basic goods and services, the one billion people who command low wages or small income streams are largely non-participants in the consumer market. At a general level, these observations raise serious concerns about the impact of the lack of decent jobs and, by extension, alert us to the uncertain future sustainability of business that relies on this narrow consumption-driven domestic market. To put it another way, making it easy for businesses to produce from the supply side ignores demand. If businesses want to grow and the nation wants to boast about its economic standing in the world, to whom will businesses sell their goods? A small, narrow middle class or elite market, which is a product of inequality, cannot sustain long-term growth and diversification.[19]

The inability of the economy to generate adequate decent jobs in the absence of social protections suggests that most labor is engaged in precarious

[18] At a low level of per capita income, as in India, the disproportionate growth in services also points to inequality in consumption in services such as education, health, telecommunication (Nayyar 2019: 485).

[19] Economies in Latin America, especially the Brazilian economy of the 1960s illustrated the limits of highly unequal and narrow elite markets for long term growth.

work, often driven by survival instincts. The implicit disguised unemployment (or underemployment) found in many MSMEs, and increasingly in the organized sector, means that more people are hired or self-employed than needed, leading to low-productivity jobs. It also means that wages, the going market rate for the price of labor, will be commensurate with low productivity levels. Under these circumstances, the goal to exhaust surplus labor is only a pipe dream. There appears to be a vicious circle: low income from poor quality jobs, lower effective demand, limited economic expansion and diversification, and even more growth of the informal sector without commensurate growth in purchasing power. This vicious circle jars with the other reality of the high-growth Indian economy: the increasing presence of upwardly mobile middle classes comprising professionals, tech entrepreneurs, profitable business owners, and political fixers, and the phenomenal rise of the billionaire (in US dollars) class.

Of course, this uneven development or inequality is not an anomaly; it is integral to the workings of contemporary capitalism. With the rise of the modern factory, the separation between owners of capital and workers and the inherent inequality in the relationship are a given. However, public redistributive policies have kept the inequality gap somewhat checked. With deregulation, globalization, cutbacks in social protections, and huge winner-takes-all rewards from new technologies managed by oligopolistic firms, the gap between profits of the former and the incomes of the latter has widened wealth gaps globally to unprecedented levels (Table 6.2, see also Chancel, Piketty, Saez, and Zucman 2022). A lid on income and wealth growth through taxes, redistributive measures, including social protections for all residents, are some of the ways by which European nations, Japan, and a few others have maintained a greater degree of equality. Could India, Inc. learn some institutional and policy lessons from these countries if they want to avoid becoming a victim of their own success?

Granted, India is a poor country, and following the much-referred Kuznets' inverted U-shaped curve that postulates that inequality worsens with growth before becoming better with more growth, can we anticipate more egalitarian outcomes down the road? There is no evidence of this happening. The Kuznets hypothesis was based on the experience of the early industrializers; it does not hold true for today's wealthy economies and certainly not for developing countries.[20] For example, in early January 2025, the market capitalization of the big seven tech companies, all American, was an astounding

[20] Even relatively egalitarian Sweden, Japan, and South Korea have been experiencing creeping inequality (see Federal Reserve Bank of St. Louis 2019, Koo 2019, Stiglitz 2012).

Table 6.2 Wealth Inequality Trends, 2000–2022, Selected Markets

	Wealth Gini Coefficient							Wealth Share of the Top 1%						
	2000	2005	2010	2015	2020	2021	2022	2000	2005	2010	2015	2020	2021	2022
Australia	63.7	63.1	63.0	64.9	65.5	66.2	66.3	20.5	20.0	19.2	20.5	20.6	21.8	21.7
Brazil	84.5	82.7	82.1	88.7	88.9	89.2	88.4	44.2	45.0	40.2	48.7	49.5	49.3	48.4
Canada	74.9	73.3	71.7	71.8	71.8	72.6	72.3	29.1	25.9	22.4	23.3	23.6	25.0	24.3
Mainland China	**59.5**	**63.8**	**70.0**	**71.2**	**70.5**	**70.1**	**70.7**	**20.7**	**24.2**	**31.5**	**31.7**	**30.8**	**30.5**	**31.1**
France	69.7	67.0	69.8	69.9	70.0	70.2	70.3	25.5	21.0	21.0	22.3	21.9	22.3	21.2
Germany	81.2	82.7	77.4	79.2	77.9	78.8	76.9	29.1	30.4	25.7	32.1	29.2	31.7	30.0
India	**74.6**	**80.9**	**82.1**	**83.3**	**82.3**	**82.3**	**82.6**	**33.2**	**41.9**	**41.4**	**42.3**	**40.5**	**40.6**	**41.0**
Italy	60.4	59.4	63.1	66.9	66.4	67.2	67.8	22.0	18.2	17.4	22.6	21.9	23.3	23.1
Japan	64.5	63.1	62.5	63.6	64.4	64.7	64.8	20.4	18.8	16.7	18.2	18.1	18.7	18.8
Korea	69.7	70.1	74.7	72.4	67.7	68.2	67.9	21.3	21.8	26.0	26.9	23.4	24.0	23.1
Spain	65.5	62.2	61.4	69.5	69.1	69.1	68.3	24.1	18.7	18.5	24.1	22.7	23.1	22.4
Taiwan	64.7	67.8	72.6	70.5	70.7	70.7	70.5	24.3	23.6	29.8	26.9	27.3	26.6	26.4
United Kingdom	70.5	67.6	69.1	73.0	71.7	70.6	70.1	22.1	20.6	23.6	25.0	23.1	21.1	20.7
United States	80.6	81.1	84.1	84.9	85.0	85.0	83.0	32.9	32.8	33.4	34.8	35.3	35.1	34.2

Source: James Davies, Rodrigo Lluberas, and Anthony Shorrocks, Global Wealth Databook 2023 in UBS (Credit Suisse 2023). *Global Wealth Report 2023: Leading Perspectives to Navigate the Future*, p. 33

$11.7 trillion (Pai, Pagaria, Savithiri, and Trehan 2025: 8), which in the next six months had climbed to a whopping $19.23 trillion. Most national GDPs, including India's, are nowhere near this size. In other words, capital has become highly concentrated through globalization and the rewards to capital have grown by leaps and bounds compared to labor. Their political influence has also magnified.

The story is similar in India, where deregulation and oligarchic favoritism have contributed to the rise of big firms, wealthy entrepreneurs, political influence, and massive inequality (Crabtree 2018). These stand in contrast to the regression of labor as they are informalized. The measure of income inequality is the GINI coefficient, an index that measures the degree of (income) inequality with a number between 0 and 1, with 1 being completely unequal.[21] What is interesting is that India's GINI coefficient was in the 0.2s for the first few decades following Indian independence. Far from 1.0, this is a very good number by any standard. Income data is hard to come by, and most informal workers have incomes too meager to file tax returns. About 94% of the adult population (Alvaredo et al. 2018: 31) do not pay taxes, while *quid pro quo* arrangements involving the wealthy allow them to avoid reporting their true taxable income (see D'Costa 2023).[22] Today, India's GINI coefficient for wealth distribution has worsened, ranking almost toward the top, worse than the United States and slightly better than Brazil (see Table 6.2). In 1990 and 2015, India's GINI was estimated to be 0.297 and 0.3915, respectively, signaling worsening of income distribution (Our World in Data 2025).

To put the Indian wealthy in a global context: just 14 people in the world had collective wealth of $2 trillion, 12 individuals $50–100 billion, and 2600 individuals $1–$50 billion (UBS (Credit Suisse) 2023: 33). In 2023 there were 6,013,282 millionaires in China; 2,827,956 in Japan, and *868,671 in India* (UBS 2024: 21, 23, 30). India's per capita income was just $2697 in current dollars. An earlier quick estimate showed that the *collective* wealth of the Indian millionaires increased from $110 *billion* to $2.86 *trillion*, or an average of $3.76 *billion* per millionaire (D'Costa 2023, based on Credit Suisse (2019: 147) data). This was higher than China's average of $3.33 billion per millionaire and only slightly lower than the US average of $4.05 billion (see D'Costa

[21] GINI coefficient is designed to see how income distribution deviates from the line of perfect equality by capturing income distribution by deciles, that is how much income accrues to each of the ten groups in the population. In acutely inegalitarian societies, the top 10% of the wealthy population can be expected to corner a disproportionately much higher share of income than 10%, possibly 50–60%.

[22] India's former Finance Minister Arun Jaitley had remarked that India was "non-tax compliant" and "tax evasion was a way of life" (*Times of India*, February 1, 2017).

2023). There is no denying that Indian business is doing well in the formal sector compared to its informal counterpart.

As Piketty demonstrates, the rate of return on capital (r) has been historically greater than the income growth rate (g) of the economy (Piketty 2017: 25–27, 2014: 354), thereby contributing to increasing inequality over time. Since wealth can be deployed to produce more income, setting off increasing inequality (r > g), progressive taxes on wealth and other redistributive measures become necessary. Under capitalism, wealth, when deployed strategically, creates income growth, which in turn adds to further wealth. This mechanism is reflected by India's sharp divide between formal and informal workers, corporate business and MSMEs, and the rise of the immensely wealthy in a system of a persistent informal sector.

India also remains significantly poorer than all the countries listed in Table 6.2. For example, Brazil had a per capita income in current dollars of $10,283 in 2024, the United States $85,810, India $2697, and China $13,303 (World Bank Group 2025a). India's per capita income represented 26.2% of Brazil, 3.1% of the United States, and 20.3% of China (World Bank Group 2025a). Based on $3.65 per day as the poverty line income, extreme poverty in India has fallen from 61.8% to 28.1% between 2011–2012 and 2022–2023, lifting 378 million people.[23] This is impressive, but it needs to be noted that given the abysmally low consumption threshold for people at the poverty line, they are vulnerable to any movements in prices and incomes. For example, any reduction in the quantity of foodgrains the poor receive through the Public Distribution System, loss of wage income earned, or fewer days of guaranteed employment under the rural employment program (Mahatma Gandhi National Rural Employment Guarantee Act (MNREGA)) will be devastating. India's poverty line still conveys a life of destitution and deprivation, a far cry from the immense wealth that has been generated on the backs of India's poor and the informal sector.

There is no easy remedy to this conundrum. At the minimum, to improve income distribution (if not wealth) a two-pronged approach is needed: investments in productive economic activities that will create a diverse portfolio of jobs in which business will have a major role, while the state must ensure redistributive policies such as redesigning existing policies of affirmative action, increasing women's labor force participation, and providing social support (Rajan and Lamba 2023: 182–193). But as India's labor markets have revealed, these will not be enough. As the recent decades have demonstrated,

[23] The extent of the decline is contested and so are the yardsticks used to measure them (see Sandefur 2022).

economic growth is unhinged from growth in good jobs, which is a source of worsening inequality. There has to be a complete rethink of the type of sectors that will contribute not just to growth but also to employment. In this rethinking, the degree of international market exposure in specific sectors, the type of education and skills development, and the composition of international trade and investment partners must be recalibrated. These are, by all reckoning, a tall order. Furthermore, as the next section illustrates, late industrialization for all its advantages is also subject to international competition that can wreak havoc with local production systems, especially if business responses to external challenges remain weak. This is another way of saying that businesses tend to adopt "convenient" strategies that meet their commercial business interests and not social goals.

6.6 The China Factor and India's Employment Predicaments

One of the reasons for the continued expansion of the informal sector is India's weak manufacturing capabilities and narrow home markets that limit product diversification and employment. This is reflected in the premature deindustrialization trap, where the share of manufacturing employment has reached a plateau. India's premature deindustrialization is not a recent phenomenon; international competition and technological change have been typical characteristics of the world economy. What has changed is that Asian economies, particularly China's, have become formidable economic and manufacturing forces. Deregulation has opened the floodgates of imports from China and other countries and exposed India's manufacturing weakness. What is worse, imports are competing with India's labor-intensive sectors such as footwear, textiles, and diamond polishing, in which presumably India has competitive advantages.

It is beyond the scope of this chapter to disentangle the many sides of this import surge. Suffice to say, open markets, Chinese competitiveness (even dumping as a countercyclical strategy), India's manufacturing weakness, and the penchant for Indian business to find the path of least resistance by not responding strategically with investment are all responsible for this state of affairs. Indian businesses are selling imported products in the domestic market and/or using them as inputs to add value to domestic production or exports. Both activities have their legitimate place in the business world. But from a macro point of view, simply reselling imports such as consumer products has limited multiplier effects in the areas of production, technological

Table 6.3 India–China Bilateral Trade (in USD Billions)

Financial Year	India's Export to China	India's Import from China	India's Trade Deficit	Total Trade	% Change in Trade
2014–2015	11.96	60.41	48.45	72.37	9.82
2015–2016	9.01	61.71	52.70	70.72	−2.28
2016–2017	10.17	61.38	51.11	71.45	1.03
2017–2018	13.33	76.38	63.05	89.71	25.56
2018–2019	16.75	70.32	53.57	87.07	−2.94
2019–2020	16.61	65.26	48.65	81.87	−5.97
2020–2021	21.19	65.21	44.02	86.40	5.53
2021–2022	21.56	94.57	73.01	116.13	34.41
2022–2023	15.31	98.51	83.20	113.82	−1.99
2023–2024	16.66	101.74	85.08	118.40	4.02
2024–2025	14.25	113.46	99.21	127.71	7.86

Source: Government of India, Ministry of Commerce and Industry, Department of Commerce (2025). Trade and Economic Relations, https://eoibeijing.gov.in/eoibejing_pages/MjQ.

spillovers, and employment. The second type of activity does have its merits for economic development if import dependency does not become a permanent feature. To ensure this, there must be significant efforts to integrate backward and/or forward to diversify and add economic value.

Trade between India and China has expanded substantially, with China's exports to India expanding faster than China's imports from India (Table 6.3). India's trade deficit with China has roughly doubled from $48.45 billion in 2014–2015 to $99.21 billion in 2024–2025. A simple disaggregation of Chinese imports for 2023 shows that over $44 billion comprised electricals and electronic equipment (Government of India, Ministry of Commerce and Industry, Department of Commerce 2025). The rest were other manufactured products such as machinery, nuclear reactors, and boilers ($24.7 billion), organic chemicals ($13.27 billion), plastics ($5.93 billion), and optical, photo, technical, and medical apparatus ($2.63 billion). While many of these sectors are large-scale, capital-intensive operations, many others, such as electric and electronic components manufacturing and assembly operations (the principal import), are not, albeit in the Chinese context, these are also known to be large-scale but labor-intensive assembly operations.

In contrast, the composition of India's exports to China reveals a mix of low value items (which is also reflected in India's overall merchandise trade): these include ores, slag, and ash (natural resources and byproducts of smelting or refining ore to extract metal: $3.42 billion); fish, crustaceans, mollusks, and aquatic invertebrates (marine products: $1.25 billion); and organic chemicals; apparel; pearls, precious stones, metals, and coins (about $1 billion each). The inability to compete with China and Southeast Asian economies was indirectly observed in 2019 when India pulled out of the Regional Comprehensive Economic Partnership (RCEP), a free trade bloc involving the ten ASEAN nations and their five free trade partners, which included Australia, New Zealand, Japan, South Korea, and China.

The fifteen-nation partnership is a formidable group of countries that can outcompete India in a number of business sectors, with the first two strong on the agricultural/primary goods front. The latter three East Asian economies have different areas of competence, each having moved up the manufacturing value chain ladder successively, which includes chips and semiconductors, electronics assembly and manufacturing, automobiles, machinery, and so on. South Korea and Japan are at the high end of electronics and the automotive sector, with China narrowing the gap by moving quickly into EVs as a frontrunner. In this context, India is just barely into these broader high-technology areas. In addition, Indian agriculture is vulnerable to competition from large agri-business, a legitimate fear of small farmers in India. Similarly, India feared losing manufacturing jobs had it signed onto RCEP, even though some businesses could have found niche opportunities for exports and gained economies of scale. The paradox is that withdrawing from the free trade agreement has not really helped India's employment situation. Instead, the trade deficit with China has gotten worse, with no reversal of the manufacturing decline at home. Business and government responses appear to be feeble (see Chapter 7 for a quick overview).

China is a daunting factor. It has honed its production processes to lean systems and scale economies, staying abreast of innovations. Assuming that the Chinese wage advantage will erode relative to India's (total wage costs may not due to the superior productivity of Chinese manufacturing), it is still an open question how quickly Indian businesses can translate the opportunity into actual competitiveness. Since India's economic liberalization, businesses have opted for increasing cheaper imports, encouraging consumerism, and, where possible, leveraging these imports for exports. This increasing import intensity of exports (value of imported inputs as a share of export value) was already quite high in 2013–2014 for some sectors such as petroleum products (91.4%), drugs and pharmaceuticals (38.92%), and gems and jewelry (63.2%) (Paul and Kumar 2020: 15). Of these three broad sectors, petroleum products and gold and diamond roughs are not available domestically. Hence, it is understandable that imported content is high for them. But the pharmaceutical sector that was assiduously developed with local active pharmaceutical ingredients (APIs) over the years has now become alarmingly dependent on Chinese APIs (see Chapter 3, Nagaraj 2025: 12). Adding local value for domestic and foreign markets is the right strategy but the rewards of too high an import intensity of exports can be destabilizing in the current volatile climate in geopolitical developments (see Chapter 7). In fact, India does not have the domestic capacity to produce the APIs it needs.

India's sizeable imports of electrical and electronic components from China could be offset by relocating electronics production to India as US pressure on American companies operating out of China mounts. Already, India is the largest assembler and exporter of Apple's iPhones to the US market. Consequently, Apple's suppliers from Taiwan, such as Foxconn, Pegatron, and Wistron (now Tata Electronics), have all established a presence in India with an estimated direct employment, mostly women, of about 90,000 and another 100,000 among other suppliers (Staffing Industry Analysts 2024).[24] Indirect employment could be three times more. There are also Chinese smartphone companies in India that are adding to the employment. Their production is most likely for the Indian market since Chinese brands are popular in India and cheaper than either Korean or American phones. From an employment as well as industrial development perspective, this is a good development in a labor surplus economy. If sustained, such employment can have an intergenerational impact of better livelihood prospects for the workers' children and possibly some spinoffs through backward integration with government intervention. But that is in the future.

In the meantime, there are three issues that could derail this positive development. First, production and exports remain vulnerable to geopolitics, nationalist policies in liberal markets, and other low-cost competitors such as Vietnam. For example, the Trump administration of 2025 is using tariffs to coerce American businesses to reshore manufacturing back to the United States. While this is a lofty goal, Apple remains a target and India remains vulnerable to such a possible relocation. Second, tariffs on India's exports to the United States could be high and could hurt Apple's exports from India unless a trade deal is negotiated fairly and alternative markets for India's other exports are established quickly. Made in India Apple products could face higher (transshipment) penalties than elsewhere and another round of manufacturing relocation for Apple, though unlikely, cannot be ruled out. Third, given Apple's production in China with Taiwanese suppliers, Chinese labor in 2012 secured about 2% of the selling cost or $15 per phone (Economic

[24] However, these assembly jobs are not high value adding activities since almost all the components are imported and the high market value of the product is captured at the consumer end in the United States.

Policy Institute 2012). Given that even if assembly work is labor-intensive, with increasing automation and India's lower wages, it does raise the question of how much manufacturing value will be locally retained through labor payments.

Electronics assembly work is relatively simple, workers are easily trainable, and automation is routine. Adding local content through imported components to create higher value exports could help foster decent jobs, learning the nuts and bolts of production and competitiveness, diversifying economically, and paying for imports to make the trade deficit manageable. However, electronics assembly work is at the bottom of the value chain. What is crucial is a long-term national and business strategy that will create backward integration, much like Dhirubhai Ambani's petrochemical project (see Chapter 3). It would mean establishing a viable ecosystem of the electronics industry, including upstream industries in semiconductors, chips, and so on.

The goal is to ensure a gradual reduction in import intensity, not necessarily elimination, of those products that need not all be sourced from abroad, such as pharmaceutical APIs, simple electronics, and automobile parts and components. Since there is no domestic input supply option for petroleum, gems, and jewelry, these sectors should continue to leverage their import intensity through local value addition, given abundant, narrowly skilled labor. However, the additional 25% US tariff for importing Russian oil had pushed India into a corner. The challenge is to identify those segments of global value chains where Indian manufacturers can competitively enter, install large-scale production, and meet international quality standards in a resilient way. The world economy offers plenty of opportunities, but businesses and export sectors must also guard against external market volatility and diversify markets. The electronics sector is intergenerationally promising if high-volume employment could be sustained and its effects spill over into other related sectors, lead to increased real demand, and raise the standard of living for workers in these units. With external markets notoriously crowded and the electronics industry highly competitive, entry barriers can be overcome with a long-term strategic investment partnership between business and government rather than a simple one-shot passive gamble of landing transnational production.

6.7 Conclusion

The previous chapters surveyed specific business sectors to illustrate how they contribute to economic development, especially job creation. In contrast, this chapter addressed why creating jobs is so difficult for India in the twenty-first century. Rather than list possible hurdles to employment (a long list could be enumerated), it offered a political economy framework of compressed capitalism to highlight the structural impediments associated with late industrialization, including the evolution of a particular form of state–business relationship. While not new or unique to India, such a relationship has detracted from the serious attention needed to create decent work and reduce the pervasive form of precarious informal employment.

Important as they may be, such as spending on physical infrastructure and robust institutions for tax and contract enforcement, supply-side factors must be complemented by aggregate demand that will get the jobs machine humming. An uncritical focus on labor rigidity to increase investment and growth misses the point that the vast informal sector is the most flexible labor market institution that India has available. What is needed is the right kind of education, training, re-skilling, and skill development that matches the different sectors where employability of available workers is low.[25] But businesses must also shoulder some of the responsibility of employment creation by investing in labor-absorbing regular jobs. The point is that it is not a lack of economic growth, rather it is the quality of that growth that needs to reconnect job creation and income redistribution.

Inequality and the persistent informal sector have significantly dampened effective demand. Businesses appear to be content with catering to narrow markets or importing rather than making in India, thereby missing out on the "learning by making" experience. The burgeoning trade deficit with China, resulting from the imports of simple labor-intensive manufactured products, adds to India's current employment predicament. When combined with other structural features of the Indian economy and new geopolitical threats, such lopsided trading arrangements with China reinforce premature deindustrialization and depress employment. These are no doubt small pieces in the larger puzzle of India's employment dilemma. But the governance dysfunctionality of the Indian business system and its relationship to the state in late industrializing India leaves a vast number of workers and would-be job seekers in a dismal place.

In the next chapter, government responses to India's manufacturing and employment shortcomings are identified to see how they might address the problems. This is followed by a rudimentary, partial strengths, weakness, opportunities, and threats (SWOT) analysis that emphasizes current threats

[25] Given the scarcity of jobs, higher education, especially engineering that is sought by many is based on hope and in practice a form of deferred unemployment.

and advantages facing labor-intensive business sectors that have been covered in this book. At a minimum, these sectors must be sustained and expanded if the vast army of the unemployed and underemployed is to have some modicum of a decent livelihood. At the same time, India will need to engage with new sectors, technologies, and geographic markets to get out of the structural stalemate and override new external threats. The chapter concludes with a quick recap of the employment narrative as seen through the relationship of Indian businesses and their contributions to economic development.

7
Is the Future of Jobs Already Here?

7.1 Introduction

In this final chapter, I provide a quick review of key government initiatives in Section 2. The purpose is to see whether these initiatives aimed to address India's manufacturing woes and employment challenges are on track to tackle the bigger problem of surplus labor and the persistence of the precarious informal sector. On the surface, these schemes have the right spirit, but in practical terms, they have yet to show visible results that make a big impact on employment. I acknowledge that some of these investments have a long gestation period, that is, a long time to bear fruit, but the bigger questions rest on the degree of business response, the type of investment, and ultimately its impact on employment. In Section 3, I undertake a brief review of the twenty-first-century dilemma in creating employment.[1] I revisit some characteristics of the labor-intensive business sectors that were examined in this book in terms of threats they confront in the second quarter of the twenty-first century. Section 4 concludes with a quick recap of the employment narrative as seen through late industrialization, the relationship between Indian business and the state, and their contributions to economic development.

7.2 Government Response to the Structural Impasse

To recap, since the economic reforms of the 1990s, the Indian economy has experienced high economic growth, not driven by industry or manufacturing. Instead, the broadly defined services sector picked up the momentum. As amply demonstrated, outside of the large corporate sector, much of the employment in agriculture, industry, and services is informal. Barring some recent developments, such as a reversal of the progression of declining employment in agriculture and an overall decline in female participation in

[1] The review is inspired by the standard strengths, weakness, opportunities, threats (SWOT) framework that is typically applied to assess individual businesses. Since business sectors and not firms are the object of inquiry, the review carried out in the chapter pertains only to the threats and advantages of the sectors in question.

Indian Business, Economic Development, and the Jobs Dilemma in the Twenty-first Century. Anthony P. D'Costa, Oxford University Press. © Anthony P. D'Costa (2026). DOI: 10.1093/9780198948407.003.0007

the labor force, the structural story of agriculture has changed little. It remains a large employer of unorganized family and wage labor. Its contribution to GDP has fallen considerably, but the size of agricultural employment has not budged much.

Clearly, these interconnected and layered developments are not easy to disentangle to find an approach to resolve them at the same time. The government overall has taken a deregulatory approach to economic activities and has correctly identified stagnant manufacturing, revealed by its low and unchanging share of GDP, as the main culprit. The share of industry fell from 31.1% in 2009 to 24.5% in 2024 (World Bank Group 2025c). The share of manufacturing to GDP is roughly 13%; the goal is to raise the share of manufacturing to 25% of GDP.[2] Comparative figures show that China's value of manufacturing is $5 trillion, which is roughly 10 times India's and the per-worker gross revenue is roughly $50,000 for China compared to $17,000 for India (Shastry 2024: 4).

The manufacturing gap and productivity difference between the two countries is enormous, but India's challenge continues to be chasing the employment gap. It is not obvious, but it is possible that China, having mostly addressed the surplus labor problem, may now confront a new dilemma of employment as productivity increases with aggressive upgrading to higher-value-added economic activities. These activities are capital- and technology-intensive, but they come on the heels of over three decades of relentless export-oriented labor-intensive industrialization, which could offset some of the jobs lost with continued diversification of the economy, up to a point. However, in a classic case of compressed capitalism and not having gone through a primary phase of widespread labor-intensive manufacturing, India is once again trying to leapfrog to new kinds of capital- and technology-intensive production. It will probably address some of the manufacturing capability gap, but the need for widespread employment may go unfulfilled. That India is between a rock and a hard place underscores the twenty-first-century dilemma.

To shore up Indian manufacturing, and by extension tackle poverty and employment, the government introduced the Make in India (MII) program in 2014 and the Productivity Linked Incentive (PLI) Scheme in 2020.[3] The idea

[2] The category of industry is not the same as manufacturing. The former also includes construction activity, which in recent years has experienced unusually high growth accompanying income growth and urban development but subsequently falling substantially during the pandemic era. This is also an urban-based sector that temporarily absorbs a lot of migrant workers from the countryside, with the agricultural sector continuing to act as a buffer against job losses when the construction projects are completed.

[3] In 2025 the government also introduced an Employment-Linked Incentive (ELI) scheme aimed to create formal jobs by offering a provident fund (a retirement savings scheme) to first time employees.

behind both is to encourage domestic and foreign businesses to invest in manufacturing with government incentives, add local value, and generate employment. They are both nationalist industrialization strategies that are similar to but also different from past industrial policies. For example, in the 1950s, the phased manufacturing program (PMP) under the Tariffs Commission called for a mandatory increase in local content for imported automobiles (D'Costa 2005: 82). The PMP, just like the MII of today, was a national industrialization strategy of self-reliance aimed to build up domestic capabilities. Unlike PMP, MII covers fifteen manufacturing and twelve service sectors and does not subject them to the restrictive regulatory licensing aspects of the earlier PMP.[4] The list is a mix of mid-level technology, essential, capital-intensive, infrastructural, labor-intensive, and export-oriented sectors. The services list includes a mix of IT, medical, tourism, and various business services that are increasingly becoming tradable through the Internet.

Both MII and PLI are policies aimed at self-reliance with a twist. Unlike the PMP of the past, these new efforts are open to foreign investment, acknowledging that in the twenty-first century, economies are largely open, India's technological competence is behind the international frontier, and the geography of supply chains is no longer just national. It also suggests ownership does not matter as long as production and employment are local, akin to Deng Xiaoping's cat metaphor mentioned in Chapter 1. However, multinational production poses challenges for India because of weak technological capabilities and the difficulties (and thus unwillingness) to integrate backward over time through diversification and adding more value to production. Most Indian businesses do not do research and development (R&D) and instead rely on foreign suppliers of technology, industrial knowledge, imported raw materials, and components as inputs to manufacturing. Multinationals do more R&D, but given their global operations, not every manufacturing location becomes their R&D hub, and in the absence of a host country R&D ecosystem, there is little incentive. To put this dilemma in its proper context, between 1998 and 2023, the gross expenditure on R&D (GERD) for China increased from 0.7 to 2.6% of GDP, while India's GERD slightly fell from 0.7 to 0.65 in 2020 (OECD 2025).[5] South Korea had the highest GERD ratio at 5%. In any case, not all imports are bad and indeed cannot be avoided for

This is a form of formal financial inclusion bringing informal workers under social protection. Incentives are also offered to employers to hire workers. It is too early to assess the impact of this scheme.

[4] Make in India (2025). "Sectors," https://www.makeinindia.com/sectors

[5] OECD (2025). Science, Technology and Innovation Scoreboard: Explore the Data, https://www.oecd.org/en/data/datasets/science-technology-and-innovation-scoreboard.html See also OECD (2021).

some specific sectors at certain times, but the practice must not become pervasive and indefinite. However, in the absence of other dynamic sectors, the multiplier effects of these activities are likely to be truncated because of the weak R&D ecosystem and technological capabilities.

The Productivity Linked Incentive scheme lists fourteen sectors seen as promising for future growth and tapping export markets. There is an overlap of some of the sectors with the MII list, but there are important differences. For example, under PLI, electronics and pharmaceuticals (APIs) have been identified for strategic intervention since India's import dependence on China for these products has become extensive. Other traditional sectors, such as autos and textiles, are targeted for diversification to higher-value items. These include electric vehicle (EV) battery technologies and hydrogen fuel and specialized applications of textiles in medical, defense, and industrial safety.[6]

The Productivity Linked Incentive program in form is similar to the 2015 Made in China (MIC) Chinese industrial policy. In substance, however, MIC has been far more ambitious and has accomplished much. It has aimed to diversify away from labor-intensive, cheap manufacturing industries to high-value-added, high-tech ones. While China has been transitioning by upgrading from successful labor-intensive industrialization to more innovation-driven output, India is now skipping ahead to high-value diversified output, relying on foreign technologies and playing catch-up without raising the level of basic manufacturing output and employment. At one level, this is structurally anticipated as compressed capitalism pushes late industrializers to be at the forefront of technologies and dynamic sectors without having addressed some of the legacy problems of agriculture and petty commodity production. However, leapfrogging, while advantageous in some areas, does not fundamentally address India's employment problems overwhelmed by a persistent informal sector. What is noteworthy is that these recent government policies parallel the earlier, difficult capital-intensive import-substituting industrialization of the 1950s, when labor was plentiful and the economy closed. Today, surplus labor still exists with a stagnant industrial sector and an open economy, making technological catch-up difficult. The dilemma is self-evident: what kind of industrialization strategy to pursue in the twenty-first century when there is a labor surplus and the global technological frontier has moved forward significantly?

[6] DHL (2025). Guide to Production-Linked Incentive (PLI) Schemes: What Are They, How They Work, https://www.dhl.com/discover/en-in/logistics-advice/logistics-insights/what-is-a-pli-scheme

The Productivity Linked Incentive scheme has not been effective thus far (Nagaraj 2025: 12). The goal to incubate globally competitive industries through this policy may be an oversell. Early evidence of success in the electronics industry shows that imports of finished mobile phones fell from $3.5 billion to $1.5 billion and exports shot up from $0.2 billion to $4.7 billion during the 2017–2018 to 2021–2022 period. However, during the same period, the imports of electronics components increased from $15.7 billion to $25.9 billion (Nagaraj 2025: 12), implying a transference of import dependence from finished products to imports of inputs. On the surface this is a good development as some value is added locally by Indian labor by making the finished products with imports. However, if this import dependence remains a permanent feature with little upstream manufacturing (backward integration), India's electronics manufacturing will remain underdeveloped. By 2023, total imports from China surged to $122 billion, with electronics and electronic equipment at $44.15 billion, machinery at $24.07 billion, and chemicals at $14.52 billion (Shastry 2024: 7). At the same time, PLI spending by the government aimed at incentivizing business has fallen far short of what was allocated by the government. Between 2021–2022 and 2023–2024, government spending and allocations on the scheme were just 6% of the committed spending (Dhar 2024), reflecting not only a divergence of public and private interests but essentially disinterest on the part of private business.

It is evident that rising imports are due to the lack of backward integration. Indian and foreign-invested businesses are not moving upstream (due to a lack of competence or business interest) to make the raw materials or components used by the downstream sectors. Interestingly, the PLI scheme anticipates that the medium-, small-, and micro-sized enterprises (MSMEs) will lead the backward integration effort (see Dhar 2024). But this is not an easy task for smaller enterprises, as modern production requires scale and establishing an entire manufacturing ecosystem for the twenty-first century. Also, if multiple firms in the same business sector are supported through the PLI scheme, the chances of industry fragmentation will be high. It is also counterproductive to the whole effort at backward integration. Long supply chains for integrated production mean that the MSMEs must be tightly linked to other producers, who may not all be in the same country. In the meantime, the world economy has become highly volatile with arbitrary protectionism and widening productivity gaps in manufacturing, raising new threats for many Indian export-oriented businesses.

The forward-looking policy of promoting advanced technology sectors such as EVs, batteries, telecom, phones, semiconductors, and pharmaceutical

APIs is broadly in line with the manufacturing thrust toward upgrading and diversification. For example, the nearly $9 billion government commitment for India's semiconductor effort, that is, fabrication, design, and manufacturing, is in the right direction as anticipated applications are in a wide range of sectors such as healthcare, transport, communications, defense, and space. These sectors represent much-needed diversification. However, semiconductors and related manufacturing, such as phones and telecom, are mostly capital-, technology-, and skill-intensive industries (Nayyar and Nayyar 2024: 8). More importantly, technologies in these sectors are controlled by large global firms. In the absence of robust R&D by Indian businesses, this discourages backward integration. Electronics assembly is labor-intensive and Apple's recent decoupling from China, prompted by US government pressure, has introduced its major suppliers from Taiwan, such as Hon Hai Precision or Foxconn, Wistron, and Pegatron, to India. India's Tata Electronics has also been included as an Apple supplier. But this kind of "friendshoring" could be short-lived if Apple's India-made iPhones face the same tariffs against Indian exports to the United States (see the next section).

In any case, for now, if investments for electronics assembly become routine, expansive, and encourage more local suppliers, and geopolitics do not undermine the emerging electronics assembly operations in India, it is a good development for employment. There are also Chinese smartphone and other electronics companies, such as Xiaomi, OPPO, and Lenovo (formerly Motorola), that have responded to India's MII program through local manufacturing. However, at this time, components for Apple iPhones as well as for Chinese smartphones are imported from elsewhere, including China. Tata's engagement in iPhone assembly and repair of certain Apple products could be a good beginning. But whether these early results can be sustained without significant efforts at assimilation of imported technologies and backward integration remains an open question. Curiously, outside of electronics assembly production, MII and PLI might reproduce the structural effects of an earlier capital-intensive self-reliant import substitution industrialization strategy, namely, disproportionately less employment relative to investment. One final point to note is that by adding more sectors to the original list of twenty-seven in the MII list, the strategic focus of MII has been considerably diluted. According to one assessment, the MII has not lived up to its promise of creating 100 million new jobs by 2022 (Shastry 2024). While it is true that all sectors need to advance simultaneously, there are limits to the effectiveness of such efforts if resources are spread thinly and without a coherent strategy for secondary economic development effects.

7.3 Threats Facing Labor-intensive Business Sectors

This book stays away from policy prescriptions for the simple reason that late industrialization for a large country such as India has structural legacies and institutional barriers that are not easily overcome. At the same time, I recognize that at least some basic responses to the grim employment reality cannot be avoided. In that spirit, a key focus for industrialization and job creation should be increased spending on quality education, training, and skill development across the board. Important as it is, it is also a typical supply-side recommendation along with infrastructure investment, a business-friendly environment, and labor flexibility. The government has responded to these shortcomings over the years. I have also made the point that labor is not rigid because the bulk of workers are found in the flexible informal sector. However, given India's poor track record on the employability of workers, including tertiary educated students, the goal ought to be an aggressive policy toward raising the quality and increasing the access to pre-college skill-based education. Such training must anticipate and keep track of the types of industrial and service jobs that are either emerging or have potential in the market. The training institutions should be benchmarked with international standards and be linked to actual production facilities through apprenticeship, internships, and trainee programs. Beyond this rather generic approach, the core of the employment problem remains, namely, how to create enough decent jobs for the growing labor force.

In the meantime, there are two looming threats. The first is technological, namely the rapid development and applicability of artificial intelligence (AI) and machine language (ML) in a number of occupations and tasks, namely, routine, predictable, coding types of clerical work (Dewan, Kashyap, and Meyers 2025: 10, Awasthi and Yagnik 2025). The second is geopolitical, namely, protectionist tariff policies, mainly by the United States, that could significantly impact successful export sectors and their employees. As of writing, the United States has implemented 50% tariffs on India's exports to the United States, 25% as "reciprocal" tariffs, and another 25% as penalties for purchasing Russian oil. Recently, tariffs against India have been negotiated downward to 18% by pledging less imports of Russian oil, only to be cornered with high oil prices and restricted supplies of natural gas (used for household cooking, manufacturing, and running business operations) from the Middle East. Iran has choked off the shipping passage for oil tankers through the Strait of Hormuz as a response to US and Israeli aggression. Without getting bogged down on the merits of these tariffs, it is evident that they are being used to extract trade concessions and pry doors open to US exporters in certain Indian markets, such as agriculture. With trade negotiations between India and the United States progressing, these draconian tariffs have come down. Nevertheless, these sudden idiosyncratic protectionist sentiments in a world largely accustomed to the free movement of goods signal the vulnerability of Indian exporters of labor-intensive products such as textiles and gems and jewelry. Foreign investment in India's export-oriented garments sector could withdraw if the tariffs remain, which can be expected to inflict pain on the employees of the garments business that rely heavily on the US market.[7] Already, there are reports that India's labor-intensive exports, such as textiles and jewelry, have taken a big hit, with predicted GDP growth declining by 0.5 to 0.6% (Saha 2025). The lesson here is to diversify export markets. The EU-India Free Trade Agreement of February 2026 is aligned with this export market diversification strategy.

In Table 7.1, I present an approximate set of features of market threats and advantages for each of the labor-intensive business sectors examined in this book. The goal is to alert readers and policymakers that, without having resolved the employment challenge, new threats are on the horizon in the very sectors where India has a labor and cost advantage, and they have done well. These are not capital-intensive sectors. With low entry barriers for business and employees, even where tertiary technical education is needed, India has enjoyed considerable advantage due to the supply of workers available. However, new technologies such as AI and protectionist policies abroad could significantly impact employment in India. Below, I briefly outline the technology and market threats for broadly labor-intensive, export-oriented sectors that have been included in this study. These are: agriculture; textiles and handlooms; software services and IT; diamond polishing and jewelry; e-commerce and digital platform economy (DPE). This exercise is mainly to illustrate how difficult job creation has become in the twenty-first century and to pre-empt further destabilization of an already stressed labor market. We have already made several references to China and its competitive strengths as an illustration of how the world is different from earlier epochs of late industrialization and developmental outcomes. To this I add the looming technological threats, driven by the idea of capitalist efficiency and productivity, and the growing protectionist world in which India finds itself.

The characteristics of the different business sectors presented in Table 7.1 are self-explanatory. However, three points are worth noting. First, Indian

[7] Other businesses, such as Mahindra & Mahindra, whose tractor exports to the United States may also be hit hard by these tariffs.

agriculture is a vulnerable sector, subject to low productivity, vagaries of weather, climate change, and prices. At the household level, there have been existential threats of various sorts, but the US pressure to pry open Indian agricultural markets with the threat of tariffs would wreak economic, social, and political havoc. If prices fell with increased agricultural output through productivity gains, the sector could be overwhelmed with further price pressure because of large-scale agricultural exports from the United States. Already, some mixed outcomes of contract farming (a form of large-scale farming) have exposed the vulnerability of small farmers.

Productivity-led agricultural growth could be supported by export markets. However, this is one sector where governments around the world, for food security and domestic political and cultural reasons, are quite protective of their agricultural sectors. With nearly 160 million agricultural workers in the country, it is inevitable that the Indian political leadership must responsibly negotiate this external pressure. It cannot afford to put the lives of millions of farmers at risk and contribute to rural misery and, in the absence of decent non-farm work, a bloated urban informal economy. Where will the rural workers go because of declining prices and falling incomes if the nonagricultural sector, namely, manufacturing and services are not ready for this transition? What the government might give up in exchange for reduced tariffs when negotiating with the United States is hard to tell, but it certainly cannot open agricultural markets to international competition. Farmers want higher minimum support prices from the government so that cultivation remains economically viable, especially when alternative sources of livelihoods are scarce. As Table 7.1 illustrates, the export exposure to the US market is quite high for several labor-intensive industries. These are some of the sectors where rural workers find non-farm employment. The impact of tariffs, if they stick, will certainly be harsh from a jobs point of view, exacerbating an already difficult situation in finding decent urban employment for the growing mass of surplus workers.

Second, AI technology presents a significant threat to India's software sector, a primary driver of its export success in recent decades. As large language models and generative AI catch on, many tasks currently done by humans will be automated. Tasks involving high-level cognitive functions are expected to continue, but work that entails a large number of repetitive tasks, using large volumes of data, including errors to avoid, will be accomplished using AI. As more data becomes available, the AI models will be self-correcting with higher reliability. Within the software service value chain, many functions and tasks will be hit. Furthermore, should AI substitute technical workers on a large

Table 7.1 The Twin Threats of Changing Technologies and Tariffs on Labor-intensive Business Sectors

Business/ Economic Sector	Current Technologies	Technology Threats	Current Markets	Market Threats	US Market Exposure (share of total exports)	Advantages/ Vulnerabilities
Agriculture	Simple	Limited automation	Limited globalized	Liberalizing domestic markets to international competition, tariffs	11%	Select tropical products/cash crops Price competition
Textiles and handlooms	Capital-intensive, artisanal	Automation/limited threat/product substitution	Globalized/limited globalized	International competition, changing tastes and preferences, high cost of artisanal products relative to substitutes, tariffs	33%	Abundant labor Artisanal labor Tariff threats
Software services and IT	Knowledge-based, human capital	Automation/AI	Globalized	International competition, reshoring due to AI, rising labor costs, immigration policies	55%	Technical labor with long international industry experience Visa restrictions
Diamond polishing and jewelry	Simple, labor-intensive, specialized non-transferable skills	Lab diamonds	Globalized	Reliance on imported diamonds, imports from China	30%	Abundant labor, industry ecosystem, international networks, craft workers Tariff threats
E-commerce and DPE	Capital-intensive/software/labor-intensive	Automation/AI	Limited globalized	Limited impact	N/A	Abundant unskilled workers, technical workers

Notes: Limited globalized = little international exposure, India's US market exposure in the pharmaceutical products sector is roughly $8.7 billion, and it is an importer of Chinese API.

Source: Compiled by the author

scale, it is possible that many of these jobs could disappear or be reshored to the export markets.

In a recent Reuters article, Tata Consultancy Services, one of India's largest software services companies, announced laying off over 12,000 jobs. While the job cuts are not attributed to AI per se, it is evident that the company is moving ahead with AI to enhance productivity (Ishwarbharath and Suresh 2025). About half a million software jobs are predicted to disappear in the next few years, with ripple effects on declining consumption of tourism, luxury shopping, and real estate, all part of the narrow elite markets that Indian businesses have come to rely on. Fortunately, other than the export-oriented software sector, for now, the many jobs that AI can displace are not found extensively in the Global South. But India is already touting its AI ambitions with policy interventions for encouraging firms to spearhead various applications and learning opportunities (IBEF, IT and BPM 2025: 5).[8] Therefore, the possible boomerang effect of AI on future employment in India should not be lost sight of.

Third, the anti-immigrant, America First Policy, aimed at local hires by curbing foreign technical professionals from working in the United States, could impact the Indian software sector (Pager and Aleaziz 2025). The threats of future tariffs and immigration regulations could impact direct and indirect employment of the very people who have boosted India's capabilities in software exports. As of now, services are not part of the reciprocal tariffs. But American firms have become very dependent on Indian companies and technical professionals. Through the H-1B employer-sponsored work visa program such workers with science, technology, engineering, mathematics (STEM) backgrounds are recruited to work for IT companies based in the United States (D'Costa 2025a: 15). Most of the H-1B visas are for IT professionals, and most of them have been secured by Indian citizens (D'Costa 2016b: 73).[9] On January 21, 2020, the total number of H1B visa petitions was 421,276. Of this, 74.5% were by Indians. China was a distant second with 11.8% or under 16% of India's share (US Citizen and Immigration Services 2020).[10] Such visibility of Indian professionals has mobilized anti-immigrant sentiments against H1B visas in every election season, but particularly intense

[8] In the world of AI, the United States has 73% of large models, China 15%, and the rest of the world just 12% (Dewan, Kashyap, and Meyers 2025: 19).

[9] Most major Indian firms in the United States serving American clients are known to bring in professionals from India. For example, Infosys and TCS, the two highest Indian employers of H1B visa holders, had 8137 and 7566 H1B visa staff respectively (Suresh and Ishwarbharath 2025).

[10] H-1B Petitions by Gender and Country of Birth Fiscal Year 2019, https://www.uscis.gov/sites/default/files/document/data/h-1b-petitions-by-gender-country-of-birth-fy2019.pdf

ones in the current political climate in the United States.[11] Naturally, given the high exposure, industry observers had already noted the importance of market diversification for innovation reasons (see D'Costa 2002, D'Costa 2003a, D'Costa 2009) but now it has become a political issue. If the tariff tensions are not resolved satisfactorily, India may be pushed closer to Russia and China, with which it has several unresolved issues pertaining to the national border, trade relationship, and damming rivers upstream.

While the hope is that the tariff issue will be resolved through negotiations, high single-market exposure needs to be derisked as part of an employment strategy along with other measures. Preparing for the imminent AI technological transition will be key, with education, digital literacy, and skill development, plus the necessary energy infrastructure (GIZ 2022).[12] But it is a catch-22 situation. With a stalled agrarian transition and premature deindustrialization, India is now faced with yet another transition challenge with AI (Albrieu 2022: 4). New technologies imply "...greater difficulty for latecomers in attaining sectoral upgrading and may limit their scope for industrialization to low-wage and less dynamic (in terms of productivity growth) manufacturing sectors. This could seriously stifle these countries' economic catch-up and leave them with stagnant productivity and per capita income growth" (Mayer 2018: 13). To this, the dignity of work, which in status-conscious India is low for physical work, must be added. This attitudinal shift is necessary and may come about over the longer term with increasing wages and formalization of work, attracting also the educated unemployed to accept factory-type production jobs.

7.4 Late Industrialization and the Jobs Dilemma

This book examined the understudied relationship between business and economic development in India. Mediated by the state, the goal has been to open a window on the question of why creating jobs in India is so difficult today. This is all the more vexing as the country displays one of the highest economic growth rates in the world. For all the corporate expansion, as evidenced by the capital-, technology-, and skill-intensive business sectors surveyed in this book, there is a large underbelly of MSMEs of informal or unorganized workers who are outside the purview of labor regulations.

[11] Granted, there may be some abuse of the visa program by bringing in cheaper professionals from India (see D'Costa 2011: 243), the issue is more about the national background of the professionals. See Sampath (2024).

[12] AI uses enormous amount of electricity to run large generative and language models.

The mostly household-based agricultural sector is also part of this unorganized sector that has become a permanent feature of contemporary Indian capitalism. Newer sectors such as modern retail, e-commerce, and the digital platform economy are generating new types of jobs, but most of these service jobs are not yet covered by social protections. Broadly, the absence of social protection is one source of worsening inequality and precarity for a large fraction of the workforce. It also points to an alternative understanding of a depressed economy, mainly, the lack of effective demand.

There are several reasons for India's employment predicaments. Most of these allegedly relate to lack of supply-side support mechanisms such as infrastructure, lack of skilled workers, technological lethargy, institutional dysfunctionality, ease of doing business, and labor rigidity. While there is some truth to all of these, especially the institutional dysfunctionality resulting from crony capitalism and *quid pro quo* arrangements between agents of the state and business, I offer a more structuralist interpretation. Late industrialization, the path-dependent nature of the economic development process, and a changed world have created a very different ecosystem for contemporary industrialization and conditions for catch-up dynamics. Many of the earlier development options are now foreclosed. For example, rather than being directed toward labor-intensive production, investments are instead flowing mostly to more profitable capital- and skill-intensive sectors. These are structural and strategic responses by both domestic and foreign oligopolistic corporate businesses to enter particular markets, while government policies aimed to tackle import competition of capital-intensive production, mainly from China is also promoting sectors that are investment and technology intensive. Under the current set of incentives and policy environment, such business behavior is difficult to regulate. All said and done, the outcomes do not contribute to what is really needed, namely, tackling India's surplus labor through large-scale employment. Hence, employment generation must be made a key goal of economic policy (Deshpande 2023: 959).

The predicaments are not new and can be structurally attributed to compressed capitalism, whereby selective leapfrogging by capitalist advances is possible in a milieu of small-scale production and an incomplete agrarian transition. The resulting inherent structural stalemate in an open economy becomes more sinister in an open economy with few guardrails. For example, large corporate and small informal businesses face considerable competition as well as opportunities to take the easy way out to import parts and components for production and skip the backward integration effort. This truncated or enclave form of development is also not new (see D'Costa 2011). Fast forward to the second quarter of the twenty-first century, and we now have automation, AI, and global protectionism as additional threats to India's employment future. The ability to export surplus labor has receded even further as anti-immigration and deglobalization sentiments become stronger, even though global labor markets remain mismatched between labor supply and demand in different types of occupations (D'Costa 2025c).

We do know what the results of policy ought to be, namely, labor-absorbing economic activities in India on a large scale. But how to get there has flummoxed experts since the problem is a structural-institutional one that is not amenable to easy solutions. The growth problem seems to have been resolved for now, but no amount of tinkering will address job scarcity and the bloated informal sector. Instead, issues of limited domestic demand resting on inadequate jobs, low informal wages, and international competition must be addressed simultaneously to avoid a vicious trap. Otherwise, to whom will businesses sell their goods? A small, narrow middle class or elite market, which is a product of inequality, cannot sustain long-term growth and employment. Concerted efforts must be made in diversifying production by creating higher-paying jobs in different sectors, including shedding low-productivity agricultural and urban-based services work through increasing productivity. Diversification demands increased investment, education and skill development, new technologies, and organizational change, all of which appear to be weak except in certain pockets in the corporate business sector. Since business accumulation strategies are self-serving, both government and society need to step up in a concerted effort to refocus India's institutions to actively shape the country's employment future.

The ultimate litmus test of development is the rising average material standard of living and social well-being. These outcomes are significantly dependent on how big and fast a dent is made in reducing India's massive labor surplus through expanding employment opportunities and rising wages in diverse economic activities. But with premature deindustrialization, it is difficult to know where to begin. Employment as a policy goal must be made a priority by repurposing the political economy of the Indian business system and its relationship to the state. Otherwise, late industrialization, as it has unfolded in India, will leave a vast pool of workers and would-be job seekers in a dismal place for the foreseeable future.

References

Abraham, R. and Kesar, S. (2025). "Trajectories of Labour Market Transitions in the Indian Economy," *World Development*, 195: 1–19, https://doi.org/10.1016/j.worlddev.2025.107029.

Abraham, V. (2019). "The Dynamic Nature of Jobless Growth in India," in Sundar, S. (ed.), *Globalization, Labour Market Institutions, Processes and Policies in India: Essays in Honour of Lalit K. Deshpande*, Singapore: Springer Singapore Pte. Limited, pp. 443–470.

Addison, T. and Roe, A. (2024). *Resources Matter: Ending Poverty While Protecting Nature*, Oxford: Oxford University Press, UNU-WIDER Studies in Development Economics.

Agarwala, R. (2019). "The Politics of India's Reformed Labor Model," in Jaffrelot, C., Kohli, A. and Murali, K. (eds.), *Business and Politics in India*, New York: Oxford University Press, pp. 95–123.

AICTE (2025). *Statistics*, https://www.aicte-india.org/, accessed May 23, 2025.

Albrieu, R. (2022). *Technology and the Future of Work (FoW): Artificial Intelligence*, New Delhi: JustJobs Network Inc.

Alvaredo, F., Chancel, L., Piketty, T., Saez, E., and Zucman, G. (2018). *World Inequality Report (2018)*. World Inequality Lab. accessed May 16, 2022. https://wir2018.wid.world/files/download/wir2018-full-report-english.pdf.

Aronowitz, S. and DiFazio, W. (2010). *The Jobless Future: Charting a Major Change in the Nature of Paid Work in the United States*, Minneapolis: University of Minnesota Press.

Arthur, W.B. (1994). *Increasing Returns and Path Dependence in the Economy*, Ann Arbor: University of Michigan Press.

Athreye, S., Kale, D. and Ramani, S.V. (2009). "Experimentation with Strategy and the Evolution of Dynamic Capability in the Indian Pharmaceutical Sector," *Industrial and Corporate Change*, 18 (4): 729–759.

Awasthi, D. and Yagnik, J. (2025). "Digitisation, Automation and 'Jobs at Risk': A Comparative Analysis of BRIS Countries, and a Detailed Analysis of the Indian Scenario," *The Indian Journal of Labour Economics*, 68: 417–450.

Ayres, C.E. (1991). "Economic Development: An Institutionalist Perspective," in Dietz, J. (ed.), *Latin America's Economic Development*, Boulder: Lynne Rienner Publishers, pp. 89–97.

Azim Premji University (2018). *State of Working India, Centre for Sustainable Employment*, Bengaluru: Azim Premji University.

Azim Premji University (2023). *State of Working India: Social identities and Labour Market Outcomes, Centre for Sustainable Employment*, Bengaluru: Azim Premji University.

Bain & Company and Center for Innovation, Incubation, and Entrepreneurship (2017). *Indian Farming's Next Big Moment: Farming as a Service*, Johannesburg, New Delhi, and Ahmedabad: Bain & Company and CIIE.

Bain and Company and Antwerp World Diamond Center (2013). *The Global Diamond Report 2013: Journey through the Value Chain*, Antwerp: AWDC.

Bain and Company and Antwerp World Diamond Center (2021). *The Global Diamond Industry 2020–21: Brilliant Under Pressure*, Antwerp: AWDC.

Balakrishnan, P. (2006). "Benign Neglect or Strategic Intent? Contested Lineage of Indian Software Industry," *Economic and Political Weekly*, 41 (36): 3865–3872.

Banik, N. and Padalkar, M. (2021). "The Spread of Gig Economy: Trends and Effects," *Foresight and STI Governance*, 15 (1): 28–38, https://doi.org/10.17323/2500-2597.2021.1.19.29.

Bardhan, P. (2019). "Merchants of Hype and Hate: A Political-Economic Evaluation of the Modi Regime," in Chatterji, A.P., Hansen, T.B. and Jaffrelot, C. (eds.), *Majoritarian State: How Hindu Nationalism Is Changing India*, Oxford: Oxford University Press, pp. 177–192.

Bardhan, P. (1984). *The Political Economy of Development in India*, Oxford: Basil Blackwell.

Barrett, C.B., Reardon, T., Swinnen, J. and Zilberman, D. (2019). *Structural Transformation and Economic Development: Insights from the Agri-food Value Chain Revolution*, [Cornell University, unpublished paper].

Basole, A. and Basu, D. (2011). "Relations of Production and Modes of Surplus Extraction in India: Part I – Agriculture," *Economic and Political Weekly*, 46 (14): 41–58.

Bessen, J. (2018). "AI and Jobs: The Role of Demand," *National Bureau of Economic Research*, (Working Paper No. 24235), http://www.nber.org/papers/w24235.

Bhaduri, A. (1983). *The Economic Structure of Backward Agriculture, India*, Macmillan.

Bhalla, S.S., and Bhasin, K. (2024). *India Eliminates Extreme Poverty, Brookings*, March 1, 2024, https://www.brookings.edu/articles/india-eliminates-extreme-poverty/

Bharadwaj, K. (1985). "A View on Commercialisation in Indian Agriculture and the Development of Capitalism," *Journal of Peasant Studies*, 12 (4): 7–25.

Bhattacharya, A.K. and Guha Thakurta, P. (2019). "Contours of Crony Capitalism in the Modi Raj," in Chatterji, A.P., Hansen, T.B. and Jaffrelot, C. (eds.), *Majoritarian State: How Hindu Nationalism Is Changing India*, Oxford: Oxford University Press, pp. 193–214.

Bhattacharya, R. and Sen, S. (2018). "*Pride and Prejudice: The Condition of Handloom Weavers in West Bengal*," Azim Premji University, Centre for Sustainable Employment, State of Working India 2018, Background Paper – 16.

Bhattacharyya, S., Abraham, M. and D'Costa, A. (2013). "Political Economy of Agrarian Crisis and Slow Industrialisation in India," *Social Scientist*, 41 (11/12): 43–63.

Bhide, S., Malik, P. and Nair, S.K.N. (2010). Private Sector Participation in the Indian Power Sector and Climate Change, Agence Française de Développement, (Working Paper No. 99).

Bhowmik, M.R. (2019). "Fourth Handloom Census: Government's Claims Belie Ground Reality," *Economic and Political Weekly*, 54 (49): 7, https://www.epw.in/engage/article/fourth-handloom-census-government-claims-belie-ground-reality.

Binswanger-Mkhize, H.P. (2013). "The Stunted Structural Transformation of the Indian Economy: Agriculture, Manufacturing and the Rural Non-Farm Sector," *Economic and Political Weekly*, 48 (26/27): 5–13.

BioSpectrum (2024). *Can India Reclaim API Throne from China?* September 1, 2024, https://www.biospectrumindia.com/features/73/25074/can-india-reclaim-api-throne-from-china.html, accessed June 26, 2025.

Black, R. (2013). *A Brief History of Climate Change*, https://www.bbc.com/news/science-environment-15874560, accessed May 12, 2024.

Buchal, C., and Sinn, H-W (2019). "Decarbonizing Mobility: Thoughts on an Unresolved Challenge," *European Physical Journal Plus*, 134 (599): 1–9.

Carley, S. and Lawrence, S. (2014). *Energy-Based Economic Development*, London: Springer-Verlag, https://doi.org/10.1007/978-1-4471-6341-1_2.

Castells, M. and Portes, A. (1989). "World Underneath: The Origins, Dynamics, and Effects of the Informal Economy," in Portes, A., Castells, M. and Benton, L. (eds.), *The Informal Economy: Studies in Advanced and Less Developed Countries*, Baltimore: Johns Hopkins University Press, pp. 11–37.

Chakraborty, A. (2015). "Reforming Labour Markets in States: Revisiting the Futility Thesis," *Economic and Political Weekly*, L (20): 39–51.

Chakraborty, A., Chowdhury, S., Banerjee, S. and Mahmood, Z. (2019). *Limits of Bargaining: Capital, Labour and the State in Contemporary India*, Cambridge: Cambridge University Press.

Chakraborty, A. and Sen, A. (2015). *Re-positioning the Traditional Handloom Sari Heritage of Bengal: Studying the Role of "Geographical Indications"*, http://www.researchgate.net/publication/281898957, accessed 02/17/2017.

Chakraborty, S. (2025). "Vedanta Eyes 'Strategic' Indian Rare-earth Production Within 5 Years," *Nikkei Asia*, July 1, 2025.

Chancel, L., Piketty, T., Saez, E. and Zucman, G. (eds.) (2022). *World Inequality Report*, World Inequality Lab, Cambridge: Harvard University Press.

Chatterjee, E. and McCartney, M. (2020). "Revisiting the Political Economy of Development in India," in Chatterjee, E. and McCartney, M. (eds.), *Class and Conflict: Revisiting Pranab Bardhan's Political Economy of India*, Oxford: Oxford University Press, pp. 3–27.

Chatterjee, P. (2008). "Democracy and Economic Transformation in India," *Economic and Political Weekly*, 43 (16): 53–62.

Chodorow-Reich, G., Gopinath, G., Mishra, P. and Narayanan, A. (2018). "Cash and the Economy: Evidence from India's Demonetization," *National Bureau of Economic Research*, (Working Paper No. 25370), http://www.nber.org/papers/w25370.

Christopher, T., Stanton, C.T. and Thomas, C. (2025). "Who Benefits from Online Gig Economy Platforms?" *American Economic Review*, 115 (6): 1857–1895.

Cioffi, J.W., Kenney, M. and Zysman, J. (2022). "Platform Power and Regulatory Politics: Polanyi for the Twenty-First Century," *New Political Economy*, 27 (5): 820–836.

Cornish, S., Singh, J., and Ruehl, M. and Ruehl (2022). How a Teaching App Feted by Silicon Valley was Left Chasing the Indian Dream, *Financial Times*, 2 October https://www.ft.com/content/8d998d44-3937-4931-8ee1-f963f6a8b253.

Crabtree, J. (2018). *The Billionaire Raj: A Journey Through India's New Gilded Age*, New York: Tim Duggan Books.

Credit Suisse (2019). *Global Wealth Databook 2019*, No place: Credit Suisse.

Credit Suisse (2021). *India Market Strategy: 100 Unicorns: India's Changing Corporate Landscape*, Singapore: Credit Suisse AG.

Credit Suisse (2023). *Global Wealth Report (2023)*, Credit Suisse AG, a UBS Group Company.

Curtis, E.M. and Marinescu, I. (2022). "Green Energy Jobs in the US: What Are They, and Where Are They?," *National Bureau of Economic Research*, (Working Paper No. 30332).

D'Costa, A.P. (1998a). "Coping with Technology Divergence Policies and Strategies for India's Industrial Development," *Technological Forecasting and Social Change* 58: 271–283.

D'Costa, A.P. (1998b). "An Alternative Model of Development? Cooperation and Flexible Industrial Practices in India," *Journal of International Development*, 10 (3): 301–321.

D'Costa, A.P. (1999). *The Global Restructuring of the Steel Industry: Innovations, Institutions, and Industrial Change*, London: Routledge.

D'Costa, A.P. (2000). "Capitalist Maturity and Corporate Responses to Liberalization: The Steel, Auto, and Software Sectors in India," special issue on Corporate Capitalism, *Contemporary South Asia*, 9 (2): 141–163.

D'Costa, A.P. (2002). "Export Growth and Path-Dependence: The Locking-in of Innovations in the Software Industry," *Science, Technology and Society*, 7 (1): 51–89.

D'Costa, A.P. (2003a). "Uneven and Combined Development: Understanding India's Software Exports," *World Development*, 13 (1): 211–226.

D'Costa, A.P. (2003b). "Institutions and Industrial Governance in India: Learning Cooperation the Japanese Way," *Asian Business and Management Journal*, 2 (1): 63–89.

D'Costa, A.P. (2005). *The Long March to Capitalism: Embourgeoisment, Internationalization, and Industrial Transformation in India*, Basingstoke: Palgrave Macmillan.

D'Costa, A.P. (2006). "ICTs and Decoupled Development: Theories, Trajectories and Transitions," in Parayil, G. (ed.), *Political Economy & Information Capitalism in India: Digital Divide, Development Divide and Equity*, Basingstoke: Palgrave Macmillan, pp. 11–34.

D'Costa, A.P. (2009). "Extensive Growth and Innovation Challenges in Bangalore, India," in Parayil, G. and D'Costa, A.P. (eds.), *The New Asian Innovation Dynamics: China and India in Perspective*, Basingstoke: Palgrave Macmillan, pp. 79–109.

D'Costa, A.P. (2011). "Geography, Uneven Development and Distributive Justice: The Political Economy of IT Growth in India," *Cambridge Journal of Regions, Economy and Society*, 4 (2): 237–251.

D'Costa, A.P. (2013). "Globalization, the Middle Class and the Transformation of the Indian State in the New Economy," in Bhattacharya, S. (ed.), *Two Decades of Market Reform in India: Some Dissenting Views*, London: Anthem Press, pp. 125–141.

D'Costa, A.P. (2014a). "Compressed Capitalism and Development: Primitive Accumulation, Petty Commodity Production, and Capitalist Maturity in India and China," *Critical Asian Studies*, 6 (2): 317–344.

D'Costa, A.P. (2014b). "Compressed Capitalism and the Challenges for Inclusive Development in India," in Dutta, D. (ed.), *Inclusive Growth and Development in Two Emerging Economic Giants of China and India in 21st Century*, Singapore: World Scientific and Imperial College Press, pp. 161–189.

D'Costa, A.P. (2016a). "Compressed Capitalism and the Fate of Indian Development," in Sita Venkateswar, S. and Sekhar Bandyopadhyay, S. (eds.), *Globalization, Economy and Challenges of Development in Contemporary India*, New Delhi: Springer, pp. 19–39.

D'Costa, A.P. (2016b). *International Mobility, Global Capitalism, and Changing Structures of Accumulation: Transforming the Japan-India IT Relationship*, London: Routledge.

D'Costa, A.P. (2017). "A Point of No Return? Changing Structures and Jobless Growth in India," ESRC (UK) and Global Challenges Research Fund (UK) sponsored *Structural Change, Inequality and Inclusive Growth: Tensions and Trade-offs* panel, EADI Nordic Conference 2017, Globalisation at the Crossroads: Rethinking Inequalities and Boundaries, Bergen, Norway.

D'Costa, A.P. (2019). "Compressed Capitalism and a Critical Reading of the State's Employment Challenges," in D'Costa, A.P., and Chakraborty, A. (eds.), *Changing Contexts and Shifting Roles of the Indian State: New Perspectives on Development Dynamics*, Singapore: Springer, pp. 127–153.

D'Costa, A.P. (2022). "Capitalist Progress and Moral Economy: Sustaining Employment in India's Handloom Sector," *Journal of Asian and African Studies*, 57 (2): 269–288.

D'Costa, A.P. (2023). "Closed Loop, Open Borders: Wealth Inequality and Uneven and Combined Development in India, *Journal of Contemporary Asia*", 53 (4): 668–692.

D'Costa, A.P. (2025a). "State, Business Association, and Diaspora: The Structure of Governance in the Indian IT-BPM Sector," *Studies in Comparative International Development*," 60: 412–440, https://doi.org/10.1007/s12116-025-09459-1.

D'Costa, A.P. (2025b). "The Making of a "New" Space Economy," in D'Costa, A.P. (ed.), *The Oxford Handbook of the New Space Economy*, Oxford: Oxford University Press, pp. 3–26.

D'Costa, A.P. (2025c). "Structures of Inequality and International Mobility of the Wealthy and Talent from Asia," *Fudan Journal of the Humanities and Social Sciences*, 1–27, https://doi.org/10.1007/s40647-025-00455-2.

D'Costa, A.P. (2027a). "Forever Amby," in Garimella, A. (ed.), *Designing India: 1947 to the Present*, (forthcoming).

D'Costa, A.P. (2027b). "Chetan Maini's Eco-Minimalism," in Garimella, A. (ed.), *Designing India: 1947 to the Present*, (forthcoming).

D'Costa, A.P. and Chakraborty, A. (eds.) (2017). *The Land Question in India: State, Dispossession, and Capitalist Transition*, Oxford: Oxford University Press.

Datt, R. (1994). "Jobless Growth: Implications of New Economic Policies," *Indian Journal of Industrial Relations*, 29 (4): 407–427.

Deloitte (2018). *Industry 4.0 in Food Industry: India Food Report*, Bengaluru: Deloitte.

Deshpande, A. (2023). "Long-Term Impact of COVID-19 on the Indian Labour Market," *The Indian Journal of Labour Economics*, 66: 951–959.

Dewan, S., Kashyap, P. and Meyers, Z. (2025). *Navigating the Revolution: Policy Recommendations for Inclusive AI*, Issue Paper, Brussels: Centre on Regulation in Europe (CERRE).

Dezan Shira and Associates (2025). *A Guide to Minimum Wage in India in 2025*, May 21, 2025, https://www.india-briefing.com/news/guide-minimum-wage-india-19406.html/, accessed July 12, 2025.

Dhar, B. (2024). "PLI: On the Way to Another Failed Incentive Scheme?" *The India Forum*, February 2024.

DHL (2025). *Guide to Production-Linked Incentive (PLI) Schemes: What Are They, How They Work*, https://www.dhl.com/discover/en-in/logistics-advice/logistics-insights/what-is-a-pli-scheme.

Domhoff, G.W. (2006). *Who Rules America: Power, Politics, and Social Change*, New York: McGraw Hill.

Donner, J. and Locke, C. (2019). "Platforms at the Margins," in Graham, M. (ed.), *Digital Economies at Global Margins*, Cambridge: MIT Press, pp. 39–41.

Economic Policy Institute (2012). *Apple's iPhone Profits Dwarf Its Labor Costs*, April 18, 2012, https://www.epi.org/blog/apple-iphone-profits-dwarf-labor-costs/, accessed November 5, 2023.

Economic Times, April 24, (2022). *India's Oil Import Bill Doubles to $119 Billion in FY22*, https://economictimes.indiatimes.com/industry/energy/oil-gas/indias-oil-import-bill-doubles-to-usd-119-bn-in-fy22/articleshow/91049349.cms.

Engelshoven, M. (1999). "Diamonds and Patels: A Report on the Diamond Industry in Surat," *Contributions to Indian Sociology*, 33 (1&2): 353–377.

Ethiraj, G. (2024). "The Future of Electric Mobility with Chetan Maini," *The Core Report*, YouTube, July 12, 2024, https://www.youtube.com/watch?v=vuB9hQ0hnj0, accessed March 24, 2025.

Eximpedia (2025). India's Crude Oil Import Data: A Detailed Analysis (2025), September 25, 2024. https://www.eximpedia.app/blog/crude-oil-import-in-india, accessed October 18, 2024.

Export-Import Bank of India (2018). Indian Handloom Industry: Potential and Prospects, (Working Paper No. 80), September 2018.

Fairwork India (2020). *Fairwork India Ratings 2020: Labour Standards in the Platform Economy*, https://fair.work/en/fw/homepage/

Federal Reserve Bank of St. Louis. 2019. *GINI Index for Sweden, Economic Data.* https://fred.stlouisfed.org/series/SIPOVGINISWE, accessed November 19, 2019.

Ford, M. (2015). *Rise of the Robots: Technology and the Threat of a Jobless Future*, New York: Basic Books.

FRED (2025). *Real Gross Fixed Capital Formation for India*, https://fred.stlouisfed.org/series/NFIRNSAXDCINQ, accessed August 10, 2025.

Furtado, C. (1963). *The Economic Growth of Brazil: A Survey from Colonial to Modern Times*, Berkeley: University of California Press.

Furtado, C. (1964). *Development and Underdevelopment: A Structural View of the Problems of Developed and Underdeveloped Countries*, Berkeley: University of California Press.

Furtado, C. (1976). *Economic Development of Latin America*, Cambridge: Cambridge University Press.

Gandhi, A. and Walton, M. (2012). "Where Do India's Billionaires Get Their Wealth?," *Economic and Political Weekly*, 47 (40): 10–14.

Gautam, M. and Yu, B. (2015). "Agricultural Productivity Growth and Drivers: A Comparative Study of China and India," *China Agricultural Economic Review*, 7 (4): 573–600.

Gerschenkron, A. (1962). *Economic Backwardness in Historical Perspective: A Book of Essays*, Cambridge: Harvard University Press.

Ghose, A.K. (2016). *India Employment Report 2016: Challenges and the Imperative of Manufacturing-Led Growth*, Institute for Human Development, Delhi: Oxford University Press.

Ghosh, J. (2025). *The FDI Reversal and the Message*, June 11, 2025, IDEAS, https://www.networkideas.org/2025/06/11/the-fdi-reversal-and-the-message/

GIZ (Deutsche Gesellschaft für Internationale Zusammenarbeit (GIZ) GmbH) (2022). *Digitalisation and the Indian Labour Market: Trends, Challenges, and Opportunities*, Bonn: GIZ.

Gnanaraj, C. and Mohapatra, S. (2014). "Internal and International Remittances in India: Implications for Household Expenditure and Poverty," Presented at the KNOMAD International Conference on Internal Migration and Urbanization held in Dhaka on April 30–May 1, 2014.

Government of India, Ministry of Commerce and Industry (2022). *Trade Statistics*, https://commerce.gov.in/trade-statistics/, accessed March 2, 2023.

Government of India, Ministry of Commerce and Industry, Department of Commerce (2025). *Trade and Economic Relations*, https://eoibeijing.gov.in/eoibejing_pages/MjQ.

Government of India, Ministry of Communications, Press Information Bureau (2024). *Highlights of Telecom Subscription Data as on 31st October, 2024*, https://www.pib.gov.in/PressReleasePage.aspx?PRID=2087254, accessed February 18, 2025.

Government of India, Ministry of Finance (2004). *Economic Survey 2004*, New Delhi: Ministry of Finance.

Government of India, Ministry of Power (2022). *Power Sector at a Glance, All India*, https://powermin.gov.in/en/content/power-sector-glance-all-india, accessed May 23, 2022.

Government of India, Ministry of Textiles (2015). *Note on Handloom Sector, Office of the Development Commissioner (Handlooms)*, pp. 1–28. http://handlooms.nic.in/writereaddata/2486.pdf.

Government of India, Ministry of Textiles (2019). *Fourth All India Handloom Census 2019–20*, New Delhi: Office of the Development Commissioner for Handlooms Ministry of Textiles Government of India.

Government of India, National Commission on Enterprises in the Unorganised Sector (NCEUS) (2007). *Reports on the Financing of Enterprises in the Unorganised Sector and Creation of National Fund for The Unorganised Sector*, New Delhi: National Commission on Enterprises in the Unorganised Sector, https://dcmsme.gov.in/Report_on_NCEUS_NAFUS.pdf, accessed April 12, 2018.

Government of India, National Commission on Enterprises in the Unorganised Sector (2007). *Reports on the Financing of Enterprises in the Unorganised Sector and Creation of National Fund for the Unorganised Sector*, New Delhi: Government of India, http://nceuis.nic.in/Report_on_NCEUS_NAFUS.pdf, accessed September 15, 2012.

Government of India, National Commission for Enterprises in the Unorganised Sector (2009). *Report on Conditions of Work and Promotion of Livelihoods in the Unorganised Sector*, New Delhi: National Commission on Enterprises in the Unorganised Sector, https://dcmsme.gov.in/condition_of_workers_sep_2007.pdf.

Government of West Bengal (2017). *Biswa Bangla: Tanna Poren*, Kolkata: Department of Industry, Commerce, and Enterprises.

Goyal, D. (2025). *Zomato Delivery Partners Earn Rs. 28,000 Monthly on Average*, February 4, 2025, https://yourstory.com/2025/02/zomato-delivery-partners-earn-rs-28-000-monthly-gig-workers-deepinder-goyal, accessed April 19, 2025.

Goyal, T.M., Kukreja, P. and Kedia, M. (2022). *MSMEs Go Digital: Leveraging Technology to Sustain during the Covid-19 Crisis*, New Delhi: India Council for Research on International Economic Relations (ICRIER).

Griffith, B. (2011). "Middle-Income Trap," in Nallari, R., Yusuf, S., Griffith, B. and Bhattacharyaa, R. (eds.), *Frontiers in Development Policy: A Primer on Emerging Issues*, Washington DC: World Bank Publications, pp. 45–48.

Gulati, A., Ganguly, K. and Wardhan, H. (eds.) (2022). *Agricultural Value Chains in India: Ensuring Competitiveness, Inclusiveness, Sustainability, Scalability, and Improved Finance*, Singapore: Springer Nature.

Halal, W., Kolber, J. and Davies, O. (2016). "Forecasts of AI and Future Jobs in 2030: Muddling Through Likely, with Two Alternative Scenarios," *Journal of Futures Studies*, 21 (2): 83–96.

Hall, P.A. and Soskice, D. (eds.), (2001). *Varieties of Capitalism: The Institutional Foundations of Comparative Advantage*, Oxford: Oxford University Press.

Heeks, R. (1996). *India's Software Industry: State Policy, Liberalisation and Industrial Development*, New Delhi: Sage.

Heeks, R. (2010). *Indian IT Sector Statistics: 1980–2009 Time Series Data, ICTs for Development*, https://ict4dblog.wordpress.com/2010/01/05/indian-it-sector-statistics-1980-2009-time-series-data/

Himanshu, L. L. and Philipp Schirmer, P. (2025). "Prices, Poverty Lines, and Poverty in 2022–23," *Economic & Political Weekly*, LX (10): 34–42.

Hindustan Motors Limited, Department of Economics and Market Research (1966). *The Automobile Industry in India: A Study*, Calcutta: Hindustan Motors Limited.

Hirway, I. (2009). *Losing the Sparkle: Impact of the Global Crisis on the Diamond Cutting and Polishing Industry in India*, New Delhi: United Nations Development Programme (UNDP), India.

Hoogvelt, A.M.M. (2001). *Globalization and the Postcolonial World: The New Political Economy of Development*, Baltimore: Johns Hopkins University Press.

IBEF Agriculture (2023). *Agriculture in India: Information About Indian Agriculture & Its Importance*, https://ibef.org/industry/agriculture-india, accessed January 27, 2024.

IBEF Auto Components (2025). *Auto Components Industry in India*, https://ibef.org/industry/autocomponents-india, accessed July 19, 2025.

IBEF Automobiles (2025). *Automobile Industry in India*, https://ibef.org/industry/india-automobiles, accessed July 20, 2025.

IBEF Gems and Jewellery (2021). *Gems and Jewellery Industry in India*, https://ibef.org/industry/gems-jewellery-india, accessed April 20, 2023.

IBEF Gems and Jewellery (2025). *Gems and Jewellery Industry in India*, https://ibef.org/industry/gems-jewellery-india, accessed February 20, 2025.

IBEF IT and BPM (2025). *IT and BPM Industry in India*, https://ibef.org/industry/information-technology-india, accessed June 22, 2025.

IBEF Oil and Gas (2021). *Oil and Gas Industry Report*, https://www.ibef.org/industry/oil-gas-india, accessed July 19, 2024.

IBEF Pharmaceuticals (2025). *Indian Pharmaceutical Industry*, https://ibef.org/industry/pharmaceutical-india, accessed August 27, 2025.

IBEF Power (2022). *Power Sector in India*, https://ibef.org/industry/power-sector-india, accessed July 19, 2024.

IBEF Power Industry (2022). *Power Industry Report*, https://www.ibef.org/industry/power-sector-india, accessed July 19, 2024.

IBEF Steel (2025). *Iron and Steel Industry in India*, https://ibef.org/industry/steel, accessed April 10, 2025.

IBM (2022). *What Is Industry 4.0?*, https://www.ibm.com/topics/industry-4-0, accessed October 25, 2024.

IBS Center for Management Research (2003). *Dhirubai Ambani and Reliance*, Hyderabad: IBS Center for Management Research, LDEN011.

ILO (2025). *Decent Work*, https://www.ilo.org/topics-and-sectors/decent-work, accessed August 12, 2025.

IMF (2025). *India: Profile*, https://www.imf.org/external/datamapper/profile/IND, accessed August 1, 2025.

India Brand Equity Foundation (IBEF) (2025). IT and BPM Industry Report. [Online]. https://www.ibef.org/, accessed July 2, 2025.

India Today (2003). *Indian Automobile Exports Zoom, Thanks to World-Class Technology, Innovation, Pricing*, September 1, 2023, https://www.indiatoday.in/magazine/economy/story/20030901-indian-automobile-exports-zoom-thanks-to-world-class-technology-innovation-pricing-792211-2003-09-01, accessed August 17, 2024.

Indian Pharmaceutical Alliance (2019). *The Indian Pharmaceutical Industry: The Way Forward*, Mumbai: Indian Pharmaceutical Alliance.

Indian Pharmaceutical Association (2019). *The Indian Pharmaceutical Industry and Global Market*, https://www.ipa-india.org/wp-content/uploads/2019/09/The-Indian-Pharmaceutical-Industry-global-market-September-2019-IIM-A.pdf, accessed September 24, 2024.

International Bank for Reconstruction and Development/The World Bank (2019). *Doing Business 2019: Training for Reform*, Washington DC: International Bank for Reconstruction and Development/The World Bank.

International Energy Agency (2021). *India Energy Outlook 2021, World Energy Outlook Special Report*, IEA, https://iea.blob.core.windows.net/assets/1de6d91e-e23f-4e02-b1fb-51fdd6283b22/India_Energy_Outlook_2021.pdf, accessed March 2, 2024.

Ishwarbharath, S. and Suresh, H. (2025). *India Tech Giant TCS Layoffs Herald AI Shakeup of $283 Billion Outsourcing Sector*, August 7, 2025, https://www.reuters.com/business/world-at-work/india-tech-giant-tcs-layoffs-herald-ai-shakeup-283-billion-outsourcing-sector-2025-08-08/?utm, accessed August 31, 2025.

Jaffrelot, C. (2019). "Business-Friendly Gujarat Under Narendra Modi: The Implications of a New Political Economy," in Jaffrelot, C., Kohli, A. and Murali, K. (eds.), *Business and Politics in India*, New York: Oxford University Press, pp. 211–233.

Jaffrelot, C. (2021). *Modi's India: Hindu Nationalism and the Rise of Ethnic Democracy*, Princeton: Princeton University Press.

Jaffrelot, C., Kohli, A. and Murali, K. (eds.) (2019). *Business & Politics in India*, New York: Oxford University Press.

Jalote, P. and Natarajan, P. (2019). "The Growth and Evolution of India's Software Industry," *Communications of the ACM*, 62 (11): 64–69.

Jenkins, R. (1999). *Democratic Politics and Economic Reform in India*, Cambridge: Cambridge University Press.

Jenkins, R. (1987). *Transnational Corporations and Uneven Development: The Internationalization of Capital and the Third World*, London: Routledge, Kegan and Paul.

Jose, S. and Hussain, S. (2025). "Is Poverty in India Really Down to 5% as Estimated by the World Bank?," *The Wire*, https://thewire.in/economy/is-poverty-in-india-really-down-to-5-as-estimated-by-the-world-bank, accessed July 3, 2025.

Kaldor, N. (1967). *Strategic Factors in Economic Development*, Ithaca: Cornell.

Kannan, K.P. and Raveendran, G. (2009). "Growth Sans Employment: A Quarter Century of Jobless Growth in India's Organised Manufacturing," *Economic and Political Weekly*, 44 (10): 80–91.

Kapoor, R. (2014). "Creating 'Good Jobs': Assessing the Labour Market Regulation Debate," *Economic and Political Weekly*, XLIX, 46: 16–18.

Kapur, M., Dawar, S. and Ahuja, V.R. (2014). "Unlocking the Wealth in Rural Markets," *Harvard Business Review*, R1406J-PDF-ENG: 1–6.

Kathuria, R., Kedia, M. and Bagchi, K. (2021). *India's Platform Economy and Emerging Regulatory Challenges*, New Delhi: India Council for Research on International Economic Relations (ICRIER), (Working Paper No. 407).

Kaushik, K. and Jayaram, K. (2024). *What were India's Electoral Bonds and How Did They Power Modi's Party?* February 16, 2024, https://www.reuters.com/world/india/what-were-indias-electoral-bonds-how-did-they-power-modis-party-2024-02-16/, accessed July 11, 2025.

Kenney, M., Bearson, D. and Zysman, J. (2021). "The Platform Economy Matures: Measuring Pervasiveness and Exploring Power," *Socio-Economic Review*, 19 (4): 1451–1483.

Khasnabis, R. and Nag, P. (2001). "Labour Process in the Informal Sector: A Handloom Industry in Nadia District," *Economic and Political Weekly*, 36 (52): 4836–4845.

Khera, R. (2018). "The Aadhaar Debate: Where Are the Sociologists?," *Contributions to Indian Sociology*, 52 (3): 336–342.

Kochanek, S.A. (1974). *Business and Politics in India*, Berkeley: University of California Press.

Kohli, A. (1990). *Democracy and Discontent: India's Growing Crisis of Governability*, Cambridge: Cambridge University Press.

Kohli, A. (2009). "India's Fragmented-Multiclass State and Protected Industrialization," in Kohli, A. (ed.), *Democracy and Development in India: From Socialism to Pro-Business*, New Delhi: Oxford University Press, pp. 107–139.

Koo, H. (2019). "Rising Inequality and Shifting Class Boundaries in South Korea in the Neo-Liberal Era," *Journal of Contemporary Asia*, 51 (1): 1–19.

Krishnan, J., Mischke, J. and Remes, M. (2018). *Solving the Productivity Puzzle: The Role of Demand and the Promise of Digitization*, McKinsey Global Institute, International Productivity Monitor, Number 35, http://www.csls.ca/ipm/35/Remes-Mischke-Krishnan.pdf, accessed May 9, 2025.

Lakha, S. (2019). "Social Protection and the State in India: The Challenge of Extracting Accountability," in D'Costa, A.P. and Chakraborty, A. (eds.), *Changing Contexts and Shifting Roles of the Indian State: New Perspectives on Development Dynamics*, Singapore: Springer, pp. 105–125.

Lewin, A.Y., Kenney, M. and Murmann, J.P. (2016). "China's Innovation Challenge: An Introduction," in Lewin, A.Y., Kenney, M. and Murmann, J.P. (eds.), *China's Innovation Challenge: Overcoming the Middle-Income Trap*, Cambridge: Cambridge University Press, pp. 1–31.

Lewis, W.A. (1954). "Economic Development with Unlimited Supplies of Labour," *The Manchester School*, 22 (2): 139–199.

Luce, E. (2008). *In Spite of the Gods: The Rise of Modern India*. New York: Anchor Books.

Macrotrends (2022). *China Poverty Rate 1990 to 2022*, https://www.macrotrends.net/countries/CHN/china/poverty-rate, accessed July 11, 2024.

Mamidipudi, A., Syamasundari, B. and Bijker, W. (2012). "Mobilising Discourses: Handloom as Sustainable Socio-Technology," *Economic and Political Weekly*, XLVIII (25): 41–51.

Marathe, S.S. (1989). *Regulation and Development: India's Policy Experience of Controls Over Industry*, New Delhi: Sage Publications.

Marjit, S. and Kar, S. (2011). *The Outsiders: Economic Reform and Informal Labour in a Developing Economy*, New Delhi: Oxford University Press.

Matthess, M. and Kunkel, S. (2020). "Structural Change and Digitalization in Developing Countries: Conceptually Linking the Two Transformations," *Technology in Society*, 63, https://doi.org/10.1016/j.techsoc.2020.101428, accessed March 19, 2025.

Mayer, J. (2018). "Robots and Industrialization: What Policies for Inclusive Growth?" Working Paper commissioned by the Group of 24 and Friedrich-Ebert-Stiftung New York, August 2018.

Mazumdar, S. (2025). "The Ugly Underbelly of 'Emergence': Indian Capitalism in the Era of Globalization," Trajectories of Declining and Destructive Capitalism, *Research in Political Economy*, 40: 199–213.

McNeil, D.G. (2001). "Indian Company Offers to Supply AIDS Drugs at Low Cost in Africa," *New York Times*, February 7, 2001, https://www.nytimes.com/2001/02/07/world/indian-company-offers-to-supply-aids-drugs-at-low-cost-in-africa.html, accessed March 3, 2023.

Michael and Susan Dell Foundation and Boston Consulting Global (2021). *Unlocking the Potential of the Gig Economy in India*, Boston Consulting Global.

Miklian, J. (2013). "Rough Cut," *Foreign Policy*, 31–35, https://foreignpolicy.com/2013/01/02/rough-cut/.

Mistree, D. (2019). "From Produce and Protect to Promoting Private Industry: The Indian State's Role in Creating a Domestic Software Industry," *Stanford Law School*, (Working Paper No. 07-2018). Updated 06-2019.

Mody, A. (2023). *India Is Broken: A People Betrayed, Independence to Today*, Stanford: Stanford University Press.

Mohanty, P. (2022). *An Unkept Promise: What Derailed the Indian Economy*, New Delhi: Sage Publications.

Money, D. (2025). "Synthetic Stones Are Sinking Botswana's Diamond-Based Economy," *World Politics Review*, accessed June 12, 2025.

Mukherjee, A. (2025). "The Great Unease of Doing Business in India: How Make in India Is Losing its Way in a Bureaucratic Maze," *Economic Times*, January 17, 2025, https://economictimes.indiatimes.com/news/economy/policy/the-great-unease-of-doing-business-in-india-how-make-in-india-is-losing-its-way-in-a-bureaucratic-maze/articleshow/117318837.cms?utm_source=contentofinterest&utm_medium=text&utm_campaign=cppst, accessed May 12, 2025.

Mukherji, R. (2013). "Ideas, Interests, and the Tipping Point: Economic Change in India," *Review of International Political Economy*, 20 (2): 363–389.

Murali, K. (2019). "Economic Liberalization and the Structural Power of Business," in Jaffrelot, C., Kohli, A. and Murali, K. (eds.), *Business and Politics in India*, New York: Oxford University Press, pp. 25–49.

Myrdal, G. (1957). *Rich Lands and Poor: The Road to World Prosperity*, New York: Harper and Row.

Nagaraj, R. (2007). "Are Labour Regulations Holding Up India's Growth and Exports? A Review of Analysis and Evidence," *Paper Prepared for National Commission on Enterprises in the Unorganised Sector (NCEUS), New Delhi.*

Nagaraj, R. (2025). "India's Premature Deindustrialization and Falling Investment Rate in the 2010s," *World Development*, 191: 1–16, https://doi.org/10.1016/j.worlddev.2025.106954, accessed August 5, 2025.

National Bureau of Statistics, UN Population Fund, and UNICEF (2018). *Domestic Migrants in China (2018): Trends, Challenges and Recommendations*, https://china.unfpa.org/en/report/20190816, accessed July 23, 2024.

Nayar, B.R. (1990). *The Political Economy of India's Public Sector: Policy and Performance*, Bombay: Popular Prakashan.

Nayyar, D. (2008). "The Internationalization of Firms from India: Investment, Mergers and Acquisitions," *Oxford Development Studies*, 36 (1): 111–131.

Nayyar, D. (2019). "India's Path to Structural Transformation: An Exception," in Liu, J.Y. and Monga, C. (eds.), *The Oxford Handbook of Structural Transformation*, Oxford: Oxford University Press, pp. 465–488, https://doi.org/10.1093/oxfordhb/9780198793847.001.0001.

Nayyar, D. and Nayyar, G. (2024). "Made in India: Industrial Policy in a Changing World," *Journal of Industry, Competition and Trade*, 24 (13): 1–27, https://doi.org/10.1007/s10842-024-00417-6.

NITI Aayog (2022). *India's Booming Gig and Platform Economy: Perspectives and Recommendations on the Future of Work*, New Delhi: National Institution of Transforming India.

NITI Aayog and Rocky Mountain Institute (2021). *Mobilising Finance for EVs in India: A Toolkit of Solutions to Mitigate Risks and Address Market Barriers*, New Delhi: NITI Aayog.

Norton, A. (2017). Automation and Inequality: The Changing World of Work in the Global South, International Institute for Environment and Development, Issue Paper 217.

OECD (2021). *Economic Outlook for Southeast Asia, China and India 2021: Reallocating Resources for Digitalisation*, Paris: OECD.

OECD (2025). *Science, Technology and Innovation Scoreboard: Explore the Data*, https://www.oecd.org/en/data/datasets/science-technology-and-innovation-scoreboard.html.

Organisation of Pharmaceutical Producers of India, with Boston Consulting Group (2019). "Leapfrogging Health Outcomes in India," Mumbai.

Our World in Data (2025). https://ourworldindata.org/grapher/gini-index-around-2015-1990-2015-countries-vs-gini-index-around-1990-1990-2015-countries, accessed August 29, 2025.

Pager, T. and Aleaziz, H. (2025). "Trump Says the U.S. Will Institute $100,000 Fee for Skilled Worker Visas," *New York Times*, September 19, 2025, https://www.nytimes.com/2025/09/19/us/politics/trump-h-1b-visas-fee.html, accessed September 19, 2025.

Pai, S., Pagaria, A., Savithiri, N. and Trehan, D. (2025). *Indus Valley Annual Report 2015*, Blume Ventures.

Parthasarathy, B., Srinivasan, J., and Bilahari, M., et al. (2025). "The Developmental Possibilities of Gig Work on Digital Platforms: The Limits to the Hope and Hype in India," *The Indian Journal of Labour Economics*, 68: 569–587.

Pathak, A.A. and Kandathil, G. (2020). "Strategizing in Small Informal Retailers in India: Home Delivery as a Strategic Practice," *Asia Pacific Journal of Management*, 37: 851–877.

Paul, M. and Kumar, R.A. (2020). "*Import Intensity of India's Manufactured Exports: An Industry Level Analysis*," Institute for Studies in Industrial Development, New Delhi, (Working Paper No. 220).

Piketty, T. (2014). *Capital in the Twenty-first Century*, Cambridge: Harvard University Press.

Piketty, T. (2017). *Capital in the Twenty-first Century*, Cambridge: Harvard University Press.

Pingali, P., Aiyer, A., Abraham, M. and Rahman, A. (2019). *Transforming Food Systems for a Rising India*, Cham, Switzerland: Palgrave Macmillan.

Pistilli, M. (2025). *Rare Earth Reserves: Top 8 Countries*, February 5, 2025, https://investingnews.com/daily/resource-investing/critical-metals-investing/rare-earth-investing/rare-earth-reserves-country/, accessed June 12, 2025.

Prahalad, C.K. and Hammond, A. (2002). "Serving the World's Poor, Profitably," *Harvard Business Review*, Reprint R0209C.

PwC (2019). *The Indian Steel Industry: Growth, Challenges and Digital Disruption*, https://www.pwc.in/assets/pdfs/consulting/technology/the-indian-steel-industry-growth-challenges-and-digital-disruption.pdf, accessed April 19, 2025.

Pyper, J. (2021). *How Long Will Coal Remain King in India?* Greentech Media, Part III, https://www.greentechmedia.com/articles/read/coal-king-india, accessed July 15, 2024.

Rajan, R.G. and Lamba, R. (2023). *Breaking the Mold: India's Untraveled Path to Prosperity*, Princeton: Princeton University Press.

Rajdou, N., Prabhu, J. and Ahuja, S. (2012). *Jugaad Innovation: Think Frugal, Be Flexible, Generate Breakthrough Growth*, San Francisco: Jossy-Bass.

Rajeev, M. (2017). "Changing Structure of Non-Performing Loans: The Case of Indian Public Banks," in Scherrer, C. (ed.), *Public Banks in the Age of Financialization: A Comparative Perspective*, Cheltenham: Edward Elgar, pp. 212–229.
Ramamurti, R. (1987). *State-owned Enterprises in High Technology Industries: Studies in India and Brazil*, Ann Arbor: University of Michigan Press.
Ramphal, N. (2022). Zomato, PayTM, Nykaa: How Investors Have Lost Big Time After These Big Tech IPOs, *The Print*, https://theprint.in/economy/zomato-paytm-nykaa-how-investors-have-lost-big-time-after-these-big-tech-ipos/1056410/, accessed May 18, 2024.
Rao, I. and Bhatnagar, D. (2009). "Surviving the Recession: Venus Jewel -A Case Study from the Indian Diamond Industry," *Vikalpa*, 34 (3): 79–99.
Rao, I. and von Glinow, M.A. (2012). "The Emergence of the Informal Sector Firms in International Business: The Globally Distributed Indian Diamond Industry," *Indian Management Journal*, 3 (4): 18–30.
Reserve Bank of India (2025). *Foreign Investment Flows, RBI Bulletin*, https://rbi.org.in/scripts/BS_ViewBulletin.aspx?Id=23489, accessed August 19, 2025.
Richman, B.D. (2009). "Ethnic Networks, Extra-legal Certainty and Globalisation: Peering into the Diamond Industry," in Volkmar, G. (ed.), *Contractual Certainty in International Trade: Empirical Studies and Theoretical Debates on Institutional Support for Global Economic Exchanges*, Oxford: Hart Publishing, pp. 31–47.
Rifkin, J. (1995). *The End of Work: The Decline of the Global Labor Force and the Dawn of the Post-Market Era*, New York: Putnam Publishing.
Robinson, J. (1962). *Economic Philosophy*, Harmondsworth: Pelican Books.
Rodrik, D. (2016). "Premature Deindustrialization," *Journal of Economic Growth*, 21: 1–33.
Roy, T. (1998). "Development or Distortion? 'Powerlooms' in India, 1950–1997," *Economic and Political Weekly*, 33 (16): 897–911.
Roy, T. (n.d.). *Indian Handlooms in the 20th Century*, http://www.digitalis.uni-koeln.de/JWG/jwg_146_129-139.pdf, Accessed 02/13/2017.
Saez, L. (2014). "India: From Failed Developmental State Towards Hybrid Market Capitalism," in Witt, M.A. and Redding, G. (eds.), *The Oxford Handbook of Asian Business Systems*, Oxford: Oxford University Press, pp. 55–78.
Saha, S. (2025). "India's Distressed Farmers Limit Modi's Leeway in Trump Trade Talks," *Nikkei*, November 1, 2025, https://asia.nikkei.com/spotlight/big-in-asia/india-s-distressed-farmers-limit-modi-s-leeway-in-trump-trade-talks?utm.
Saikia, D. (2009). "Agriculture-Industry Interlinkages: Some Theoretical and Methodological Issues in the Indian Context," *Munich Personal RePEc Archive*, (MPRA Paper No. 27820).
Saldinger, A. (2018). "How India Became a Leader in Low-Cost, High-Quality Eye Care," Devex, *Gates Foundation*, October 31, 2028, https://www.devex.com/news/how-india-became-a-leader-in-low-cost-high-quality-eye-care-93749, accessed January 12, 2025.
Samaddar, R. (2008). *Primitive Accumulation and Some Aspects of Work and Life in India in the Early Part of the Twenty-first Century*. Mahanirban Calcutta Research Group. www.mcrg.ac.in/pp20.pdf, accessed October 7, 2012.
Sampath, K. (2024). The Visa That Divided MAGA, *Juggernaut*, December 31, 2024, https://www.thejuggernaut.com/h1b-indian-immigrants-racism-musk-maga-civil-war?s=cmfutlpry000rs601byqjsfpg, accessed September 12, 2025.
Sandefur, J. (2022). "The Great Indian Poverty Debate, 2.0," *Center for Global Development* April 19, 2022, https://www.cgdev.org/blog/great-indian-poverty-debate-20, accessed April 25, 2022.
Sanyal, K.K. (2007). *Rethinking Capitalist Development: Primitive Accumulation, Governmentality and Post-colonial Capitalism*. New Delhi: Routledge India.
Sarma, M. and Krishna, V.V. (2010). "State and the Software: Public Policies in the Shaping of the Indian Software Sector," *The Service Industries Journal*, 30 (1): 25–42.

Schaede, U. and Shimizu, K. (2022). *The Digital Transformation and Japan's Political Economy*, Cambridge: Cambridge University Press.

Sen, A. and Ghosh, J. (2017). "Indian Agriculture after Liberalisation," *Bangladesh Development Studies*, XXXX (1&2): 53–71.

Sen, K. (2025). "Labour Market Inequality in India over Three Decades," *Economic & Political Weekly*, LX (23): 44–51.

Sen, K., Kar, S. and Sahu, J. (2018). "The Stroll, the Trot, and the Sprint of the Elephant: Understanding Indian Growth Episodes," in Pritchett, L., Sen, K. and Werker, E. (eds.), *Deals and Development: The Political Dynamics of Growth Episodes*, Oxford: Oxford University Press, pp. 250–284.

Sen, P. (2005). *Task Force to Explore Options other than Price Control for Achieving the Objective of Making Available Life-saving Drugs at Reasonable Prices*, Delhi: Submitted to the Department of Chemicals & Petrochemicals, Government of India.

Sen, S. (2006). *Diversification Strategies in Emerging Markets with Special Reference to Indian Business Groups*, PhD Thesis, Department of Business Administration, Faculty of Management Studies and Research, Aligarh Muslim University, Aligarh (India).

Sethu, C.A., Abhinav Surya, L.T. and Ruthu, C.A. (2024). "Poverty in India: The Rangarajan Method and the 2022–23 Household Consumption Expenditure Survey," *Review of Agrarian Studies*, 14 (2): 3–22.

Sharma, A.N. and Mehta, B.S. (2024). "India's Growth and Employment Patterns: A Four-decade Perspective (1983–2024)," *Economic and Political Weekly*, LIX (50): 38–53.

Sharma, D. (2009). *The Long Revolution: The Birth and Growth of Indian IT Industry*, New Delhi: HarperCollins Publishers.

Shastry, V. (2024). *Roadblocks to India's Manufacturing Renaissance*, Hinrich Foundation Report, 1–17.

Siddiqui, D.M. (2025). "What's Happening in Bangladesh's Garment Industry?" *Economics Observatory*, March 26, 2025, https://www.economicsobservatory.com/whats-happening-in-bangladeshs-garment-industry, accessed April 3, 2025.

Singh, J. (2020). "Small Farmers and Organised Retail Chains in India," *Economic and Political Weekly*, 55 (26–27), https://www.epw.in/journal/2020/26-27/review-rural-affairs/small-farmers-and-organised-retail-chains-india.html.

Sinha, A. (2005). *The Regional Roots of Developmental Politics in India*, Bloomington: Indiana University Press.

Sinha, A. (2019). "India's Porous State: Blurred Boundaries and the Evolving Business-State Relationship," in Jaffrelot, C., Kohli, A. and Murali, K. (eds.), *Business and Politics in India*, New York: Oxford University Press, pp. 50–92.

Sitharaman, N. (2025). *Social Security, Healthcare Schemes to Benefit 1 Crore Gig Workers*, February 1, 2025. https://yourstory.com/2025/02/social-security-healthcare-gig-workers-budget-nirmala-sitharaman, accessed May 24, 2025.

Speake, J. (2015). *Oxford Dictionary of Proverbs*, Oxford: Oxford University Press, 6th edition.

Sridharan, E. (1996). *The Political Economy of Industrial Promotion: Indian, Brazilian and Korean Electronics in Comparative Perspective 1969–1994*, New York: Prager Publishers.

Staffing Industry Analysts (2024). *Apple's India Expansion Could Generate Over 600,000 Jobs*, August 27, 2024, https://www.staffingindustry.com/news/global-daily-news/apples-india-expansion-could-generate-over-600000-jobs#:~:text=August%2027%2C%202024,being %20women%20and%20first%2Dtimers, accessed September 4, 2025.

Statista (2021). *Value of Cut and Polished Diamonds Exported from India Between Financial Year 2009 and 2021*, https://www.statista.com/statistics/896611/india-cut-and-polished-diamonds-export-value/, accessed June 1, 2022.

Statista (2022). *Distribution of Gross Domestic Product (GDP) Across Economic Sectors in the United States from 2000 to 2019*, https://www.statista.com/statistics/270001/distribution-of-gross-domestic-product-gdp-across-economic-sectors-in-the-us/, accessed March 25, 2024.

Statista (2025). *Number of Registered Unorganized Workers In India In 2025, By Sector*, https://www-statista-com.eu1.proxy.openathens.net/statistics/1456696/india-registered-unorganized-workers-by-sector/, accessed April 17, 2025.

Statistics Bureau of Japan (2022). *Japan Statistical Yearbook 2022*, Statistics Bureau of Japan, https://www.stat.go.jp/english/data/nenkan/index.html, accessed March 25, 2024.

Stiglitz, J. (2012). *The Price of Inequality: How Today's Divided Society Endangers Our Future*, New York: W.W. Norton.

Suresh, H. and Ishwarbharath, B.S. (2025). "Trump's H-1B Visa Crackdown Upends Indian IT Industry's Playbook," *Reuters*, September 22, 2015, https://www.reuters.com/business/finance/trumps-h-1b-visa-crackdown-upends-indian-it-industrys-playbook-2025-09-21/?utm, accessed September 22, 2025.

Sweezy, P. and Baran, P.A. (1966). *Monopoly Capital: An Essay on the American Economic and Social Order*, New York: Monthly Review Press.

Tambe, N. (2024). *MSME Statistics and Trends, Forbes Advisor*, February 6, 2024, https://www.forbes.com/advisor/in/business/msme-statistics/#:~:text=There%20are%20a%20total%20of,areas%20have%20309%20lakh%20businesses, accessed May 12, 2025.

Team Inc42 (2025). *India's Unicorn Club: Here's The Comprehensive List Of 100+ Unicorns in India*, https://inc42.com/features/indias-unicorn-club-the-comprehensive-list-of-unicorns-in-india/, accessed August 27, 2025.

Tejani, S. (2015). "Jobless Growth in India: An Investigation," *Cambridge Journal of Economics*, 40: 843–870.

Thomas, J.J. (2012). "India's Labour Market during the 2000s: Surveying the Changes," *Economic and Political Weekly*, XLVII, 51: 39–51.

Thomas, J.J. (2013). "Explaining the "Jobless" Growth in Indian Manufacturing," *Journal of the Asia Pacific Economy*, 18 (4): 673–692.

Tirodkar, A. (2025). "US Tariffs Deepen the Crisis in Gujarat's Diamond Industry," *Frontline*, September 13, 2025, https://frontline.thehindu.com/economy/gujarat-diamond-industry-crisis-us-tariffs-russia-ukraine-war/article70044655.ece?utm_source=frontline_search&utm_medium=organic&utm_campaign=search_results&utm_term=diamond_industry, accessed September 16, 2025.

Todaro, M.P. and Smith, S.C. (2020). *Economic Development*, Harlow: Pearson Education Ltd., 13th edition.

UBS (2024). *Global Wealth Report*, https://www.ubs.com/content/dam/assets/wm/static/noindex/wm-germany/2024/doodownload/Global-Wealth-Report-2024.pdf.

United Nations Centre on Transnational Corporations (1983). *Transnational Corporations in the International Auto Industry*, New York: United Nations.

United Nations Development Program (UNDP) (various years). *Human Development Report*, New York: UNDP.

US Citizen and Immigration Services (2020). *Characteristics of H-1B Specialty Occupation Workers Fiscal Year 2020 Annual Report to Congress*, Washington DC: Homeland Security, https://www.uscis.gov/sites/default/files/document/reports/Characteristics_of_Specialty_Occupation_Workers_H-1B_Fiscal_Year_2020.pdf.

US Energy Information Administration (2021). "*International Energy Outlook Narrative*," https://www.eia.gov/outlooks/ieo/pdf/IEO2021_Narrative.pdf.

Vir, A. and Sanghi, R. (2021). *The Internet Country: How India Created a Digital Blueprint for the Economies of the Future*, Tigerfeathers, https://tigerfeathers.substack.com/p/the-internet-country, accessed September 2, 2023.

Walton, M. (2020). "An Indian Gilded Age? Continuity and Change in the Political Economy of India's Development," in Chatterjee, E. and McCartney, M. (eds.), *Class and Conflict: Revisiting Pranab Bardhan's Political Economy of India*, Oxford: Oxford University Press, pp. 224–255.

Whitley, R. (1999). *Divergent Capitalisms: The Social Structuring and Change of Business Systems*, Oxford: Oxford University Press.

Williams, G. (2025). *Top 10 Cobalt Producers by Country*, https://investingnews.com/where-is-cobalt-mined/, February 19, 2025, accessed July 11, 2025.

Witt, M.A. and Redding, G. (2014). "Introduction," in Witt, M.A. and Redding, G. (eds.), *The Oxford Handbook of Asian Business Systems*, Oxford: Oxford University Press, pp. 1–8.

World Bank (2019). *Doing Business 2019: Training for Reform*, 2. https://doi.org/10.1596/978-1-4648-1326-9. https://www.worldbank.org/content/dam/doingBusiness/media/Annual-Reports/English/DB2019-report_web-version.pdf.

World Bank Group (2025a). *GDP Per Capita*, https://data.worldbank.org/indicator/NY.GDP.PCAP.CD, accessed September 1, 2025.

World Bank Group (2025b). *Labor Force, Total, India*, https://data.worldbank.org/indicator/SL.TLF.TOTL.IN?locations=IN, accessed September 29, 2025.

World Bank Group (2025c). *Industry (Including Construction), Value Added (% of GDP) – India*, https://data.worldbank.org/indicator/NV.IND.TOTL.ZS?locations=IN, accessed September 29, 2025.

Yelvington, K.A. (2019). "The Misery of Being Exploited by Capitalists Is Nothing Compared to the Misery of Not Being Exploited at All? A Predicament for Applied Anthropology," *Dialectical Anthropology*, 43: 397–403.

Index

For the benefit of digital users, indexed terms that span two pages (e.g., 52–53) may, on occasion, appear on only one of those pages.

Tables, figures, and boxes are indicated by an italic *t*, *f*, or *b*.